KARL POLANYI'S POLITICAL AND ECONOMIC THOUGHT

KARL POLANYI'S POLITICAL AND ECONOMIC THOUGHT

A CRITICAL GUIDE

Edited by Gareth Dale, Christopher Holmes and
Maria Markantonatou

agenda
publishing

First published in 2019 by Agenda Publishing

Agenda Publishing Limited
The Core
Bath Lane
Newcastle Helix
Newcastle upon Tyne
NE4 5TF
www.agendapub.com

ISBN 978-1-78821-089-8 (hardcover)
ISBN 978-1-78821-090-4 (paperback)

British Library Cataloguing-in-Publication Data
A catalogue record for this book is available from the British Library

Typeset by JS Typesetting Ltd, Porthcawl, Mid Glamorgan
Printed and bound in the UK by TJ International

CONTENTS

THE CONTRIBUTORS

MICHAEL BURAWOY teaches at the University of California, Berkeley. He is the author of *Symbolic Violence: Conversations with Bourdieu* (2019).

GARETH DALE teaches at Brunel University. His books include *Reconstructing Karl Polanyi* (2016) and *Karl Polanyi: A Life on the Left* (2016).

MATHIEU DESAN is Assistant Professor of Sociology at the University of Colorado Boulder.

KURTULUŞ GEMICI teaches at the National University of Singapore. His publications include "Karl Polanyi and the Antinomies of Embeddedness" (*Socio-Economic Review*, 2008) and "The Neoclassical Origins of Polanyi's Self-Regulating Market" (*Sociological Theory*, 2015).

RANDALL GERMAIN is Professor of Political Science at Carleton University. His teaching and research explores the political economy of global finance and the evolution of theories of international political economy.

SANDRA HALPERIN is Professor of International Relations at Royal Holloway, University of London. Her research areas include global development, the historical sociology of global relations, the causes and conditions of war and peace, and Middle East politics.

CHRISTOPHER HOLMES is a Lecturer in International Political Economy at King's College, London. He is the author of *Polanyi in Times of Populism: Vision and Contradiction in the History of Economic Ideas* (2018).

SAMUEL KNAFO is a Senior Lecturer in International Relations at the University of Sussex. He is the author of *The Making of Modern Finance: Liberal Governance and the Gold Standard* (2013)

MARIA MARKANTONATOU received her PhD in 2005 from Albert Ludwigs University, Freiburg, Germany. She is an Assistant Professor in political sociology at the University of the Aegean, Lesvos, Greece, and is currently working on the crisis in Greece.

HÜSEYIN ÖZEL is Professor of Economics at Hacettepe University, Turkey. His doctoral dissertation, at University of Utah, was on the social theory of Karl Polanyi. His current research is on globalization and the social/economic consequences of neoliberalism.

TILMAN REITZ is a professor of sociology at the University of Jena, Germany. He received his PhD in philosophy in 2001 and has been working in both disciplines since 2009.

PAULA VALDERRAMA is a philosopher and economist. She wrote her doctoral thesis on the social philosophies of Karl Polanyi and Friedrich Hayek at Free University Berlin.

DAVID YARROW is a research fellow at the University of Edinburgh, having completed his PhD at the University of Warwick in 2018. He is currently researching post-growth statistical and accounting systems in global governance.

INTRODUCTION

Christopher Holmes

This book is designed to offer something to anyone with an interest in Karl Polanyi's work, whether a newcomer or a seasoned scholar. Each chapter offers a comprehensive description and discussion of his major theses and ideas in relation to ten themes essential to his work, followed by an afterword which considers the insights offered by the book as a whole. The chapter themes span the range of Polanyi's political and economic interests, from the importance of economic ideas, the various facets of the international economic system and the role of the state, to his understanding of class, fascism and democracy. By reading the whole volume, the reader can expect to come away with a full overview of Polanyi's political and economic thought and one which clearly unpacks the relevance of his ideas to subsequent scholarship and contemporary issues.

The reader should not, however, expect to be presented with a single, unified picture of Polanyi's intellectual contribution, because none exists. This is in part because Polanyi was a writer and a polymath rather than a straightforward academic labourer, confined within the bounds of a particular discipline. Following training as a lawyer in Budapest, he spent formative years as a journalist in Vienna writing for the widely-read periodical *Der Österreichische Volkswirt*. After that, he moved to Britain, supplementing continuing journalism with often precarious work tutoring for various universities and adult education institutions. These two periods were critical to Polanyi's intellectual formation and are capped by the publication of his celebrated historical analysis of industrial capitalism, *The Great Transformation*, in 1944. Only after this point did Polanyi secure permanent academic posts in the United States, first at Bennington College, then Columbia University. From there, Polanyi wrote or contributed to a number of academic articles and books focused largely on issues of ancient economic anthropology.

It is striking how different Polanyi's writing is during each of these periods, speaking to different audiences with different aims, often using the vocabulary of different disciplines. On this basis, a case could perhaps be made for attempting to divide one's presentation of his work biographically, into distinct phases of output, emphasizing the situatedness of each period with the associated intellectual terms of debate. Yet this would give a somewhat artificial picture, because common interests and strains of argumentation weave across these periods. Moreover, such an approach would discourage comparison between the varied ways in which Polanyi articulated key ideas over time, which is arguably one of the most intellectually productive ways of examining his work. Reflecting these points, many of the chapters in this book explicitly attempt to connect the dots between Polanyi's different periods of output, identifying both key continuities, and key changes, in his views. Some of these take the form of innovative arguments about well-known issues of interest: international political economy, the gold standard, commodification, etc., while others piece together a picture of Polanyi's thought on less well-appreciated themes such as knowledge and money theory.

This polymathism leads to a second reason: such is the success of Polanyi's conceptual contributions to scholarship that parts of it now feature in the standard lexicon of thought in a variety of social scientific disciplines. With that success has come a variety of different perspectives on its strengths and its weaknesses. Some of this variety can be traced to a not inconsiderable amount of ambiguity in Polanyi's formulation of key ideas, but it is also due to the fact that there are a series of ongoing debates within the community of Polanyi scholars on a variety of questions, including the proper interpretation of key concepts, the degree of importance one should assign to other traditions of thought in understanding his ideas (particularly neoclassical economics and Marxism), the relationship between his early political economy and his later anthropology and the extent to which his ideas can be translated into contemporary contexts meaningfully. Rather than seeing these as debates that can be settled "once and for all", one should see them as indicative of strength in the Polanyian tradition. This book as a whole, in which his thought is relayed by thirteen leading experts in the field, avoids closing down any of these questions. Instead, it provides the reader with a wide range of perspectives on them, inviting the reader to formulate their own views.

This relates to the third, and most important reason why one should not search for an overly unified picture of Polanyi's work. This is that, beyond questions of interpretation, critique of Polanyi's work itself has become intrinsic to the tradition of Polanyian thought. A considerable proportion of the many academic articles and books devoted to applying Polanyi's ideas to contemporary issues are hedged with caveats about the limitations of his conceptual scheme, or the ways in which it should be altered or refined. Many authors ostensibly sympathetic to Polanyi's normative aims and/or some of his broad analytical insights, have found the power of his work to depend precisely on engaging, rather than avoiding, its difficulties, ambiguities and inconsistencies.

The essentiality of critique to the Polanyian tradition is abundantly demonstrated in this volume, and provides an instructive theme upon which to briefly introduce the contents. Some contributions seek to whittle away the weaker aspects of Polanyi's central theses so as to focus on the parts of most value. For example, considering Polanyi's critique of the market view of economy, Christopher Holmes and David Yarrow (Chapter 1) recognize the empirical inaccuracies and misleading generalizations that arose when Polanyi translated that critique into a narrative of human history. Yet, they argue, his underlying thesis on the conceptual blindspots that the market view engenders still stands regardless, and remains relevant to understanding the way notions of "economy" are used in policy today. In their chapter, Maria Markantonatou and Gareth Dale (Chapter 3) achieve similar goals in relation to Polanyi's theory of the state. Polanyi, they argue, did provide a strong and novel critique of the idea of the *liberal* state and its impact on the way people think about the appropriate roles of political authority in economic life, yet he never developed a fully coherent theory of the state in general, nor any account of its origins or evolution, omissions which sit alongside sometimes sanguine approaches to the use of state power.

In other chapters, critique takes the form of more forthright rejection. Sandra Halperin (Chapter 4), for example, takes Polanyi to task for his failure to reflect on the role of class in shaping the politics of Europe during the nineteenth century. Whilst, for Halperin, Polanyi clearly and extensively documents the harms arising from industrialization during the period, he completely ignored the role of political repression by ruling classes in driving that industrialization and enforcing the very social systems which produced those harms. Samuel Knafo (Chapter 5) also focuses on the nineteenth century, examining Polanyi's analysis of the gold standard monetary system and its pivotal role in his critique of liberal economic governance in general. Polanyi, Knafo argues, ignored the fundamental role of British political institutions – parliament and the Bank of England in particular – in underpinning the system, and thereby misunderstood its actual workings. For Knafo, as for Halperin, too much is hung by Polanyi on the economic, not enough on the political, in his explanation of outcomes in nineteenth-century European history.

Other authors seek to deepen or extend Polanyi's arguments in relation to the theme in question so as to refine Polanyi's approach. Perhaps the most ambitious attempt at extension comes from Germain (Chapter 2) in his analysis of Polanyi's contributions to international political economy. Here, Germain senses ambiguities in Polanyi's work on the role of the inter-state system and the international monetary system in shaping processes and outcomes in the global economy. To address those ambiguities, Germain complements Polanyi's analysis with E. H. Carr's international relations theory and Fernand Braudel's analysis of money, in so doing fortifying Polanyi's approach to the historical evolution of international economic order. Another case in point is Gemici's analysis of Polanyi's thought on money. Gemici (Chapter 6) presents the notion of "commodity fiction" as a way to join the dots between Polanyi's somewhat disparate thoughts on money theory in economics, history, sociology and anthropology. Likewise, in the following chapter, Özel (Chapter 7) identifies the weaknesses in Polanyi's notion of commodification – which is central to his theses in *The Great Transformation*, yet somewhat underspecified as an actual process – and suggests that they can be resolved by bringing that notion into conversation with the Marxist labour theory of value. In his chapter, Tilman Reitz (Chapter 10) picks up on the same lack of clarity, but uses it instead as a platform to investigate how far Polanyi's notion of land, labour and money as "fictitious commodities" can plausibly be extended to include other institutions such as that of the chapter title, "knowledge".

A final method of approach is to draw connections between the various parts of Polanyi's output so as to tease out his approach, or approaches, to a theme of underlying importance across his writing. For example, together, Gareth Dale and Mathieu Desan's contribution on "Fascism" (Chapter 8) and Paula Valderrama's subsequent chapter on "Democracy" (Chapter 9) provide a thorough and nuanced account of Polanyi's approach to traditional political questions about representation and tyranny, as reflected in his overriding sense of a tension between capitalism and democracy in liberal democratic socie-ties. Both chapters recognize, in different ways, an abstract, philosophical bent in Polanyi's approach to politics, and, echoing something of Knafo's contribu-tion, one which sometimes skips over the details of how outcomes are actually arrived at through political process. Valderrama takes this approach on its own terms and finds much of value, whereas Dale and Desan, whilst respecting its innovation, see it as indicative of Polanyi's failure to relate his political ideas to the specific struggles of his day.

Taking a step back, Michael Burawoy's afterword (Chapter 11) thinks through the strengths and limitations of Polanyi's political and economic thought as a whole, considering its explanatory power in the long-run history of industrial capitalism right up to the present day. In so doing, he puts his finger upon an issue which, as we have seen, reverberates loudly across the breadth of this volume: the tendency of Polanyi to hang too much of the explanatory burden directly on economic ideas in public life, at the expense of questions about mechanisms of power and domination as exercised through political means. Burawoy documents this issue both in Polanyi's writings and in the other chapters of this book, yet, exemplifying the aims of the volume as a whole, Burawoy uses this weakness as a platform for productive engagement. By bring-ing Polanyi's thought into conversation with Antonio Gramsci, amongst others, he emphasizes that, despite such weaknesses, Polanyi's specific insights on the social struggles that arise from processes of commodification remain power-fully relevant today, especially given the diminishing structural power of the primary axis of Marxist-style struggle: the working class.

In sum, the approaches taken in this book demonstrate that, rather than thinking of Polanyi's political and economic thought as something fixed, as something that must be sided "with" or "against", it is better to think of it as a conceptual language. This language offers us a set of ideas, approaches and case studies which enable us to think about perennial questions of political economy today and as manifest in the past but, like all conceptual languages, it presents a particular view of the world which foregrounds some issues and not others. By robustly probing at its limits, one is able to drive debate forward not only on Polanyi's legacy, but on the appropriate way of thinking through the relationship between polity, economy and society itself. Indeed, the question of this relation-ship was fundamental to all of Polanyi's political and economic thought, and it is therefore fitting that his work should continue to inspire so much scholarship on it.

1

ECONOMIC IDEAS

Christopher Holmes and David Yarrow

INTRODUCTION

What is the economy and how should we understand its place in society? This question is central to many of Karl Polanyi's key contributions to political economic thought, and it developed into an explicitly stated research focus in the later stages of his academic career. The way in which he approached the issue can be broadly understood as resulting from his engagement with the neoclassical understanding of the economy which had come to prominence during his youth. Under strict neoclassical assumptions, individuals are materially self-interested without limit, yet resources are scarce, and so they must trade in order to maximize utility.[1] This sort of behaviour is the only "economic" behaviour, and so from this perspective, "the economy" is coterminous with "the market". And to the extent that these assumptions are pitched as inherent to human nature, they are applicable to economic activity in all times and places. Although Polanyi sometimes reproduced elements of neoclassical thought in his analysis of capitalism,[2] he strongly rejected its universalist pretensions, seeing them as fitting in to a longer tradition of essentialism[3] in liberal economic thought, particularly the laissez-faire theories of nineteenth-century political economists such as Thomas Malthus and David Ricardo.

In this chapter, we consider the various ways in which Polanyi's desire to challenge market-centric representations of the economy permeated his most important theoretical interventions, considering strengths and weaknesses along the way. Firstly, we examine the critique of laissez-faire market ideology that Polanyi presented in *The Great Transformation*[4] (*TGT*). Here, Polanyi argues that a market-centric reading of the history of capitalism occluded both the role of politics in creating and sustaining market orders, as well as failing to recognize adequately the way in which markets can generate various types of harm and conflict. After demonstrating how that critique fits into the broader framework of the book, we note weaknesses both in terms of a failure to

7

recognize relevant precedents to nineteenth-century laissez-faire thought, and in terms of the way in which the theoretical premises of economic liberalism are relied on too directly in his narrative of real-world economic history. In the second section, we move on to consider Polanyi's books published subsequently to *TGT*. In them, he sought to demonstrate that a market-centric view of economy could not be universally valid by finding empirical examples of economies – usually ancient – not organized primarily along market lines. In response, he developed a "substantivist" economics which represented the economy in institutional terms and which did not assume market-like characteristics of people. After outlining this theory, we discuss the fact that he never applied this substantivism to market society directly, noting the various ways in which this omission has been approached in the literature.

In regard to both arguments, we conclude that there are clearly problems in the way in which Polanyi executed his critique of market-centric accounts of economy. He had a tendency to pile ideational and historical levels of analysis on top of one another, which meant that the complexity of the history of both economies and economic ideas sometimes got glossed over. Nevertheless, to think that these problems undermine his critique of market-centrism itself would be to throw the baby out with the bathwater. Instead, it is a question of thinking more cautiously about how market-centrism manifests itself, who purveys it, and what impact it has in particular contexts. With this in mind, the final section of this chapter surveys some examples of the contemporary relevance of Polanyi's challenge to market-centrism both in academic economics and in recent debates over the limitations of the UN System of National Accounts (SNA), which, since the 1950s, has provided the most authoritative and widely deployed representation of "the economy" in policy-making, and one which is couched strictly in market terms.

ECONOMIC LIBERALISM IN THE GREAT TRANSFORMATION

In *TGT*, Polanyi argued that the industrial revolution provided the initial impetus for a range of efforts to organize increasing spheres of economy and society according to the logic of the market, because markets were able to organize production and allocate resources with a degree of efficiency that previous economic systems could not.[5] Via the price mechanism, markets were capable of facilitating the rapid development and expanding consumption and production that industrialization entailed, first in England, then internationally through trade as supported by an integrated international monetary system (the gold standard). The book moves on to illustrate some of the perils of this new system. He categorized this aspect of his thesis in terms of the effects of marketization on three "fictitious commodities":[6] land, labour and money, or in non-commodity terms, nature, people and the monetary system.

For example, over the eighteenth century, the increasing organization and allocation of labour through markets rather than manorial ties and feudal order proved to be far more efficient and much better suited to the ever-changing requirements of production in the modern industrial economy. But those ever-changing requirements also meant periods of unemployment as production changed form and location far more rapidly. For Polanyi, unemployment affected people in ways that could not be captured when thinking of them in commodity terms: "the alleged commodity 'labor power' cannot be shoved about, used indiscriminately, or even left unused, without affecting also the human individual who happens to be the bearer of this peculiar commodity. In disposing of a man's labor power the system would, incidentally, dispose of the physical, psychological and moral entity 'man' attached to that tag".[7] In a precursor of today's general awareness of the scale of human destruction of the environment, he makes the same argument about the commodity "land": what is an economically productive use of natural resources might negatively affect nature as a habitat for people to exist within through effects like pollution, soil depletion, deforestation, etc.[8] Finally, the organization of the international economy through deeply integrated financial markets and a unitary monetary system enabled a highly productive allocation of capital across national borders, and therefore huge international economic growth, but it also gave rise to a situation in which the livelihoods of individuals in one place were made much more sensitive to economic cycle effects anywhere else in the system, a dynamic which, for Polanyi, eventually played out in the 1929 US stock market crash and ensuing Great Depression.

Polanyi argues that the effects of the marketization of these fictitious commodities produced social "countermovement[s]"[9] of one sort or another designed to mitigate or offset these harms by interfering with the principle of market self-regulation, a process he sometimes describes as the "protection of society".[10] In some instances, these countermovements were progressive in nature. In the case of labour, for example, he argues that workplace legislation and the recognition of unions served to protect workers' livelihoods, and in the case of land, he discusses the role of legislation in slowing down urbanization and providing for allotments and other green spaces to improve life in the new industrial centres of England. However, in the case of the gold standard, Polanyi argues that societal self-protection took the form of a rejection of the international economic system as a whole, which, in the form of trade and currency protectionism, fused with nationalist sentiments in some countries, laying the ground for the growth of fascist ideologies in the run up to the Second World War.

The target of Polanyi's critique in this analysis was thus not markets per se. He respected the productivity that markets enabled and, at the end of *TGT* where he tentatively suggests some ideas about what a better economic system would look like, he argues only for the abolition of the principle of market self-regulation in regard to the fictitious commodities.[11] Also, Polanyi's earlier attempts to provide an ideal model for the organization of economic life in industrial society reserved a place for valuation of goods via markets.[12] The problem was specifically a worldview which sought to understand human affairs in general from within the parameters of the market self-regulation idea only: not just the production of widgets, but the relationships between people, the relationship between people and nature and the organization of the economy as a whole.

Fred Block and Margaret Somers have aptly described this view as "market fundamentalism".[13] What made it fundamentalist was the way in which it was built upon a particular account of human nature as solely self-interested and materialist, and therefore acquisitive – in other words as *homo economicus*, or "economic man".[14] The emergence of this idea, in Polanyi's narrative, takes place during a period of experimentation with the provision of welfare in England under the Speenhamland system between 1795 and 1830. He charts the influence of a number of prominent pamphleteers during that time, who argued against the provision of aid-in-wages (a system which topped up worker wages if they fell below a certain level) because it interfered with the incentives provided by the market, which worked on self-interested motives inherent to human nature in their view, namely "the pangs of hunger on the one hand" and "the scarcity of food on the other".[15]

This "biological"[16] or "naturalis[t]"[17] way of justifying the marketization of labour and the abolition of government protection through welfare provision, for Polanyi, was then appropriated wholesale in the dominant economic theory of the day, especially that of Thomas Malthus, in his "law" of population and Ricardo in his "law" of diminishing returns. These intellectual moves served to present "the market" not only as something distinct and separate from society, but moreover as a natural way for humans to organize. Hence interference with it – welfare provision, regulation of industry, protectionism, etc. – was unnatural. In this way, despite starting out as "only a first vigorous attempt at adjustment"[18] of society to the demands of industrialization, the price mechanism came to be seen not as a pragmatic solution to the organization of industrial production, the costs and benefits of which might be judged depending on the particular issues and circumstances in question, but rather as the necessary matrix of all human relationships in general. To characterize this belief system, Polanyi regularly draws parallels between this "liberal economic" view and the theism which had been so central to the organization of European societies in medieval times.[19]

The "vision of perfectibility"[20] offered in the laissez-faire view produced a cock-eyed way of understanding both processes of marketization and responsive social protection, in Polanyi's view. On one hand, because it suggested that markets were the natural manifestation of fundamental propensities in human nature, it occluded the fact that, in the real world, the establishment of market systems depended on political effort, whether in terms of definite acts of legislation which had the effect of marketizing parts of the economy,[21] or in terms of the role of broader power-shifts amongst the social classes of societies.[22] On the other hand, the market fundamentalist view suggested that all the types of social protection which grew to mitigate the effects of marketization over the nineteenth and early twentieth centuries should be recognized merely as unnecessary barriers to the efficient operation of the market in respect of the fictitious commodities. Anything that got in the way of the workings of markets was, by this account, at best counterproductive or, at worst, indicative of a "collectivist conspiracy" working against the inalienable economic freedom of individuals.[23] The dominance of the economic liberal view had produced misapprehensions in regard to the rise of fascism in the inter-war period, too. "Economic liberals", in his view, looked at increasing global integration – particularly monetary integration via the gold standard – as a purely economic phenomenon, and a greatly beneficial one at that. From this perspective, fascism could only be understood as a "political" interruption to the "normal" logic of market-led international economic integration.[24] For Polanyi, by contrast, fascism was, at root, an economic ideology: it was one answer – the worst possible answer – to the question of how to reconcile economy and society in an industrial system. This was a question which, for him, the ideology of economic liberalism had failed to answer.

As a critique of the laissez-faire idea in the abstract, Polanyi's account is powerful and innovative. However, inevitably given the sweeping style in which he presents his thesis, it can be found wanting in the details. For example, although some ideological antecedents are occasionally noted, the book often implies that *laissez-faire* ideology appeared very abruptly, emerging from nothing to fully-formed during the 1795–1830 period.[25] This way of presenting the history of economic ideas is problematic because it hides all the complexities and subtleties with which earlier scholars of political economy debated and conceptualized the commercial society emerging around them. For example, Matthew Watson has highlighted Polanyi's handling of Adam Smith. Polanyi often[26] seems to treat Smith's political economy simply as a forerunner of the *homo economicus* idea via the famous notion of a human "propensity to truck, barter and exchange",[27] but, as Smith scholars have comprehensively demonstrated in recent decades, this is a highly selective reading of Smith, which does not do justice either to the complexity of Smith's account of political economy in general, or to the way in which he situated economic concerns in relation to civic and moral ones. As Watson argues, Polanyi tended to view Smith through "Ricardian" eyes, which meant that he barred himself from drawing on a wealth of material in Smith's political economy that would be consistent with Polanyi's wider aims to find ways to think about economy, society and polity as conceptually conjoined.[28]

Going further back, as Gareth Dale has shown, Polanyi's narrative ignores strong evidence from historians – some of which would have been available to Polanyi at the time of writing *TGT* – that suggests the *homo economicus* idea was already firmly established in the public consciousness in seventeenth-century England.[29] Moreover, the concept of market self-regulation was not the first time that scholars of political economy had attempted to think through the notion of economy as something distinct, subject to its own laws derived from nature. Some of the most important episodes of this story centred on the development of the concepts of private property and of contract in the work of natural lawyers in the seventeenth century, particularly Samuel Pufendorf, Hugo Grotius and John Locke. The economic theses of these scholars were critical to establishing the conceptual languages upon which the notion of the market could be built in the Enlightenment period and beyond,[30] yet they are barely mentioned in Polanyi's history of economic ideas.

If Polanyi's history of ideas lacks detail on the antecedents of the Speenhamland period, then there is a different problem pertaining to his account of economic thought from that time on. Although his discussion of economic thought in the 1795–1830 period contains a variety of illuminating (and sometimes amusing) details, elsewhere in the book, he tends only to refer to "economic liberalism", or "laissez-faire" in general. It might be reasonable, if still lacking nuance, to say that the canon of subsequent liberal economic scholarship up until the time of writing *TGT* did reflect broadly laissez-faire assumptions established by Malthus and Ricardo, but by trying to explain such a huge range of real-world economic history in terms of the weaknesses of that single idea, economic liberalism becomes something of an autonomous force in his analysis, one which both people and economic institutions simply either embody (labour markets, the monetary system, etc.), or reject (the state, society, nations, etc.).

This style inevitably crowds out the complexity of the historical events to which he applies the thesis. For example, as Block and Somers have shown, advances in our knowledge of the Speenhamland episode itself show that things were a lot more complex than Polanyi had accounted for, with differences between English regions, the results of technological change, war, and the effects of England's return to the gold standard all playing significant roles in shaping the fortunes of workers during the period. Their study undermines Polanyi's characterization of the period solely in terms of the opposition of the incentives of the labour market and the provision of aid-in-wages.[31] The same might be said about Polanyi's analysis of the gold standard. Polanyi sometimes implies that the monetary system did actually function according to the logic of supply and demand, with states only acting in response to it, so as to cushion or prevent the effects of that logic on the domestic population. As Knafo shows in this volume, this view overlooks, or at least mishandles, how the interests of particular states and classes within states, rather than price, drove the establishment and expansion of the system in the first place. In sum, by judging economic history against the yardstick of the laissez-faire idea so rigidly and directly, Polanyi left his reading of economic history open to challenge on the basis that this or that actor's actions were not actually fully defined by that idea in practice.

These weaknesses are significant, and they certainly mean that we cannot use *TGT* on its own as an accurate guide to history in the nineteenth century, nor as an accurate guide to the history of economic ideas. Nevertheless, they do not actually undermine Polanyi's critique of laissez-faire ideology in and of itself. Polanyi's primary aim on this score was to show that market-centric conception of the economy and of human life in general produced a worldview which is insensitive to certain types of harm endemic to industrial societies, and on this score, he was successful. *TGT* provides two types of argument to this effect. As we have seen, the first argument consists of a description of those harms, including the phenomenon of unemployment, the over-farming of soil and the potential for the monetary system to transmit shocks from place to place, showing in each case how they could not be conceptualized adequately from within the bounds of a laissez-faire view. The second argument, which we have only so far touched on, consists of an effort not only to describe the universalist pretensions of the laissez-faire view, but to show that they were empirically inaccurate. Although Polanyi did present an argument to this end in chapter 4 of *TGT*, it was an issue which came to define much of his published academic work subsequently, and so to understand that argument specifically, it is to that work that we now turn.

FORMALISM AND SUBSTANTIVISM

If *The Great Transformation* can plausibly be read as a critique of the laissez-faire description of the economy, then the book leaves a clear question: what would a better description look like? Polanyi tried to answer this question directly in work published after the Second World War. Here, drawing on the work of, amongst others, the forerunner of neoclassicism, Carl Menger,[32] Polanyi's critique of liberal economics as displayed in *TGT* mutated into a critique of "formalism"[33] as purveyed in the study of economic history and economic anthropology. Formalism, for Polanyi, connoted an approach to understanding economic interaction by any persons in any place and during any period of time according to neoclassical assumptions, i.e. scarcity as a material fact, human nature as self-interested and, in result, of market exchange as the institutional basis of all economic interaction.

For Polanyi, the universalism of the formalist view stood at odds with the wide variety of institutional settings and economic systems that humans can be observed actually engaging within over history. Instead, he therefore championed a "substantive" definition of economics, which did not assume particular human propensities or institutional configurations. Given this concern to demonstrate heterogeneity, his substantive definition of economy was couched in very broad terms. At its broadest, for Polanyi, it encompassed "man's dependence for his living upon nature and his fellows ... refer[ring] to the interchange with natural and social environment, insofar as this results in supplying him with the means of material want satisfaction".[34] By this account, economy is "the material organisation of man's life",[35] or put more simply, people's "livelihood".[36] Insofar as it contains anything more specific than this, it is the idea that this supply of material goods has to be "continuous",[37] implying that some notion of how an economy reproduces itself over time should be intrinsic to how we understand the economy. Bob Jessop captures this aspect well, suggesting that Polanyi "argues that societal ... conditions sustain the ... interdependence of economic movements and ensure their 'recurrence' (i.e. their continued reproduction) – without which neither the unity nor stability of the ... economic process is possible".[38]

A sizeable chunk of Polanyi's later academic writing was devoted to making the argument that formalist precepts were not held widely, if at all, in societies other than those in the post-industrial revolution West. In the edited collection of essays, *Primitive, Archaic and Modern Economies: Essays of Karl Polanyi* (1968) we can observe several versions of this argument. For example, in "Aristotle discovers the economy", an essay originally penned for inclusion in an edited collection, *Trade and Markets in Early Empires* (1957), Polanyi argued that, whilst Aristotle was familiar with markets, including of course the Athenian *agora*, outside of such settings, the fulfilment of some form of natural justice was often the guiding principle on matters of price.[39] Moreover, Aristotle's basic conception of economic activity took the autarkic household as its archetype, in which the provisions self-sufficiency and reliable subsistence, rather than self-interest, were the most fundamental economic behaviours. Where the major economic historians of the day (Polanyi mentions Joseph Schumpeter amongst others) had written off Aristotle's economic thought as irrelevant, immature or insufficiently scientific, Polanyi saw it as evidence that scarcity, self-interest and market exchange were not universal facts of life. Instead, these were concepts which people might or might not use to understand their conditions at particular times and in particular places. Beyond his coverage of ancient economies, Polanyi dwelled at length on the research of anthropologists such as Margaret Mead, Richard Thurnwald and Bronisław Malinowski who, in his view, provided descriptions of more recent non-capitalistic societies where various forms of economic activity were clearly rooted in norms other than those of self-interest and market exchange. In terms of the social structures in which economic activity is organized, Polanyi argued that market exchange was only one of four possible "forms of economic integration", the others being reciprocity, redistribution and householding.[40] Further, he suggested that market exchange was for most of human history the least important, and that where markets did exist, they did not operate according to principles of supply and demand as per formalism.[41]

Formalist economic anthropologists and others provided a number of critiques of this view which we do not have space to discuss properly here. Suffice to say, Polanyi sometimes overstated the degree to which the motive of gain was absent in ancient economic practices in his efforts to distinguish ancient market activities from modern ones, and his own conceptual scheme of "forms of economic integration" was, for some, itself overly simplistic in characterizing the wide diversity of pre-modern economic activity.[42] Nevertheless, his innovations did suggest a way of looking at the economy that would have lasting impact. Most importantly, it suggested that economic activity – in the substantive sense of the provision of material livelihood – could be driven by religious reasons, by the competition for honour or glory, by the concern to uphold custom or political control.[43] Isolating one particular motivation as fundamentally "economic" – material acquisitiveness in the neoclassical case – as the basis for our understanding of all economies was therefore arbitrary:

> Single out whatever motive you please, and organise production in such a manner as to make that motive the individual's incentive to produce, and you will have induced picture of man as altogether absorbed by that particular motive. Let that motive be religious, political, or aesthetic; let it be pride, prejudice, love or envy, and man will appear as essentially religious, political, aesthetic, proud, prejudiced, engrossed in love or envy. [...] The particular motive selected will represent "real" man.[44]

Whether or not one *can* interpret a given economic interaction from within the confines of a particular economic model, the point for Polanyi was that, without studying and understanding the motives which drive people to engage in that interaction, our knowledge of that interaction will be at best partial and at worst misleading. And since motives are only intelligible through language, reflecting prevailing social and cultural norms, one must make understanding of that language and those norms integral to our understanding of economic activity. If there is no truly universal theoretical model applicable to all economic behaviour, then study of the economy has to start instead with the actual institutions[45] of a given economy, meaning both the social structures of economic organization (families, firms, governments, legal systems, etc.) and the conceptual languages and ideological norms that guide behaviour within those structures. For some, this emphasis on motive, meaning and language is what marks Polanyi out as constructivist in theoretical orientation.[46] One way that Polanyi himself puts it is to say that economies are "embedded" in society. That is to say that there is no strict demarcation between "economic" activities and "political" or "social" activities.[47] Rather, the nature of economic interactions is governed by institutional setting (in the broad sense described above). As he puts it: "Man is not an economic, but a social being. He does not aim at safeguarding his individual interest ... but rather at ensuring social good will, social status, social assets".[48]

Here, however, we hit upon the most significant problem in Polanyi's understanding of economic ideas, and one which has become a central bone of contention for those developing or critiquing his work. The tension is this: surprisingly, given the strength with which he seeks to challenge the formalist approach to economy as coterminous with market, he consistently argues in later work that formalist assumptions *are* acceptable and appropriate for understanding the economy of market societies, i.e. those in which the market is, in fact, the dominant form of economic integration.[49] In practice, "market societies" means post-industrial revolution western economies, which are drawn in distinction to all other "non-market" societies both present and in the pre-industrial past.[50] In the former, the market has become "disembedded" from society such that the price mechanism comes to take on a life of its own, in turn structuring human affairs along market-like lines, and so the economy becomes intelligible according to formalist principles. As Gemici summarizes in his comprehensive analysis of this issue, "it is clear that [Polanyi] admits the validity of marginalist price theory for analyzing contemporary market dynamics. What he objects to is the application of neoclassical economic theories to the analysis of economic systems other than the self-regulating market under capitalism."[51]

At points in his later work, Polanyi does give fleeting hints at what a non-formalist understanding of market societies might look like. For example, when critiquing market-centric views of capitalism, he mentions un-named "realistic thinkers" who:

> emphasised the substantive meaning of *economic*. They identified the economy with industry rather than business; with technology rather than ceremonialism; with means of production rather than

titles to property; with productive capital rather than finance; with capital goods rather than capital – in short, with the economic substance rather than its marketing form and terminology.[52]

Similarly, writing at a time when large-scale national economic planning was still a common state activity in many parts of the world, Polanyi argued that formalist economic assumptions could not be relevant to societies, in which such "redistribution" was the dominant form of economic integration, in the same way that they might be for those in which the market was dominant.[53] From here we could easily extrapolate: in every capitalist nation that we have experience of, economic activity does not take place solely within markets. States allocate wealth in various ways (redistribution), gifts of one sort or another are given (reciprocity) and families organize the division of household labour (householding). It would have been a short step to apply his institutional understanding of the economy to market societies directly using the "forms of integration" terminology, but this was a step which he never took, instead consistently limiting his applications of the substantivist approach to non-industrial societies.

More broadly, why should we assume that human behaviours in markets are any less socially constituted and context-specific than those in non-market contexts? This question has become an ongoing theme in the Polanyian literature, with many seeking to draw on his conceptual language of embeddedness, but to apply it to market societies in a way that Polanyi did not. For example Mark Granovetter's seminal article on this topic sought to soften the sharp distinction Polanyi drew between embedded pre-modern economies and disembedded modern ones, arguing that most economic activity, whether modern or ancient, is embedded in networks of interpersonal relationships that debar any simple understanding of those activities either in terms of economic self-interest or in terms of social conditioning alone.[54] From a different approach, Viviana Zelizer drew on Polanyi's insights on the way in which the uses of different types of money was socially circumscribed in ancient societies.[55] Yet where Polanyi drew a sharp line between such "special purpose money" and the "all-purpose money" of modern capitalism which conformed to the principles of the market,[56] Zelizer instead showed many of the ways in which the uses of money in capitalist societies could also be circumscribed by social context, and how such restrictions in turn reflected specific power relations between people in particular locations and settings. Cultural political economists have also recently been attentive to the issue in Polanyi's work. As Jacqueline Best and Matthew Paterson have argued, Polanyi's willingness to entertain the neoclassical notion of market self-regulation prevents him from appreciating the way in which culture is used in order to maintain or destabilize market economic orders. From a more critical angle, Martijn Konings argues that the Polanyian understanding of market society overlooks the ways in which "morality, faith, power and emotion" constitute market relationships themselves in capitalism.[57] As an empirical proposition, Polanyi's notion of actually existing market societies as governed by the self-regulating logic of price can thus be shown to be as problematic as that of the "formalist" scholars who he wished to challenge.

This issue can be understood in similar terms to that which we have seen in Polanyi's analysis of laissez-faire ideas in *TGT*: what is a good critique of essentialism in economic ideas is too readily applied as historical description. In this case, formalist and substantive ways of representing economic activity are, via the distinction between embedded and disembedded economy, mapped on to an extremely broad brushed notion of economic history which pivots on a sharp separation between economic practices in post-industrial revolution western societies and those of all others. Yet despite this issue, it is reasonable to say that Polanyi was still at least partially successful in his primary analytical aims, which were to provide evidence to show that formalist assumptions of scarcity and material self-interest were not universal to human economic experience, and to provide a conceptual language to describe economic behaviour alternative to formalism.

CONTEMPORARY RELEVANCE

If Polanyi's critique of economic liberalism is at its most persuasive when "economic liberalism" is understood as a way of representing the economy rather than as a concretely existing economic system, the question is *who* exactly thinks in these terms, and what are the effects of thinking in that way? Clearly, few would express their economics in the austere language of Malthusian naturalism today, but the notion of economy-as-market is still a very important ideological force. Most obviously, it remains hegemonic in disciplinary economics, and this is important because the theories espoused by professional economists can be performative, shaping policy and public debate.[58] Public choice theory, which applies neoclassical premises to political processes, has powerfully shaped the way in which policy-makers and the broader public think about the societies they live in.[59] Under the auspices of what has become known as "economics imperialism"[60] neoclassical methodology has been applied to all manner of human activities previously not considered as "economic" in the formal sense, a process that famously began with Gary Becker's work on marriage and crime.[61]

In terms of the way economics is taught, notions which contravene the principle that markets always clear efficiently – public goods, market failure, monopoly, economic cycle and so on – are now all standard to mainstream economics textbooks, and so such books certainly cannot be described as peddling laissez-faire. Yet, at the same time, those textbooks do continue to introduce the subject to students solely as the study of exchange under conditions of scarcity[62] and whilst alternative theoretical visions are occasionally noted these days,[63] they are not incorporated into the analysis, generally being relegated to "discussion section" or "textbox" status. One cannot extrapolate to the whole of the economics profession from the view given in basic textbooks, but many world leaders, policy-makers, journalists and public intellectuals emerge from courses – Harvard's liberal arts programme, or the politics, philosophy and economics (PPE) degree at Oxford, for example – in which students often get only a brief, textbook-led introduction to the discipline, and so the influence of such introductory representations of the economy should not be sniffed at.

Moreover, since the 2008 sub-prime mortgage crisis, a litany of banking, stock market and monetary crises[64] have been experienced around the world and, in result, there has been a concomitant crisis of confidence in the economics profession. Vanishingly few mainstream economists or policy practitioners predicted these crises, and in part, this was because they were enthralled by the vision of financial markets as self-regulating systems capable of managing the economy with a minimum of state intervention.[65] In response, there have been widespread calls to "pluralize" economics curriculums beyond the restrictions of the neoclassical approach, so as to include theoretical languages which are capable of conceptualizing the possibility of crisis.[66] Keynesian and Marxist approaches have loomed largest in this respect, but Polanyi's own interventions remain a valuable alternative.

If we look towards representations of the economy in applied economics, we can see that market-centrism remains significant in the very bones of policy thought too. For example, since the 1950s, the UN System of National Accounts (SNA) has provided the most authoritative vision of "the economy" for public policy. Within the SNA, the economy is conceived of as a closed system of market flows between households, businesses and government. These flows represent the national income, given by the statistic gross domestic product (GDP), which refers to the sum of monetary transactions within markets in a given year. Thus, the SNA and its central statistical aggregate, GDP, only include as "economic" human activities which can be expressed in commodity terms through market transactions. The SNA is a global statistical framework, referred to and utilized by all national governments and economic international organizations as a basis for economic policy, and GDP has become the most widely recognized and used economic statistic: governments are voted in or out on whether they have boosted it or allowed it to flag, and countries rank themselves against one another according to it.[67]

The problems with thinking about the economy in these market-centric terms have been widely voiced, and those voices often bear a distinctly Polanyian accent. On one hand, many harms arising from market activity for society and the environment are included in GDP growth figures.[68] Famously, an environmental catastrophe such as an oil spill will show up very favourably in GDP, as it will generate many additional market transactions (the clean-up operation, insurance and legal fees, PR services to manage reputational damage). Within the SNA, these effects thus register only as increased market activity, even though they may actively erode the quality of people's lives when considered more broadly than in commodity terms. On the other hand, many "goods", which are clearly welfare-producing and economically meaningful, are excluded from the SNA and from the GDP measure. As feminists have long recognized, for example, the exclusive focus on market exchange effectively excludes all the unpaid labour performed outside the market – housework and caring, but also voluntary work – from our understanding of the economy, despite the essentiality of that labour to the successful reproduction of society and the labour force.[69] Best current estimates are that, in the UK, household labour constitutes almost 50 per cent of "the economy" if compared to output measured by GDP, for example.[70]

These critiques have been around as long as the SNA itself,[71] but again there has been a marked upswing in their volume and visibility in public debate in the last decade. For example, the Stiglitz-Sen-Fitoussi commission was convened by the French government in 2009 in order to assess how economic welfare, social progress and living standards might be better measured,[72] and its report has led to major global efforts to reform economic statistics and to include an increasing array of non-market phenomena in the definition of the economy. Consequently, there has been an increasing amount of work in statistical agencies on how non-market activities might be valued, and on what basis they might be included in representations of the economy.[73] Such debates are eminently tractable from a Polanyian perspective on economic ideas. Indeed, as some indication of the Polanyian pedigree of this effort, it is of note that one of the leaders of the commission was Joseph Stiglitz, who wrote the foreword to the 2001 edition of *The Great Transformation* and has continued to invoke Polanyi since then.

Yet, when statisticians and policy-makers have sought to put these ideas into practice, it is noteworthy that the market tends to remain the prime arbiter of value. For example, on the basis of the Stiglitz-Sen-Fitoussi commission's work, it has become common for national official statistical agencies to produce measures of household production and unpaid work,[74] which is achieved by using time-use data to calculate the hours spent on various types of such work, and then by comparing these to wage labour rates for similar activities, so that a proxy-market value can be assigned to them. Moreover, despite increasing recognition that non-market labour makes an essential contribution to the economy, there is continued resistance amongst statisticians to simply including these proxy values in official measures such as GDP on the basis that it would be too complex and would impair the clarity of national accounts.[75] Consequently, this non-market economic activity is increasingly dealt with through an ever-expanding system of so-called "satellite accounts" for household production, the sharing economy, ecosystem resources, etc., which sit outside of the core SNA framework.[76] This way of approaching the issue offers a means to respond to critiques of the SNA whilst leaving its market-centric conceptual edifice intact.

In Polanyi's original exposition, one is either a formalist or a substantivist, but such details show that arguments over appropriate representation of the economy might be better understood as an ongoing process. And whilst there is clearly recognition of the limits of market-centric accounts of "the economy" in policy thought currently, the line between market and non-market accounts is more complex in practice than Polanyi's account might suggest: even if these overt attempts to "de-marketize" our understanding of economy, is not a simple case of a substantive understanding of the economy displacing a formalist, market-based one. Rather, it is a situation in which the tools of formalist economic analysis are being manipulated in unusual ways so as to try to account for non-market human activity in quasi-market terms.

CONCLUSION

Clearly Polanyi had a proclivity for conceptual devices expressed in the form of binary opposition. Beyond Menger's "two definitions of economics",[77] Polanyi drew heavily on Henry Maine's distinction between "status" and "contractus"[78] as fundamental categories of legal system and Ferdinand Tönnies's sociological distinction between "*gemeinschaft*" and "*gesellschaft*".[79] And these binaries become represented in his own conceptual landscape, consisting of markets vs social protection, embedded vs disembedded economies, habitation vs improvement, substantivism vs formalism, etc. Such oppositions are simply too broad to be mapped on to epochal historical descriptions in the way that Polanyi sometimes did. Characterizing all western economies since industrialization simply in terms of the market view of economy occludes more than it reveals, and lends a credence to the veracity of that view which his analysis in so many other ways rejects.

Yet those oppositions did help Polanyi to provide a suite of fascinating critiques of market ideology. On one hand, *TGT* shows the power of economic ideas to shape what economic states of affairs are considered desirable or realistic, whether in terms of how economic liberalism justified the immiseration of the working classes in industrializing England or how it failed to provide intellectual resources to grasp the explosive effects of global economic integration in a system of rival nation states. On the other hand, his later work presents the reader with a powerful argument for a particular institutional approach to studying economies, as well as a suite of conceptual tools geared towards that end. Subsequent literature demonstrates that it is a straightforward matter to use those tools to understand industrial societies in a way that Polanyi did not. Given the ongoing influence of market-centric representations of the economy both in scholarly economics and in policy-thought, we think that these ideas are very likely to remain relevant for some time to come.

Notes for Chapter 1

1. A view famously summarized in Lionel Robbins' notion of economics as "the science which studies human behaviour as a relationship between ends and scarce means which have alternative uses" (Robbins, *An Essay on the Nature and Significance of Economic Science* (London: Macmillan, 1932), 15).

2. K. Gemici, "The neo-classical origins of Polanyi's self-regulating market", *Sociological Theory* 33(2) (2015), 125–47.

3. A way of thinking in which things, in this case people, have an intrinsic and unalterable essence to them which defines their nature.

4. K. Polanyi, *The Great Transformation: The Political and Economic Origins of Our Time* (Boston, MA: Beacon, 2001).

5. For example, see Polanyi, *Great Transformation*, 81 and 188.

6. *Ibid.*, 76.

7. *Ibid.*

8. *Ibid.*, 193.

9. *Ibid.*, 136.

10. *Ibid.*

11. *Ibid.*, 259–61.

12. Gemici, "Neo-classical origins", 128.

13. F. Block & M. Somers, *The Power of Market Fundamentalism: Karl Polanyi's Critique* (Cambridge, MA: Harvard University Press, 2014), 3.

14. For example, Polanyi, *Great Transformation*, 45.

15. *Ibid.*, 119.

16. *Ibid.*, 120.

17. *Ibid.*, 121.

18. K. Polanyi, *The Livelihood of Man* (New York: Academic Press, 1977), l.

19. For example, Polanyi, *Great Transformation*, 110, 141, 145.

20. *Ibid.*, 88.

21. *Ibid.*, 146.

22. *Ibid.*, 143.

23. *Ibid.*, 76.

24. *Ibid.*, 221.

25. *Ibid.*, 143.

26. For example, Polanyi, *Great Transformation*, 45, although he does distinguish Smith from later market ideology on page 117.

27. For example, Polanyi, *Great Transformation*, 45.

28. M. Watson, "The great transformation and progressive possibilities: the political limits of Polanyi's Marxian history of economic ideas", *Economy and Society*, 43:4 (2014), 603–25.

29. G. Dale, *Karl Polanyi: The Limits of the Market* (Cambridge: Polity, 2010), 81–2.

30. See Part 2 of C. Holmes, *Polanyi in Times of Populism: Vision and Contradiction in the History of Economic Ideas* (Abingdon: Routledge, 2018).

31. F. Block & M. Somers, "In the shadow of Speenhamland: social policy and the old poor law", *Politics and Society* 31:2 (2014), 283–323.

32. For his most substantial discussion of Menger, see K. Polanyi, "Carl Menger's two meanings of economic", in G. Dalton (ed.) *Studies in Economic Anthropology* (Washington, DC: American Anthropological Association, 1971), 16–24.

33. Polanyi, *Livelihood of Man*, 19; K. Polanyi [1957], *Primitive, Archaic and Modern Economies: Essays of Karl Polanyi* (New York: Doubleday Anchor, 1968), 142.

34. Polanyi, *Primitive, Archaic & Modern Economies*, 139.

35. *Ibid.*, 80.

36. *Ibid.*, 140 and Polanyi, *Livelihood of Man*.

37. Polanyi, "Carl Menger's two meanings", 19.

38. B. Jessop, "Regulationist and autopoieticist reflections on Polanyi's account of market economies and the market society", *New Political Economy* 6:2 (2001), 213–32.

39. Polanyi, *Primitive, Archaic & Modern Economies*, 96–7.

40. *Ibid.*, 148. Polanyi did not consistently include householding alongside the other three, see Dale, *Karl Polanyi*, 118.

41. Polanyi, *Livelihood of Man*, 125.

42. Some of these critiques are gathered in S. Hejeebu & D. McCloskey, "The reproving of Karl Polanyi", *Critical Review: A Journal of Politics and Society* 13:3 (1999), 285–314, and Dale, *Karl Polanyi*, 123–32.

43. Polanyi, *Primitive, Archaic & Modern Economies*, 68.

44. *Ibid.*

45. Polanyi is sometimes referred to as an institutional economist, which in essence refers to the substantive approach in his case.

46. For example, R. Abdelal, "Constructivism as an approach to international political economy", in M. Blyth (ed.) *Routledge Handbook of International Political Economy* (Abingdon: Routledge, 2009), 62–76.

47. Polanyi, *Primitive, Archaic & Modern Economies*, 66.

48. *Ibid.*, 65.

49. *Ibid.*, 61; Polanyi, *Livelihood of Man*, 20; Polanyi, "Carl Menger's two meanings".

50. *Ibid.*

51. Gemici, "Neo-classical origins", 133.

52. Polanyi, *Livelihood of Man*, 6.

53. Polanyi, *Primitive, Archaic & Modern Economies*, 119.

54. M. Granovetter, "Economic action and social structure: the problem with embeddedness", *American Journal of Sociology* 91:3 (1985), 481–510.

55. V. Zelizer, "The social meaning of money: 'special monies'", *American Journal of Sociology* 95:2 (1988), 342–77.

56. Polanyi, *Livelihood of Man*, 98.

57. M. Konings, *The Emotional Logic of Capitalism: What Progressives Have Missed* (Stanford, CA: Stanford University Press, 2015), 15.

58. See D. McKenzie, *An Engine Not A Camera: How Financial Models Shape Markets* (Cambridge, MA: MIT Press, 2008).

59. See C. Hay, *Why We Hate Politics* (Cambridge: Polity, 2007).

60. See B. Fine, "'Economic imperialism': a view from the periphery", *Review of Radical Political Economics* 34:2 (2002), 187–201; U. Mäki, "Economics imperialism: concepts and constraints", *Philosophy of the Social Sciences* 39:3 (2009), 351–80; and G. Stigler, "Economics – the imperial science?", *Scandinavian Journal of Economics* 86 (1984), 301–13.

61. For example, G. Becker, "Crime and punishment: an economic approach", in *Essays in the Economics of Crime and Punishment* (Washington, DC: National Bureau of Economic Research, 1974), 1–54.

62. For example, N. Mankiw & M. Taylor, *Economics* (Boston, MA: Cengage, 2017), 1–2.

63. *Ibid.*, 16, 31, 243.

64. For an exploration of the relevance of Polanyi's ideas to the 2010 eurozone crisis and its aftermath, see C. Holmes, "Whatever it takes: Polanyian perspectives on the eurozone crisis and the gold standard", *Economy and Society* 43:4 (2014), 582–602.

65. C. Holmes, "Seeking alpha, creating beta: charting the rise of hedge fund-based financial ecosystems", *New Political Economy* 14:4 (2009), 431–50.

66. For example, L. Fischer *et al.* (eds), *Rethinking Economics: An Introduction to Pluralist Economics* (Abingdon: Routledge, 2018).

67. D. Phillipsen, *The Little Big Number: How GDP Came to Rule the World and What to do About it* (Princeton, NJ: Princeton University Press, 2015).

68. L. Fioramonti, *Gross Domestic Problem: The Politics Behind the World's Most Powerful Number* (London: Zed Books, 2013).

69. S. Rai, C. Hoskyns & D. Thomas, "Depletion: the cost of social reproduction", *International Feminist Journal of Politics* 16 (2014), 86–105; M. Waring & G. Steinem, *If Women Counted: A New Feminist Economics* (San Francisco, CA: Harper & Row, 1988).

70. D. Webber & C. Payne, *Household Satellite Accounts, 2005 to 2014* (London: ONS, 2016).

71. Famously, even the father of modern income accounting himself, Simon Kuznets, vocalized doubts about their usefulness: S. Kuznets, "Uses of national income in peace and war" in S. Kuznets (ed.), *Uses of National Income in Peace and War* (NBER, 1942), 1–45 and S. Kuznets, "National income: a new version", *Review of Economics and Statistics* 30:3 (1948), 151–79.

72. J. Stiglitz, A. Sen & J.-P. Fitoussi (eds), *Report by the Commission on the Measurement of Economic Performance and Social Progress* (Paris: Commission on the Measurement of Economic Performance and Social Progress, 2010).

73. N. Ahmad & S.-H. Koh, "Incorporating estimates of household production of non-market services into international comparisons of material well-being", OECD Statistics Working Papers No 2011/7; "Proposals for satellite accounts" in Webber & Payne, *Household Satellite Accounts, 2005 to 2014*

74. Ahmad & Koh, "Incorporating estimates"; Webber & Payne, *Household Satellite Accounts: Valuing Informal Childcare in the UK.*

75. UN, *SNA 2008*, 6.

76. These are set to proliferate as statisticians address the problems of digital labour markets and other issues. See ONS, *The Feasibility of Measuring the Sharing Economy* (London: ONS, 2016).

77. Polanyi, "Carl Menger's two meanings", 16.

78. See Polanyi, *Primitive, Archaic & Modern Economies*, 82.

79. See *Ibid.*, 83.

2

INTERNATIONAL POLITICAL ECONOMY

Randall Germain

A social transformation of planetary range is being topped by wars of an unprecedented type in which a score of states crashed, and the contours of new empires are emerging out of a sea of blood. But this fact of demoniac violence is merely superimposed on a swift, silent current of change which swallows up the past without so much as a ripple on the surface! A reasoned analysis of the catastrophe must account both for the tempestuous action and the quiet dissolution.

Karl Polanyi[1]

KARL POLANYI AND WORLD MARKET ECONOMY[2]

For the past quarter of a century, Karl Polanyi's work has provided an important touchstone for critical analyses of the contemporary market economy, most forcefully through his magisterial book *The Great Transformation*. This text, published as the Second World War entered its crucial phase, provides a suggestive and insightful understanding of how and when, to follow Geoffrey Barraclough's evocative phrase, "humanity swings out of its old paths on to a new plane".[3] Of particular significance for the contemporary revival of Polanyi's ideas are the twin concepts "double movement" and "embedded liberalism". The idea that society would of necessity protect itself from social annihilation enabled critical scholarship to consider the many ways in which resistance to what is usually identified today as neoliberalism is both multifaceted and enduring. *The Great Transformation* provides a foundational text for much of this research.

In this chapter I consider Polanyi's contribution to one strand of political economy scholarship, that comprised by the field of international political economy, or IPE. As a field of study, IPE examines the particular way in which wealth and power are pursued and/or used to create a world market economy within which states, firms, social classes and people interact in cooperative and con-flictual ways.[4] Polanyi's work came to the sustained attention of IPE scholars in the early 1980s, when John Ruggie used the distinction between embedded and disembedded economies to identify the distinctive elements of the Bretton Woods era.[5] Ruggie argues that Polanyi's concepts enable us to grasp what is truly unique about the postwar liberal international order, namely that govern-ments finally responded definitively to the negative consequences of the "great transformation" by agreeing to subordinate international economic pressures to domestic welfare choices. Ruggie styles this innovation the "compromise of embedded liberalism", and suggests that even though the United States aban-doned the gold-exchange standard in August 1971, its commitment to the social ethos of embedded liberalism remained intact. As he puts it, the abandonment of the dollar's link to gold was a change within the Bretton Woods' regime, not a change of that regime.[6] Ruggie's use of Polanyi led many IPE scholars to deploy his work to understand the extent and degree of change in the global political economy.

In this chapter I explore how Polanyi's framework of analysis can be used by IPE scholarship to conceptualize a world market economy. Much of *The Great Transformation*, of course, focuses on explaining the origins of the great liberal experiment to release the economy from the entanglements of society, which transpired over two centuries of British political, economic and social history. Polanyi argues that to understand the collapse of the world's political economy in the twentieth century one has to recognize the contradictions contained in the efforts to consolidate an emergent market economy during the seventeenth and eighteenth centuries in relation to the operation of the British Poor Laws. But how did Polanyi understand these contradictions to be "globalized"? How did "market economy" become "world market economy", and what were the drivers and dynamics of this process? From the point of view of IPE, perhaps the most fundamental question is simply whether the features which distinguish market economy are inherently or inevitably global in scale?

My answers to these questions emphasize two important ambiguities in Polanyi's work with respect to the international or global dimension of his framework. One ambiguity concerns the role of states and the inter-state sys-tem in his analysis. Although *The Great Transformation* begins by describ-ing the four institutional foundations of nineteenth-century civilization *writ large*, the bulk of its analysis concentrates on the origins and evolution of the self-regulating market in England. Yet, the internationalization of this form of economic civilization could not occur without the operative dynamics of the balance of power system; this system is not, as Polanyi remarked, a mere "super-structural" effect.[7] Moreover, it is intimately and organically connected to the spread of empire and colonialism. Effectively, scaling up the market economy to world market economy depends upon a process of accumulation and growth which can only be delivered by an expansive state. If laissez-faire was planned, as Polanyi recognizes, such planning also took capitalism global, and in this process the state was absolutely necessary. This latter point however remains more implicit than explicit in Polanyi's schema, and in this chapter I show how, by connecting Polanyi to other historical thinkers with similar interests, we can strengthen this dimension of his analysis to reinforce the formidable critical insights that his work so rightly inspires.

Linked to the ambiguity of this scale effect is another one concerning the process by which the fictitious commodities which underlay the consolidation of a self-regulating market can in fact become globalized. Polanyi's discussion of land, labour and money assumes an equality of contribution to the scaling effect by which market economy *becomes* world market economy. However, land, labour and money are not all scalable in the same way. I argue below that land is not an inherently scalable "commodity", fictitious or otherwise, while labour is only scalable within certain specified limits. Money, on the other hand, is eminently scalable, and because modern money is also fiat money such scalability generates a significant power capacity for that state which issues world money. It turns out, in other words, that once again the state is the crucial enabling instrument for the globalization of Polanyi's fictitious commodities. By clarifying the role of the state in connection to how fictitious commodities actually become globalized, we can see more clearly why capitalism is at the same time global in character but yet anchored fundamentally to a national (i.e., state) foundation.

I unpack these ambiguities over three sections. First, I canvass how IPE has made use of Polanyi's work. The principal point I wish to make here is that IPE scholarship can profitably expand its use of Polanyi. I then reconstruct the moves Polanyi makes to go from market economy to world market economy. I focus here in particular on the globalizing effects of the fictitious commodities of land, labour and money, to demonstrate that while land remains a localized commodity, labour and money have many important international or global dimensions which quite naturally take us from market economy to world market economy. But it is empire and colonialism which effect this transition most concretely, which means that the state and the inter-state system are complicit, indeed necessary, for the emergence of world market economy. It is in the organic connection between labour and the state, but above all between money and the state, that I anchor Polanyi's most important (but under-recognized) contribution to IPE scholarship. I follow this section by connecting Polanyi's work to that of two other historical thinkers, E. H. Carr and Fernand Braudel, in order to amplify and consolidate the global dimensions of his framework. In different and useful ways their work complements and expands the way in which Polanyi's framework can be scaled towards the "global". I close by reframing how IPE scholarship might better use Polanyi's work to interrogate more deeply significant points of change and transition which appear possible in light of tensions evident in the current historical juncture. IPE scholarship has been fixated by the impending crisis of global capitalism for nearly three decades now, and it is my contention that Polanyi's work can help us to understand why global capital remains robust and vital in the face of seemingly continual crisis and instability.

IPE ENCOUNTERS POLANYI: EMBEDDED
LIBERALISM AND THE DOUBLE MOVEMENT

The impact of *The Great Transformation* on mainstream social science from its publication in 1944 to the revival of what today we call neoliberalism in the early 1980s was uneven and episodic,[8] and in this context the academic field of IPE is no exception.[9] There would no disagreement, however, on when IPE as a field of study first encountered Polanyi in a substantive and meaningful way: with John Ruggie's influential 1982 account of how to interpret the so-called breakdown of the Bretton Woods regime. Ruggie's ground-breaking analysis departed from most of his interlocutors in the regime debate by asking about the social purpose that regimes might serve. This inside-out question was expressly anchored by Ruggie in Polanyi's distinction between embedded and disembedded economies. The agreements struck at Bretton Woods refashioned the nineteenth-century authority–market relationship by re-embedding international regimes into the entanglements of welfare states as they were developing within the wartime allies.[10] This distinction thus helped Ruggie to develop what he called a "generative grammar" of liberalism to understand the evolution of international authority during this period.[11]

The idea of movement between embedded and disembedded economic structures proved very suggestive to many IPE scholars, who also paid attention to Polanyi's conception of the double movement to help account for the rise of neoliberalism beginning in the 1980s.[12] Perhaps the most complete analysis of the double movements (plural) of the twentieth century is provided by Mark Blyth, who traces the rise and demise of the welfare state in Sweden and the United States over this period.[13] Blyth goes beyond Ruggie to focus on the intersection of social purpose (rendered as ideas) and organized interest groups to argue that frameworks of ideas are constructed or built up in certain ways so as to stabilize meaning in uncertain times (such as during the 1970s when the Bretton Woods system unravelled, or during the economic collapse of the Great Depression). His major contribution here is to add a layer of ideational organization to Polanyi's rather indeterminate notion of how double movements actually form and function.[14] Blyth's work is a good representation of the principal use made of Polanyi within IPE as a field of study.

There are of course exceptions to Polanyi's use within IPE as described above. Geoffrey Underhill anticipates a key strand of my argument below, for example, when he emphasizes how Polanyi highlights the critical role of the state within the construction of the global political economy. He does this, however, within a "Polanyi-as-inspiration" model in his survey of IPE's history.[15] More critically, Hannes Lacher has taken issue with the way in which IPE scholars have taken the contradictions which Polanyi identifies within liberalism, but without see-ing the necessity of transcending the laws governing market economy entirely.[16] Contra Ruggie, Lacher argues that the idea of an embedded form of liberalism would not have been embraced by Polanyi for the basic reason that it would have maintained intact the contradictions which make liberalism a utopian enter-prise. He suggests that if we follow Polanyi's arguments we should not expect the compromise of embedded liberalism to make land, labour and money any less fictitious today than they were in the nineteenth century. Here Lacher's cri-tique in some ways parallels non-IPE scholarship on Polanyi, which tacks more closely to Polanyi's uncomfortable accommodation to postwar developments.[17]

I want to suggest that the unique contribution which Polanyi can make to IPE resides in the insights his work provides for thinking about the emergence, consolidation and organization of world market economy. As Ruggie and others in IPE recognize, Polanyi's conceptual framework provides a unique purchase on a singularly important dimension of knowledge, namely how market econ-omy was able to envelop the world and establish a cohesive structure of global political economy. Ruggie's invocation of social purpose is one way to think about this,[18] but there are other analytical levers which Polanyi offers. In the next section I move beyond the embedded/disembedded distinction and the double movement to consider the operative principles of market economy itself as a highly useful feature of Polanyi's work. If our goal is to understand how market economy becomes world market economy, we can usefully re-engage with some of the basic principles that Polanyi identified in terms of the operation of the self-regulating market.

FROM "MARKET ECONOMY" TO "WORLD MARKET ECONOMY": THE GLOBALIZATION OF FICTITIOUS COMMODITIES

The Great Transformation famously begins by outlining the four institutions of nineteenth century civilization: the balance-of-power system, the interna-tional gold standard, the self-regulating market, and the liberal state. But it is the self-regulating market that underpins these institutions: "The key to the institutional system of the nineteenth century lay in the laws governing market economy".[19] And at the heart of market economy are a trio of elements which, when bound together in a certain way, make market economy possible: land, labour and money. Polanyi calls these "fictitious commodities", because in fact throughout human history they have never been available for exchange on the basis of price as determined by the "laws" of supply and demand. Their availability for exchange has always been encoded by society's customs, needs and social hierarchies. To free the market from social entanglements, to make it self-regulating, requires nothing less than an unprecedented social experiment which Polanyi recognized to be utopian in endeavour.[20] This "great transformation" was the fatal flaw of nineteenth-century civilization, out of which came the fascist scourge.

As the heading to this chapter suggests, Polanyi's vision of nineteenth-century civilization is worldwide in scope. Market economy, although initially a British phenomenon, spread to envelop the world; for him, market economy quite naturally develops into world market economy. This is why, at several points in *The Great Transformation*, he demonstrates precisely how the plight of colonized peoples parallels the horrors visited upon English labourers in the seventeenth and eighteenth centuries; both have been forcefully subjected to the laws of market economy as applied to their land and labour.[21] In this sense, we may say that, for Polanyi, the disembedding of "land" and "labour" generates "market economy", where the agent that "releases" land and labour to transform them from social into fictitious commodities is the (liberal) state. The feature I wish to emphasize in this dynamic is the role of the state: as we will see, scaling upwards to a world market economy requires a globally-oriented or expansive state.

But how precisely can land and labour as fictitious commodities be scaled to a world market? For land, Polanyi emphasizes three ways in which the liberal experiment released it from the grip of society: by privatizing the usability of land through enclosures; by making land available for the uses of industrial capitalism (for example, by building factories and settlements in formerly rural agricultural areas); and by mobilizing colonial and foreign lands for food production destined for Britain and Continental Europe.[22] This last feature was necessitated by the rise of industrial towns and the demand from their populations for cheap food: "With this last step land and its produce were finally fitted into the scheme of a self-regulating world market".[23] However, it is important to recognize here that it is not the land itself which is scaled to a world market, but its produce. Land cannot be "globalized"; rather, it is the produce of land which is mobilized for trade. In this context, Polanyi sees an organic connection between free trade and land as a global fictitious commodity; free trade is the instrument by which a world market in land is established.[24]

We need to be cognizant here of the shift Polanyi makes from the usability of land to its produce as the key dynamic of its global mobilization. Land itself, of course, cannot be moved; it is a fixed asset. It may be bought and sold, but ownership has no choice but to respect its immobility. It is this immobility which must lead us to refuse Polanyi's suggestion that land itself can be scalable in terms of its produce; there is, technically speaking, no world market for land in the way in which we may talk (within parameters) of a world market for commodities such as oil, or even in a certain way for human capital and skills. The mobilization of the produce of land through trade, which is Polanyi's entry point to thinking about the scalability of land as a global fictitious commodity, is only weakly connected to the organization of a world market economy. As he notes elsewhere, trade and markets do not have an inherent and organic connection; trade has historically been organized through administrative means rather than through market mechanisms.[25] My claim here is that the place of land within Polanyi's framework, while useful for how we think about the origins of market economy, becomes less so for our thinking about how market economy becomes scaled towards world market economy. This is an important ambiguity to acknowledge if we are to harness his work for our understanding of IPE.

If the idea of land as a fictitious commodity contains ambiguities for assembling a conception of world market economy, how does the idea of labour as a fictitious commodity fare? Here Polanyi is on stronger ground, for labour can in fact become commodified on a global scale precisely because of its mobility. It is not only that the produce of labour – via trade – can become a globally circulating feature of market economy, but that labour itself can circulate to build, extend or advance the institutions of the market economy and the creation of value and profit. Waves of migration throughout human history have significantly affected how everyday and luxury goods have been made, bought and sold, while war and plunder have displaced and reorganized populations in important ways.[26] Mobility is the dynamic that enables labour to become a constituent foundation of world market economy, whether voluntary or forced. In this sense, and unlike the ambiguous logic Polanyi uses to connect land to world market economy, it is easy to see how labour as a fictitious commodity can be understood to help frame world market economy.

Within Polanyi's discussion of how labour as a fictitious commodity helps to underpin a self-regulating world market, or what I am calling world market economy, one attribute stands out as definitive: the push and pull of class formation.[27] Class of course is not a principal motor force of history for Polanyi, but it nevertheless occupies a central place in his explanation of the evolution of market economy. In this respect, his key claim is that although the working class and market economy were conjoined at their birth in England, the industrial working class played only a minor role in its own early formation.[28] Much more important were the roles of the landed aristocracy, the Church and the emergent industrial capitalists, whose actions to advance the market economy or protect society shaped nineteenth-century civilization. As Polanyi notes with respect to the critical decade from the repeal of the Poor Laws to the climax of the Chartist movement, "The laboring people themselves were hardly a factor in this great movement the effect of which was, figuratively speaking, to allow them to survive the Middle Passage. They had almost as little to say in the determination of their own fate as the black cargo of Hawkins' ships."[29]

Here we encounter a very interesting anomaly as we explore how Polanyi uses the idea of fictitious commodities to move from market economy to world market economy: labour, as a "commodity", is essentially inert at the very moment when it scales up to its world historical presence. Its scalability, in other words, is left rather indeterminate by Polanyi. The key agency, of course, is the state in its colonial and imperial form. British and European imperialism took its most expansive and dynamic form expressly during the period of the nineteenth century, when the agency of the working class was – according to Polanyi – effectively quiescent. What this means for labour as a constituent element of world market economy is precisely that its global form relied on the state for its shape. In this sense an important part of Polanyi's main argument – that the self-regulating market is the "fount and matrix" of nineteenth-century civilization – is reversed. The "fount and matrix" of the self-regulating market, we may say, is actually the state, at least insofar as it pertains to the organization of world market economy.

Another way of making this point is to recognize that the scalability of labour as a fictitious commodity is directly connected to the dynamism or expansiveness of the state. And it needs to be stressed that it is not only the "liberal" state that can be expansive and dynamic: it is all states. This recognition breaks down the tight link Polanyi establishes between the self-regulating market and the liberal state as key institutions of nineteenth-century civilization. In fact, non-liberal states could and did participate in "releasing" labour from the strictures of society just as much as liberal states. In other words, the origins of labour as a *global* fictitious commodity are not solely connected to the self-regulating market and its political off-shoots. Labour's scalability extends to such multi-causal phenomena as imperialism and colonialism. I pursue in the next section how this feature of labour as a fictitious commodity sits within the institution of the balance of power, but for now I simply wish to draw attention to the constrained manner in which labour can be considered a global fictitious commodity. It is scalable – unlike land – but it requires an ancillary support structure which can only be provided by the state.

I turn now to consider the final leg of Polanyi's triptych of fictitious commodities, money. The laws of market economy treat land and labour as factors of production; their combination generates whatever it is we consume as the necessities or luxuries of life. Money, on the other hand, determines the price level. It is central to the organization of business, and its availability (or scarcity) affects demand for the products of the market economy. Land and labour together generate the supply of goods on the market, while the organization and availability of money determines the demand for goods. Polanyi's principal insight here is that where money is organized on the basis of a quantity of something which has its own inherent and objective value, such as gold, this organization inevitably plays havoc with the normal operation of the economy because of the sudden and capricious volatility it imposes on the price level. His claim is that businesses cannot be sustainably profitable under such a monetary organization, and yet the classical doctrine of money maintained by political economists from Hume to Marx obscured this tension.[30] Just as with the organization of land and labour, the liberal conception of laissez-faire with respect to money makes societal intervention for the purposes of self-protection inevitable. In the case of money, the form this intervention takes is central banking.[31]

The conceptual move Polanyi makes to take our thinking about money from market economy to world market economy rests on the simultaneous involvement of central banks in both of these arenas. He fully recognizes that the classical doctrine of money is an illusion within the borders of national economies. Not only central banks but private banking institutions in fact create money by printing it – he calls this "token" money which today we would call *fiat* currency. Such an elastic (i.e., expandable) source of money and credit stabilizes how business is able to use money, and dampens to a considerable extent its price volatility.[32] Critically for Polanyi, this means that money has ceased to act solely as a commodity – as a means of exchange – and has become instead something different, namely a means of payment, or purchasing power. The reality of "token" money is that it is a claim on resources rather than simply a means to facilitate the exchange of resources.[33] And as a claim on resources, it is elastic and negotiable precisely because it is future-oriented. It is in this sense that money is political, which correspondingly means that the pursuit of monetary policy by central banks must inevitably draw them "into the sphere of politics".[34]

But token money has a limitation: it cannot function internationally due to its inability to circulate as a means of payment beyond national borders. Here a globally-acceptable form of commodity money is in fact required for foreign trade. Thus, in Polanyi's formulation, money becomes a global commodity precisely by adopting both a token and a commodity form. Central banks issue or support token money domestically even as they support the movement of gold (a globally-acceptable form of commodity money) abroad for international payment purposes. It is the necessity of this relationship between national money and international payments which makes the scalability of money as a fictitious commodity not only natural but also inevitable. Money, in other words, is entirely a global fictitious commodity. It is global because for international exchange to occur, purchasing power must be made available for that purpose. And it is fictitious because this medium of payment is also inherently political (or negotiated) by virtue of relying on central banks for its operationalization. When this operationalization breaks down, the negotiated (or fictitious) nature of international money becomes revealed as a social convention rather than as an objective, natural mechanism that operates according to the "laws" of market economy. In Polanyi's framework, money is inherently scalable, and because of this it is the most politicized feature of the world market economy.

At the same time, it is the high degree of politicization which makes money also the weakest link among his triptych of fictitious commodities. Money was the natural conductor of the new nationalism that emerged during the 1920s and 1930s, as states moved decisively to bring money under formal national control in order to refashion world market economy during this period.[35] Polanyi's account here highlights the central role of the state in the negotiation of world market economy, and we can extend this emphasis to include also the organic links between money and empire as imperialism and colonialism spread in the closing decades of the nineteenth century. In effect, the international organization of money enabled imperialism to prosper during this period, as it facilitated the subordination of colonies to their metropoles through enforced participation in financial centres controlled by imperial states.[36] Whether in Africa, the Middle East, Asia or Central and Latin America, monetary connections between imperial centres and colonial peripheries largely determined colonial development and autonomy. Here we can go beyond Polanyi to amplify the reliance of world market economy on a particular configuration of global money which surpasses the role he equated with *haute finance*. *Haute finance* was itself enabled by global money; it was not the enabler of global money.

We are now in a position to reassess the utility for IPE of Polanyi's contribution to political economy. This contribution hinges, as much IPE scholarship correctly appreciates, on his understanding of how the contemporary organization of political economy is inherently global in scale and scope. But much of this literature misconstrues the well-spring of this organization, which is less connected to the embeddedness of the economy in society and the possibilities of the double movement, and more strongly connected to the particular way in which Polanyi understands the self-regulating market to be global in form. My claim here is that even though Polanyi is correct to focus on the laws of market economy to explain the emergence of world market economy, these "laws" do not operate quite as Polanyi laid them out in *The Great Transformation*. Most importantly, his three fictitious commodities are not equally or evenly scalable to a global form. Land is simply not scalable to a global form, while labour is scalable but only under certain conditions that are uniquely determined by states. Critically, however, money is inherently scalable, but like labour only in league with states because its form and utility rest on the political foundations of state activity. And it is necessary to recognize that this relationship applies to all states, and not only "liberal" states. Polanyi's misspecification of this latter point helps us to understand how he could fail to perceive accurately the postwar direction of the global political economy. In the next section, I correct for his misspecification by connecting his work to that of two historical thinkers who, in different ways, are able to stabilize Polanyi's ambiguities in a useful manner.

POLANYI AND HISTORICAL IPE: CONNECTIONS AND COMPLEMENTARITIES

There are of course many scholars whose work might be used to complement Polanyi's conception of world market economy. I have chosen for this purpose the work of E. H. Carr and Fernand Braudel, for two sets of reasons. First, like Polanyi, both of these thinkers are historically oriented scholars who in general approach their subjects through what might be termed an historical lens. This means that they are each sensitive to the flow of historical time as a unique attribute of how we come to understand the social world. They therefore share a similar epistemological approach to the broad problem of knowledge construction in the social sciences.[37] Second, their work can clarify the ambiguities and extend with greater precision the insights of how fictitious commodities might be scaled from market economy to world market economy. In the case of Carr it is the role of the state in globalizing labour and money through instrumentalities peculiar to the state. Without abandoning the balance of power system, Carr provides a more persuasive account of how the state is integral to the scaling up of labour and money as global fictitious commodities, namely by linking the state to imperial and colonial actions as part of the effort to "control" the inter-state system. And Braudel adds an important further rationale for the natural movement of money to world market economy, namely the secular increase in the monetization of the economy. Braudel traces this over a longer time span than Polanyi works with, but his focus is entirely in agreement with Polanyi's understanding of the political nature of money as a product of the emerging nexus between money, capital and the state in the modern period. Supplementing Polanyi's framework with insights from the work of Carr and Braudel directs our attention to fundamental and enduring features of world market economy that we need to take account of even today.[38]

I have noted above the way in which Polanyi somewhat ambiguously considers the balance-of-power system to be "superstructural" in its effects. For him it is a kind of scaffolding that reinforces the more fundamental attributes of the self-regulating market at the global or international level. Bringing Carr's work into direct conversation with Polanyi corrects for this ambiguity. For Carr, who in his writings from the late 1930s through to the 1950s should be considered a scholar of historical international political economy rather than international relations,[39] the balance of power must be understood in relation to more fundamental forms of political relations which operate across both domestic and international levels. The balance of power is not an institution in its own right; rather, it is an effect of state behaviour within an over-arching inter-state system. While the balance of power between states at any single point in time might of course play a role in helping to generate political outcomes, Carr argues that it is more accurate to acknowledge that it is states themselves which fundamentally produce these outcomes. In this sense it is relations among political authorities that determine the balance of power at particular moments in time, with these relations being affected by changes in the organization and structure of states, which are in turn the preeminent form of modern political authority. This deeper and more political understanding of the connection between the balance of power within the inter-state system and the evolving structures of leading states in the first half of the twentieth century allows Carr to better capture the dynamic which enables market economy to become world market economy.

This dynamic is entirely connected to the historical advance of mass industrialization and the concomitant turn towards imperialism and colonialism by powerful states in the 50 years between 1890 and 1940.[40] It is these states and their actions which transform market economy into world market economy. The mechanism for this transformation, for Carr, is the planning for world market activity provided by great powers. In his time, he sees no real alternative to some form of great power condominium arising out of the decades long experience of global war and economic collapse. Liberalism as an organizing principle was no longer able to furnish suitable political direction either domestically or internationally. Like Polanyi, Carr could see that the liberal era was over, and that planning by the state and its agencies was necessary to repair the social and economic damage wrought by two decades of continual crisis. Such planning, he believed, demanded the supersession of the liberal form of state, and he located the principal agency for this in the mass mobilization of labour and society more generally, which he saw as a product of a growing historical consciousness on the part of the generation of people who had come of age during the "twenty years crisis". The critical point here is that Carr saw a renewed and democratized state at the centre of a new global politics which would by definition be organized outside of the established framework of traditional liberal ideas, pushed from within by the mass mobilization of a new society composed of organizations and institutions that were modern and social democratic in their social relations. Adding Carr to Polanyi thus corrects for the ambiguous place of the state in establishing world market economy. It is (all) states that stand behind world market economy, because the inter-state system is an organic (rather than a superstructural) element of the expansion of market economy. On this point Carr is crystal clear.

The value of supplementing Polanyi with Carr's analysis can be seen in a short piece published by Polanyi in 1945, in which he considers how far the international system has been transformed and its future prospects.[41] The major premise of this article is that inter-state relations will revolve after 1945 around the pursuit of regional planning in Europe by the Soviet Union and a renewed focus on liberal internationalism by the United States, with Britain facing a major choice of whom to support. Much of this piece builds on themes developed in *The Great Transformation*, but with a more clear-sighted appreciation of the depth to which the United States (and American society in general) would hue to and support the extension of liberal capitalism to a war-ravaged world. The way in which he frames Britain's choice, however, belies his underdeveloped conception of the state. For Polanyi, the choice between America and Russia for Britain involves a choice between regional planning and what he calls "universal capitalism", a choice he encourages Britons to make on the basis of the future benefits which he believes regional planning will bring to the world. There is little in his analysis, however, of how far either the British state is itself "invested" in universal capitalism, or of the capacity of the British state to deliver a postwar future without want or fear solely using its own resources. Indeed, he has a rather naïve view of the state, and this is especially evident in his assessment of the Soviet Union's postwar ambitions to be a good neighbour without imperial pretensions. Deepening the analysis of the state as the central instrument through which world market economy could be built, as Carr fully recognized, is indispensable to correct this ambiguity in Polanyi's framework of analysis.[42]

Turning to Braudel, his value-added in relation to Polanyi lies with how his work deepens the consideration of money as a fictitious commodity. While Polanyi provides a brilliant critique of money as a commodity, and nicely demonstrates the tensions at work in how central banks operate in two relatively distinct spheres (domestic and international), there is a lack of agency in his treatment of money in terms of its development over time. Specifically, there is no clear sense in Polanyi of how money is connected to world market economy as a product of political negotiation. Domestically we can see this, but not at the international level. Yet, in reality there were world monies in the nineteenth and twentieth centuries, just as there continues to be a world money in the twenty-first century, and it is states which either issue such world monies and/or enable the conditions for others to create them. In the nineteenth century it was sterling which acted as world money, while since 1945 it has been the US dollar that has acted in this capacity.[43] And as Polanyi correctly understood, in both cases these currencies are more than a means of exchange, they are also a means of payment that represent claims by their holders on resources in the real world. This is why the capacity to issue such a claim in the first place both requires and reinforces political power. There is thus an organic connection between world money and some form of world political authority: they go together as part and parcel of world market economy. Again we require a way to directly connect the state to world market economy because Polanyi's framework of fictitious commodities does not quite get us there.

This is where Braudel becomes extremely useful. Throughout his three volume work on the consolidation of world capitalism, he painstakingly follows the growth of what he calls the "world-economy", or what we more commonly call today the global political economy.[44] A key feature of this growth involves an expanded role for money, most importantly through the monetization or financialization of economic transactions. At the start of the period of his enquiry in the fourteenth century, large parts of the world-economy (or world-economies, as there were several at this time) did not require money to function. Economic exchange was organized around status and reciprocity; prices were administered by many different types of authorities. Polanyi would consider these examples of "embedded economies". However, as webs of economic exchange expanded, and most importantly for Braudel as the state was drawn into supporting different aspects of economic activity in exchange for resources, a close relationship developed between money, capital and the state. By the eighteenth century, the world-economy had become dominated by capitalists – their money and capital – and fully supported by states in general but great powers above all. There came into effect a money-capital-state nexus at the heart of the modern world-economy, even if it passed through a series of stages where it was anchored by different cities and national economies.[45] In other words, Braudel provides us with a form of agency that actively globalizes money as a fictitious commodity. With the help of his model we can easily understand how, as far as money is concerned, market economy becomes world market economy.[46]

Complementing Polanyi with the insights provided by E. H. Carr and Fernand Braudel with respect to the role of the state helps us to understand the inherently global scale and scope of market economy. It helps to clarify the ambiguities Polanyi leaves us with in terms of how the fictitious commodities of labour and money actually become *global* fictitious commodities. Together, the work of these three scholars suggests how we might explore the durability of global capitalism in our time, including why it remains cohesive and coherent despite a seemingly unending series of crises and shocks.

CONCLUSION

As other chapters in this volume testify, the extent to which Karl Polanyi's work continues to resonate with efforts to comprehend the basic structures and features of our modern political economy is remarkable. Within the field of IPE, some of the most prescient analyses of structural changes in the global political economy harbour at least some debt to the distinctions between embedded and disembedded economies and the double movement which he pioneered, and the field as a whole has certainly benefitted from the critical and holistic approach to which he adhered. But as I have argued, there are important ambiguities to note in his effort to scale up market economy to world market economy based upon the operationalization of fictitious commodities. Most importantly, this scaling effect is predicated on a reversal of what Polanyi considered to be the "fount and matrix" of nineteenth-century civilization, namely the self-regulating market. Instead, my analysis suggests that we need to understand how world market economy is itself anchored in the expansive role of the state in its general rather than only liberal form; it is the state that should be considered the "fount and matrix" of nineteenth-century civilization. Moreover, we have yet to overcome this foundational element of world market economy: to the extent that we can identify a twenty-first century civilization, the state continues to be its foundational anchor.

But to get to his point we need to complement Polanyi's framework with insights from the work of E. H. Carr and Fernand Braudel. Carr's work helps us to clarify and amplify the general role of the state by situating the balance of power not as a superstructural effect of the self-regulating market, but as a political effect of the behaviour of states, and great powers above all. For Carr, the inter-state system is a creation of great power behaviour, and it is the expansive desires of these states, and the efforts of other states to respond to great power behaviour, which explains how the balance of power operates at any given point in time. Critically, it is the response of states to the pressures of industrialization and mass political mobilization that accounts for the shape of domestic and international politics after the Second World War. Here his work aligns with Polanyi's analysis and extends it to help account for how the double movement became, for a moment, subject to the planning imperative which gripped the Allied nations in the decades immediately after 1945, and which was further extended to colonial nations in the great wave of independence movements in the 1950s and 1960s. Like Polanyi, for Carr the key to the sustainability of postwar transformations lay with advances in democratization that he saw to be the consequence of the mass political mobilization brought on by the Great Depression and war years. Neither he nor Polanyi were prepared to consider that this movement itself could stall and even be reversed.[47] Nevertheless, their conjoined framework helps us to understand that the "fount and matrix" of the contemporary world market economy is in fact those states which are also great or expansive powers.

Braudel's work further supplements Polanyi's framework by cementing his deeply insightful analysis of money as a fictitious commodity. In effect, Braudel's historical narrative firmly yokes the fictitious nature of money to the state, insofar as he demonstrates in a compelling manner how the weight of money in the economy expanded in lock-step with the growth of state power and capacity, which was in turn generated by the instantiation of capital with the state. In Braudel's bold argumentation, it was not until capital and the state became conjoined that the era of industrial capitalism took flight.[48] Here we can use Braudel's work to extend Polanyi's insights about money by linking the circulation of money as capital within not simply a market economy but the world-economy in its entirety. Braudel understands that it is world money which acts as a means of payment precisely because world money is produced by the intersection of central banks and banking networks anchored by cities that are at the heart of "their" world-economies, whether Amsterdam in the eighteenth century or New York in the twentieth century. And importantly, he is alert to how such a constellation of interlocking factors can post-date the material forces which had initially aligned to bring them into being. Guilders and sterling acted as world money long after the material economic conditions in Holland and England that had come together to enable their roles had atrophied or collapsed. This is the central point about world money that Braudel urges us to consider: the dominance of a national money acting as a world money can outlast the economic dominance of its national foundations, so long as the political influence and leverage of its issuing state persists (for whatever reason). As with Carr, turning to Braudel to complement Polanyi's work clarifies the ambiguities concerning the role of the state in his conception of how market economy becomes world market economy.

Extrapolating from the above, we can say that as a field of study, there is much more that IPE can make of Polanyi's framework of analysis. Suitably refocused and reinforced, IPE can use Polanyi to help understand some of the most significant features of the modern world market economy. If we clarify and extend his conception of the state and insert it more forcefully into how we understand labour and money as fictitious commodities came to be globalized, we will be given tools to explore the diverse ways in which key states – but America above all – shape and direct, or "superintend" as Panitch and Gindin style it, a globally expansive form of capitalism.[49] The strength of global capitalism today lies precisely in the way in which it is anchored simultaneously in the American economy and its national state; it is at once expansively global and decidedly national. Those analyses which fail to recognize the organic connection between American nationalism and global capital risk obscuring how much American society (and Americans themselves) are willing to pay to keep the world open for American business, or indeed how open American business is to non-Americans who emulate these ideals.[50]

In any event, states and above all great powers must be at the centre of our analysis. It is also my contention that IPE scholars can make more use of Polanyi's penetrating insights into the role of money as a global fictitious commodity. Eric Helleiner, in his "Polanyian" analysis of the contemporary global financial order nearly two decades ago, charted an important opening here, by adding to his consideration of the double movement also a focus on the many ways in which state policies are fundamental to any understanding of the shape and future direction of global finance.[51] His analysis, however, is muted in its consideration of how exactly the American state is necessary for the continued centrality of the dollar, which remains today's only genuine world money. It is the negotiated nature of the dollar, in the face of many who argue that America is in decline, which should be of central concern to IPE scholars today.[52] For the dollar remains very much world money, in spite of rather than because of what the current administration of US President Donald Trump actually does. Again, we need to return to the extraordinary power and capacity of the American state – which is more than just the president – and its involvement with global capital to explain the enduring status of the dollar as the world's top currency, which helps in turn to account for the enduring positon of American hegemony as the critical single feature of world market economy. Polanyi's insights into how world money acts as purchasing power rather than simply a medium of exchange is enormously fruitful here, and with a little help from the work of Fernand Braudel they offer much to build upon.

Although Polanyi rather spectacularly misread the direction of post-1945 politics, his analytical framework retains much traction for contemporary analysis. Especially promising are a modern conception of how two of his three fictitious commodities can also be understood as global fictitious commodities that have a central role to play as anchors of world market economy. But to get there we need to place his work in conversation with others in order to upgrade his understanding of the role of the state. Suitably modified and refocused, Polanyi's framework should become an important part of the analytical toolkit for critical political economy, including the field of international political economy.

Notes for Chapter 2

1. K. Polanyi, *The Great Transformation* (Boston, MA: Beacon, [1944] 2001), 4.
2. I would like to thank Ilirjan Shehu for valuable research assistance in writing this chapter.

3. G. Barraclough, *An Introduction to Contemporary History* (Harmondsworth: Penguin, 1964), 12.

4. This is a definition of IPE that builds on widely used formulations. See B. Cohen, *International Political Economy: An Intellectual History* (Princeton, NJ: Princeton University Press, 2008), 2–3; R. Gilpin, *The Political Economy of International Relations* (Princeton, NJ: Princeton University Press, 1987), 8–9; S. Strange, "International economics and international relations: a case of mutual neglect", in R. Tooze & C. May (eds), *Authority and Markets: Susan Strange's Writings on International Political Economy* (Basingstoke: Palgrave Macmillan, [1970], 2002), 187–8; and especially P. Katzenstein, R. Keohane & S. Krasner, "*International Organization* and the study of world politics", *International Organization* 52:4 (1998), 647.

5. J. Ruggie, "International regimes, transactions, and change: embedded liberalism in the postwar economic order", in Ruggie, *Constructing the World Polity* (London: Routledge, [1982] 1998), 63–84.

6. *Ibid.*, 78.

7. Polanyi, *Great Transformation*, 3. As he further explains: "In other words, only on the background of the new economy could the balance-of-power system make general conflagrations avoidable" (17).

8. F. Block & M. Somers, *The Power of Market Fundamentalism: Karl Polanyi's Critique* (Cambridge, MA: Harvard University Press, 2014), 6.

9. In most disciplinary histories of IPE, Polanyi is either absent or receives brief mention as an inspiration for pioneers of the field. Examples of Polanyi's absence include perhaps the most widely cited standard history of the field, Katzenstein, Keohane & Krasner, "*International Organization* and the study of world politics", and an influential critical alternative, J. Hobson, "Revealing the Eurocentric foundations of IPE: a critical historiography of the discipline from the classical to the modern era", *Review of International Political Economy* 20:5 (2013), 1024–54. Examples of Polanyi's inspirational role can be found in Cohen, *International Political Economy*, 18–19, and in R. Cox, "The 'British' school in global context", in N. Phillips & C. Weaver (eds), *International Political Economy: Debating the Past, Present and Future* (Abingdon: Routledge, 2009), 123–4.

10. Others have deployed Polanyi to identify the push and pull of domestic interests as against international economic pressures in connection to the failure of the interwar global economy. See, for example, B. Eichengreen, *Globalizing Capital: A History of the International Monetary System*, second edition (Princeton, NJ: Princeton University Press, 2008), 3.

11. Ruggie, "International regimes, transactions and change", 64 and 78.

12. For examples of this use of Polanyi, see E. Helleiner, "Great transformations: a Polanyian perspective on the contemporary global financial order", *Studies in Political Economy* 48 (1995), 149–64; and M. Bernard, "Ecology, political economy and the counter-movement: Karl Polanyi and the second great transformation", in S. Gill & J. Mittelman (eds), *Innovation and Transformation in International Studies* (Cambridge: Cambridge University Press, 1997), 75–89. It should be noted that Helleiner's consideration of Polanyi also includes a focus on the role of the state and its relationship to how capitalism is organized, in this case in terms of the global financial system.

13. M. Blyth, *Great Transformations: Economic Ideas and Institutional Change in the Twentieth Century* (Cambridge: Cambridge University Press, 2002).

14. *Ibid.*, 274.

15. G. Underhill, "State, market and global political economy: genealogy of an (inter-?) discipline", *International Affairs* 76:4 (2000), 820.

16. H. Lacher, "The politics of the market: re-reading Karl Polanyi", *Global Society* 13:3 (1999), 131–26. There are also those, however, who argue that Polanyi was not so much mis-read as mistaken in the fundamentals of his analysis of the tensions within global capitalism. See for example S. Halperin, "Dynamics of conflict and system change: *The Great Transformation* revisited", *European Journal of International Relations* 10:2 (2004), 263–306. Slightly less critical views are taken by Kirshner, who credits Keynes rather than Polanyi with the idea of "embedded liberalism", and Nitzan and Bichler, who remain unconvinced that Polanyi's conception of labour as a "fictitious commodity" holds much explanatory value. J. Kirshner, "Keynes, capital mobility and the crisis of embedded liberalism", *Review of International Political Economy* 6:3 (1999), 314 and 317; J. Nitzan & S. Bichler, *Capital as Power: A Study of Order and Creorder* (Abingdon: Routledge, 2009), 86–7.

17. See more generally Block & Somers, *The Power of Market Fundamentalism*. There is of course no such thing as unanimity over how precisely to interpret Polanyi among all such interlocutors, but their starting point – unlike Ruggie and much IPE scholarship – retains the ambiguity exhibited by Polanyi towards postwar developments. Some of the sources of such ambiguity are explored in G. Dale, "Karl Polanyi's *Great Transformation*: perverse effects, protectionism and *gemeinschaft*", *Economy and Society* 37:4 (2008), 495–524.

18. Indeed, as IPE as a field has come to engage with the tradition of constructivism in the social sciences, many have begun to associate Polanyi with this tradition of analysis (rather than the traditions with which Polanyi himself would normally be associated). See Ruggie, *Constructing the World Polity*, 19; and R. Abdelal, "Constructivism as an approach to international political economy", in M. Blyth (ed.), *Routledge Handbook of International Political Economy* (Abingdon: Routledge, 2009), 65 and 67.

19. Polanyi, *Great Transformation*, 3.

20. *Ibid.*, 29, 138–9.

21. *Ibid.*, 157–61, 164, 182–3.

22. *Ibid.*, 179–83.

23. *Ibid.*, 179.

24. For Polanyi, the scalability of land is directly connected to what it can produce, which means that its scalability is a function of trade: "Although the soil cannot be physically mobilized, its produce can, if transportation facilities and law permits" (*Great Transformation*, 180).

25. K. Polanyi, "Marketless trading in Hammurabi's time", in K. Polanyi, C. Arensberg & H. Pearson (eds), *Trade and Markets in the Early Empires: Economies in History and Theory* (Glencoe, IL: Free Press, 1957), 12–26.

26. E. Wolf, *Europe and the People Without History* (Berkeley, CA: University of California Press, 1982).

27. Polanyi, *Great Transformation*, Ch. 14. Polanyi's chief concern with class analysis is the non-economic sources of class formation and agency. He refuses to consider classes as the "product" of economic interests, even if their agency does bear its imprint. Instead, for him, classes are primarily a product of the organization of society (*Great Transformation*, 152–6).

28. *Ibid.*, 101.

29. *Ibid.*, 166. John Hawkins was among the earliest English sea captains to capture and run slaves from Africa to America.

30. In basic form, the classical tradition of political economy as exemplified by the writings of David Hume, Adam Smith, David Ricardo and Karl Marx, viewed money as a commodity which had a cost to produce and use. This cost, whether associated with minting bullion or printing paper, could be specified, quantified and calculated in relation to the price level. But most critically, the quantity of money circulating in an economy did not affect savings and investments. These were "real" factors of production dependent upon the production and consumption of goods. For an exposition of the classical doctrine of money see D. O'Brien, *The Classical Economists* (Oxford: Clarendon Press, 1975), ch. 6.

31. Polanyi, *Great Transformation*, 193–5.

32. *Ibid.*, 194.

33. *Ibid.*, 196.

34. *Ibid.*, 198.

35. *Ibid.*, 199.

36. This is the central argument of Herbert Feis, a work Polanyi relies on extensively for his claims with respect to *haute finance*: H. Feis, *Europe, the World's Banker, 1870–1914* (New Haven, CT: Yale University Press, 1930); see also M. de Cecco, *Money and Empire: The International Gold Standard, 1890–1914* (Oxford: Blackwell, 1974) and R. Germain, *The International Organization of Credit* (Cambridge: Cambridge University Press, 1997).

37. I have written on the question of Carr and his historical approach to international politics and IPE in R. Germain, "E. H. Carr and the historical mode of thought" in M. Cox (ed.), *E. H. Carr: A Critical Appraisal* (Basingstoke: Palgrave Macmillan, 2000), 322–36; and R. Germain, "The political economy of global transformation: Susan Strange, E. H. Carr and the dynamics of structural change", in R. Germain (ed.), *Susan Strange and the Future of Global Political Economy* (Abingdon: Routledge, 2016), 165–82. I have considered the work of Fernand Braudel in this connection in Germain, *International Organization of Credit*, 15–16. Polanyi's historical mode of thinking is not as clearly articulated as Carr and Braudel, but can be deduced from the way in which he considers change and transformation to occur, and especially in terms of how the rate of change in history can be constrained (or unleashed) by active social policy. See especially Polanyi, *Great Transformation*, 36–40.

38. It is also the case that there is something of a conversation already at work among these three thinkers, even if indirectly (they were never collaborators or participants in a collective vision of political economy). For Polanyi on Carr, see *Great Transformation*, 204 and 263, and G. Dale, *Karl Polanyi: A Life on the Left* (New York: Columbia University Press, 2016), 167, 275, 279 and 366. For Braudel on Polanyi, see F. Braudel,

Civilization and Capitalism 15th–18th Centuries, Vol. 2: The Wheels of Commerce, trans. S. Reynolds (New York: Harper & Row, 1979), 225–8. Carr on either Polanyi or Braudel is trickier, as I have found no direct citations of their work in any of his writings; and ditto for Braudel on Carr. Nevertheless, my own reading of all three sees them as participating in overlapping conversations concerning the nature of historical analysis, especially as it utilizes the "historical imagination", and the entwined evolution of capitalism and the state. See for example E. H. Carr, *What is History?* (Harmondsworth: Penguin, 1967) and F. Braudel, "History and the social sciences: the *longue durée*" in *On History*, trans. S. Matthews, (Chicago, IL: University of Chicago Press, 1980), 25–54.

39. Germain, "The political economy of global transformation", 170–1.

40. Carr's views on the post-Second World War future of world politics and especially politics in Europe, America and Russia can be found in a series of BBC lectures delivered in 1951 and published as E. H. Carr, *The New Society* (Boston, MA: Beacon Press, 1951/1957). These lectures both modify and amplify many of the views already set out in E. H. Carr, *The Twenty Years Crisis, 1919–1939* (London: Macmillan, 1939) and E. H. Carr, *Nationalism and After* (London: Macmillan, 1945).

41. K. Polanyi, "Universal capitalism or regional planning?", *London Quarterly of World Affairs* 10:3 (1945), 86–91.

42. Carr himself of course is not immune to aspects of this critique. Like Polanyi he gave Stalin and the Soviets the benefit of the doubt with respect to their postwar foreign policy ambitions, and at times his own analysis betrayed the period's fluid political directions. It should be acknowledged that very few scholarly analyses pinned down the postwar future with accuracy. For Carr's views on postwar Soviet foreign policy, see E. H. Carr, *The Soviet Impact on the Western World* (London: Macmillan, 1947), and for his views on the changing shape of the state (and the inter-state system) see Carr, *Nationalism and After*. It is almost certain that Polanyi would have been familiar with the latter publication.

43. In both eras, moreover, it was also financial institutions with preferential connections to the British and American states which were able to create credit denominated in those currencies, whether the *haute finance* of the City in the nineteenth century or the so-called "bulge bracket" Wall Street investment banks of the twentieth and twenty-first centuries. For an historical analysis of this relationship, see R. Germain, *Global Politics and Financial Governance* (Basingstoke: Palgrave Macmillan, 2010).

44. The following is drawn primarily from F. Braudel, *Capitalism and Material Life: 1400–1800*, trans. M. Kochan (London: Weidenfeld & Nicolson, 1967/1973); Braudel, *Wheels of Commerce*; and F. Braudel, *Civilization and Capitalism 15th–18th Centuries: The Perspective of the World*, trans. S. Reynolds (New York: Harper & Row, 1979/1984).

45. In Braudel's history, the modern (European) world-economy was led in turn by Antwerp, Genoa, Amsterdam and London, each of which provided a money-capital-state nexus appropriate to leading "its" world-economy. This is the extended subject of Braudel, *Perspective of the World*.

46. It must be acknowledged that there are some important tensions between Braudel and Polanyi on certain aspects of how to understand the world market economy, the most important being that for Polanyi market economy and capitalism are one and the same thing, while for Braudel they are distinct parts of a broader economic, social, political

and cultural order. For the purposes of this exposition, however, the complementarities seem to me to be more significant than the differences.

47. In important ways, both Polanyi and Carr misread the political and economic direction of the post-1945 world. Part of the reason was the emergence of the Cold War, which neither really anticipated. But equally importantly, neither recognized the limitation of mass political mobilization and its analogue, mass democracy, to counter the pressures of industrial capitalism as it reconfigured itself during this period.

48. Braudel, *Wheels of Commerce*, 374–400. It is at this point that capitalism assumes its world historical significance. In this sense, both Braudel and Polanyi would agree that capitalism became a world historical phenomenon at some point during the eighteenth century, albeit for slightly different reasons.

49. L. Panitch & S. Gindin, *The Making of Global Capitalism: The Political Economy of American Empire* (London: Verso, 2012).

50. Susan Strange provides a compatible view of how the "transnational American empire" works in precisely this manner: S. Strange, "Towards a theory of transnational empire", in Tooze &May (eds), *Authority and Markets*, 141–56.

51. Helleiner, "Great Transformations".

52. Although he does not specifically invoke Polanyi, Helleiner's recent discussions of the future of the dollar under Trump align quite well with these premises. See E. Helleiner, "Downsizing the dollar in the age of Trump? The ambiguities of key currency status", *The Brown Journal of World Affairs* 23:2 (2017), 9–27.

3

THE STATE

Maria Markantonatou and Gareth Dale

INTRODUCTION

Karl Polanyi's critique of the market economy has over recent decades attracted much attention, in the context of debates over "market society" and neoliberalism. Less consideration has been paid, however, to his political theory, including his understanding of "the state".[1] Although the interrelations among politics, the economy and society always occupied the centre of his analysis, it is true that there is little in his oeuvre that directly addresses the state. His focus, Michael Burawoy remarks, was "not politics and the bourgeois revolution but economics and the market revolution, not the formation of a national bourgeoisie but the formation of national markets".[2] His thesis that the origins of the "cataclysm" (the wars and economic crises of the early to mid-twentieth century) "lay in the utopian endeavour of economic liberalism to set up a self-regulating market system" implies no less than "that the balance of power, the gold standard, *and the liberal state* … were, in the last resort, shaped in one common matrix, the self-regulating market".[3] The liberal state, for Polanyi, was one of the four defining institutions of nineteenth-century civilization, alongside the balance of power system, the gold standard and the self-regulating market ("the common matrix"). Of these, the state is the one to which he devotes the least analysis. Despite its role in shaping the other three, it gains no systematic or separate attention. Rather, sporadic observations are sprinkled throughout *The Great Transformation*, most of which elaborate the same idea of the allegedly non-intervening, liberal state.

But this is not the end of the story. For Polanyi, as for Marx, the understanding of the modern state as an institutional correlate of the market economy (in Polanyi's case) or of the mode of production (in Marx's) was only one angle among many. Just as from Marx's reflections and historical, philosophical and journalistic remarks on the state at least six approaches can be sifted out, according to Bob Jessop,[4] so too in Polanyi's writings various perspectives emerge.

These were developed during the different historical conjunctures in which he wrote, and serve distinct arguments concerning state–economy and state–society relations. They include conceptions of the state as a structure that, although strictly "separated" from the liberal market economy, continually intervenes to create and then maintain it; a social construction, in line with *corpus artificialis* conceptions; a fascist/corporatist machine that acts on behalf of capital to crush the working class; and an institution for the conduct of war and the security of national territory as a condition for the reproduction of both the economy and the social body. In addition, there is his thesis that states, although born from conquest, have been profoundly altered by the extension of the vote – an institutional revolution that tamed political power, subjecting it through parliamentary democracy to regulation in the interests of "society".[5]

It is not the case, then, that Polanyi authored a coherent state theory in the sense of a general and comprehensive macro-analysis of the modern state, or an ideal-typical understanding of it, or a theorization of state power through a systematic account of the historical origins and evolution of states, or a detailed concretization of capitalist states' complex and heterogeneous social functions. This lack of a state theory sits alongside Polanyi's loose conceptualization of "society", which often ends up overloaded and functions, as Nancy Fraser points out, as a "black box", a "catch-all" term that "mixes together everything that is not the 'economy,' conflating important distinctions between, for example, states and civil society, families and public spheres; nations and subnational communities".[6]

Nonetheless, his writings do include a seminal thesis on the indispensable and interventionist role of the *liberal state* in creating the framework of market society. Its essence is the notion that the free-market system did not arise "naturally" but required "an enormous increase in continuous, centrally organized and controlled interventionism".[7] Moreover, the theses he formulated on the political origins and construction of the market, the relation of economy to politics, and the agendas and ideologies of liberalism, fascism and socialism brought him recurrently to consider questions of state power. All this calls for a closer examination and reconstruction of Polanyi's approach to the state – the task of this chapter. We begin by surveying his thinking on the state as it evolved in the interwar period. We then turn to his concept of the liberal state, as it is outlined in particular in *The Great Transformation*. Finally, we shall tease out some of the ambiguities and contradictions in his theorization of the liberal state, as well as briefly exploring its usefulness in relation to today's crisis in the eurozone.

STATES IN A FUNCTIONAL, PLURALIST SOCIETY

Polanyi's first significant engagement with state theory came in the immediate aftermath of the First World War. It was a phase of heightened inter-state conflict followed by the fragmentation of states (including his own, the Habsburg Empire), the revolutionary overthrow of regimes, and the calling into question, by the Bolshevik-led revolution in Russia, of the principle of state power itself. In this crucible, socialist theory thrived. The current to which Polanyi was especially attracted was guild socialism. Its appeal to him lay in part in its advocacy of radical democratization – in the twin form of workers' direct control over production (the emphasis of syndicalism) and workers' parties gaining control of the state (the emphasis of social democracy).[8] In addition, he found persuasive the "functional" theory of a prominent British guild socialist, G. D. H. Cole. As propounded by guild socialists, functional theory was pluralist. That is to say, it rejected normative accounts of the state as society's paramount institution. Instead, each organ of society should serve "its own purpose best by being relatively independent, and by working in conjunction with, but not under the authority of, any of the others".[9]

In his essay "Guild and the State" (1923), Polanyi conceptualizes the state through its legitimate purposes (or functions) and its domain as he believes it would appear in a guild-socialist order. He begins by commending guild socialism for its advocacy of the socialization, rather than nationalization, of the means of production – that is to say, it would "place them under the democratic control of the trade unions and cooperatives",[10] thereby restricting, rather than inflating, state power. He then turns to defining the state. Here he borrows critically from the tradition that understands the state as a *corpus artificiale* (artificial body). Originating with Hobbes, such approaches see the state as socially constructed, and legitimated on grounds of cohesion, appeasement and internal and external security.[11] Polanyi shares the conception of the state as a social construction, but, in sharp contrast to the English philosopher, denied the necessity of the state as a manager of social cohesion. "It is not true," Polanyi argues, "that the organic functioning of society can only be guaranteed by the state. On the contrary: *state power artificially unifies and, by so doing, impairs the natural and healthy unity of society.*"[12]

In his next step, Polanyi does not take his unmasking of the state's artificiality as a point of departure from which to scrutinize problems of state theory, or to a class analysis of state power; instead he propounds his distinctively "solidaristic conceptualization of society", as an element of what he terms a "functional social theory".[13] As he framed the theory, social institutions are constructed upon the functional requirements of the life of individuals. Individuals have material needs, and so engage in economic activity; "this is the basis of economic associations".[14] In addition, the commonality of all workers gives rise to "the second functional association: the guilds".[15] Another impulse of individuals is to cultural life, and this underpins associations of sciences, religion, education, and art. In the case of the state, its function is to ensure equality and justice for individuals who occupy a contiguous territory.

Yet that function is but one among many, and the state, Polanyi concluded, is merely one social institution among many – it should not be accorded sovereign power.[16] In a guild-socialist order there would therefore be "no need for state power as a unifying factor", because the manifold institutions of social life organizations would "operate in harmony". This does not mean that state power would become redundant. Rather, "its *authority merely becomes attenuated*. It still remains an important bearer of functions located on the municipal, regional – in other words neighbourly –scales". It would "no longer remain the single 'sovereign power', but rather simply one power on an equal footing with the other main functional power: *the guild. Free cooperation between the guild and the state* – this is the new social imaginary envisaged by the guild socialists".[17]

In other texts from the same period, Polanyi puts some flesh on his model of a guild-socialist order, but without going into detail on the projected character of the state (or "commune"). A socialist commune, he suggests, would be comparable to the modern state but "narrower" in its "sphere of influence".[18] Critically, as Johanna Bockman points out, in texts such as "Socialist Accounting" (1922) he did not consider the state "in a conventional sense, as the defender of society".[19] Rather, in a socialist "functional democracy" the state will not be preserved or abolished but sublated. It would be "not only a political organ, but also the real representative of the higher goals of the community".[20] It would, in other words, shed its character as an objectified and reified power structure.

In the 1920s, Polanyi was not a well-known figure and his writings on guild socialism made little impact. However, one point was picked up and criticized by Ludwig von Mises. The Austrian economist held against Polanyi's model of a guild-socialist society that it obfuscates the question of economic sovereignty. Who, Mises asks, really owns the means of production in the guild-socialist model: the workforce organized in guild organizations, or the state?[21] (In this, Mises anticipated the critique of Cole's guild socialism by Carl Schmitt, in *The Concept of the Political*.) That Polanyi's model assigns *ownership* to the state but reserves for worker-controlled bodies the right of *disposal* constitutes, for Mises, an insuperable contradiction, for ownership means nothing if not the right to dispose. In his published reply, Polanyi maintained that Mises erred in assuming that one institution of power must be able to trump all others.[22] In constitutional governments, for example, complex arrangements exist that involve two or three ruling organs, each of which possesses final authority in a specified range of areas but none over them all. In a socialist society, moreover, a society not fractured by class divisions, the various institutions would represent different interests of each and every citizen, rendering entrenched institutional conflict unlikely or, at worst, minor in kind.

In other essays from the mid-1920s, Polanyi developed a twin-track understanding of the state: on one hand, a liberal position, he holds it in the abstract to be a necessary feature of society; on the other, in Marxist tones, he considers its existence in modernity as an alienated form of social relations. The state, he argued in "On Liberty" (1927), is fundamentally an institution created by society "to safeguard its common interests against internal and external enemies", and yet it existed as a reified and alienated power, in virtue of the capitalist institutional structures in which it operates, in particular the separation between state and economy.[23] In his words, it was "the fragmentation into states" and the "antagonistic" character of the market economy, above all its lack of "overview", as well as the opaqueness of "the relationship between the political state and the economy" that were thwarting historical progress toward democracy and socialism. Demystified, the state was "a social relation of people to one another" and the task of socialism was to overcome "the state by resolving this social relation into a direct one that is no longer mediated by the state".[24] As long as the free market economy continued, the economy/society separation would not be overcome.

By the late 1920s, the radical movements that had stimulated debate, Europe-wide, among socialists over the nature of the state in a future society had retreated. Guild socialism in Britain faded into insignificance and its allies in Austria's social democratic party were leaching support too. Then, at the decade's end, tumbling stock markets signalled the onset of the Great Depression. In this context, Polanyi's concern with debates over a future socialist society gave way to other interests, notably in economic history. He developed his analysis of market society, in connection with which he sketched an original and radical critique of the *liberal* British state, to which we return below. But his critique of the liberal state was not taken forward into a radical interrogation of the state form *per se*. Instead, he tended to borrow from mainstream theories; his thought took a "realist turn".

POLANYI'S REALIST TURN

In the 1930s, Polanyi came to emphasize the centrality of states in constituting international order, the anarchy of that order, and with states understood as acting in terms of their self-preservation and the "national interest". This realist turn could be seen in his scorn for the belief that states might "wither" away, in his oft-repeated insistence that "power ... and coercion are inevitable in a complex society",[25] that "no society is possible in which power and compulsion are absent, nor a world in which force has no function",[26] and in one component of his critique of liberal idealism: that it fails to grasp the necessity of frontiers and of "loyalty to the State" (which he regarded as the *sine quibus non* of settled human communities).[27] It could also be seen in his sympathy for Rousseau's view that, in his paraphrase, in a free society "that which serves the survival of the people is right", and that such a society can exist only if its citizens are "prepared to sacrifice all and everything in the service of their country and its free institutions".[28]

In this period too, in which his conviction was growing that fascism must be fought by military means, Polanyi came to emphasize territoriality as the foundation of state sovereignty. This was of a piece with his turn to realism and was related to his conception of "society" as a territorially-delimited functional entity. In line with mainstream approaches to states, Polanyi explains their historical constitution in terms of economic evolution and the modernization (or "improvement") of the means of production – as responses to the exigencies of coordination in agrarian society, with its complex division of labour. States, he argues, arose during the transition from nomadic, hunter-gathering societies to agrarian ones.[29] Quoting the economist Ralph Hawtrey, he proposed that settled agriculture is crucial for community life, in contrast with the life of nomads which is "little removed from" that of animals. Settled agricultural communities require permanent loci and fixtures, and states, in turn, could hardly exist outside a well-defined territory; "Hence that *territorial* character of sovereignty, which permeates our political conceptions",[30] he concludes, again citing Hawtrey.

Polanyi's realism, however, did not go so far as to conceive of war as a transcendent necessity of human nature. "There is nothing to support the pseudo-realistic prejudice that of all our institutions war is the one which is coterminous with mankind," he held, adding that not only have there "been times in the past without war, there may be times ahead of us which will not know war".[31] However, in a complex society war, he believed, does have a place. Indeed, it is the inevitable outcome of the formation of "civilization", "community" and the state. He makes the case in the following way:

> No human community can develop any of its vital functions without having settled for a generation at least who does and who does not belong to the community. For communities are organized in states and without some loyalty to the State, the Community cannot function satisfactorily. [...] In other words, no community [...] can produce law and order, safety and security, education and morality, civilization and culture unless its frontiers are settled and there is no

reasonable danger of their becoming unsettled. Any threat to their frontiers, ever so distant, must inhibit the normal functioning of the community, and stop all higher forms of life. Incidentally, this will usually be true of both communities involved since frontiers affect them both. There must be decision, at all cost. And if no other institution is available, war must be invoked if higher forms of life be allowed to continue.[32]

The realist turn in Polanyi's thought related to several political debates of the era, on impending war, the Soviet Union, and economic globalization (or "universalism"). On war, he had in his sights above all the Christian pacifism of his day. It skirted too close to the anarchism with which he had flirted when young, in its rejection of the social necessity of institutions and its demonization not only of economic value but also of political power. It exhibited an anchoritic spirit toward the dilemmas of war, including on the pressing question of confronting Nazi Germany. On Soviet Russia, Polanyi's realism aligned with his support for Stalin's agenda, as encapsulated in the notion of "socialism in one country", which he commended as "the attempt to make Russia into an industrial country by her own means, without foreign loans and without the help of other countries".[33] Stalin's Russia was living proof that "the state can be an instrument of emancipation".[34] Relatedly, it aligned with his defence of the Comintern's realist turn in the 1930s. Against its critics on the left, he maintained that Russia, had no choice but to adopt a foreign policy which, "like that of any other country, is primarily determined by self-interest".[35]

As regards globalization, here too Polanyi's position reflected his realist approach to territorial states. His critique of capitalism, as is well known, is of its liberal-universalist form, a form that achieved its first global triumph in the nineteenth century, under the British ensign. Institutionally, it featured a shift toward free trade and the gold standard, as well as the replication, worldwide, of liberal constitutions and central banks.[36] From Polanyi's realist vantage point, he criticized liberal agendas of deterritorialized international capitalist expansion, as well as domestic liberal agendas promoting workers' "flexibility" through market-impelled geographical mobility. He took liberals to task for their refusal to properly appreciate that land forms "part of the territory of the country, and that the territorial character of sovereignty was not merely a result of sentimental associations, but of massive facts, including economic ones".[37] Territorialization, he argues, had historically been vital for the construction of society, for purposes of economic sustainability, welfare provision and social cohesion.

Let us pause to remind ourselves of the trajectory of Polanyi's state theory, as it evolved in the decades following the end of the First World War. In his guild socialist phase, the emphasis was normative, with a socialist transition in mind. States should be ordered within a "functional society". They should represent citizens in their "function" as members of a territorially-bounded community. The unification of society would arise pluralistically, through the cooperation of individuals and the plurality of social institutions that represent the various dimensions of social life. As such, the state was understood *not* as the "unifying factor" of social order but as the administrative structure representing individuals in their public lives. In his later more Fabian phase, in the 1930s and 1940s, his approach had shifted somewhat. Charismatic statesmen such as Franklin Delano Roosevelt are now lionized,[38] and the actions of democratic and "socialist" states are given a positive, at times exalted, gloss. By the war's end, Polanyi was increasingly invested in the plans of the leading states: Attlee's Britain, Soviet Russia, and New-Deal America. He proposed that they should use the opportunity afforded by the revival of national sovereignty in a world economy no longer bound to the gold standard to set new economic rules at the international level, with national growth and autonomy in economic policy prioritized and with dirigiste economic policy-making recognized as legitimate. To make this vision effective, political leaders would need to understand the deficiencies of the previous "universalist" political-economic order and the causes of its breakdown in the first half of the twentieth century. As a contribution to that goal, Polanyi wrote *The Great Transformation*. It is in that book that he presented a significant contribution to state theory, in the form of a critique of the liberal state.

MARKET SOCIETY AND THE LIBERAL STATE

Polanyi's critique of market society, in *The Great Transformation* and elsewhere, centres on the critique of the commodification of land, labour and money – in essence, the "factors of production" of classical economic theory. In the view of laissez-faire liberalism, the factors of production should be regulated by market forces alone. Viewed from one angle this appears as an "economic" idea – it addresses the mechanisms of resource allocation. Equally, it carries a political implication, that land, labour and money – and "the economy" in general – should not be regulated by states. States should instead take a minimal "nightwatchman" role, organizing military security and punishing property transgression but with benign inattention to everyday economic affairs. Whether applied to the economy or the polity, these ideas were, in Polanyi's term, "utopian".[39] They represented an experiment that liberal policy-makers and economic actors attempted to implement but which was doomed to failure because the goal was unrealizable. Polanyi illustrates his argument with reference to nineteenth-century Britain, in particular to the discrepancy between the nightwatchman state as it was conceived by laissez-faire liberals and its actual historical development. In theory:

> the liberal state was more or less separated from and independent of economics: liberalism, in its essence, rejected the unity of society. State and industry, economics and politics were kept apart: the State was supposed to keep strictly to political matters and to govern as little as possible; the industrial system, on the other hand, was allegedly controlled by laws of its own – the sacred laws of competitive prices. So long as the State did not interfere with these prices, they provided the greatest possible yield of commodities.[40]

Such was the theory, he adds, and powerfully influential it was, but "this condition of affairs never existed in actual fact".[41] The image of the "purely political" state was a myth. The liberal state's *attempted* self-restriction to a narrow role as enforcer of the rules of the market did represent a fundamental departure from all previous human history. That enforcement role, however, required the state to intervene in, and regulate, economic affairs on a grand and sweeping scale. In Polanyi's oft-quoted phrase, "laissez-faire was planned, planning was not".[42] There was nothing natural or spontaneous about the free-market system, as some had supposed; it was constructed and regulated by states. Liberal criticisms of state intervention and bureaucracy were therefore misplaced, for it was precisely by such means that the market system had been constructed.

In *The Great Transformation*, then, Polanyi compellingly debunks the myth that the industrial revolution, even in Britain, was simply a private process overseen by a hands-off state. Behind the market system, even in its laissez-faire guise, lay a programme of social engineering, steered by states that were more intrusive and muscular than any of their feudal or even absolutist predecessors. The construction of the market system, as Polanyi puts it, "was in no way the result of the gradual and spontaneous emancipation of the economic sphere from governmental control", but rather, "the outcome of a conscious and often violent intervention on the part of government".[43] By violence, Polanyi means a range of coercive state behaviour up to and including war. A case in point was the American Civil War, in which "the South appealed to the arguments of laissez-faire to justify slavery; the North appealed to the intervention of arms to establish a free labour market".[44]

As such, *The Great Transformation* should be situated in a broad current of social theory that conceives of the ascendancy of liberal capitalism as coincident with and facilitated by a far-reaching transformation in state capacity and strategy: the rise of consolidated and centralized states that sought to re-engineer the norms and behaviour of working people and the poor, fashioning them into subjects responsive to market forces. In their different ways, earlier sociologists of the transition to "modernity", notably Karl Marx, Max Weber, and Émile Durkheim, had all argued that a market system requires regulation. For Marx, states played a role as "conditions of the historic dissolution process and as makers of the conditions for the existence of capital",[45] through colonial wars, the creation of rules and institutions of private property, the management of labour, and so on. For Weber, the accent is on the role of states in regulating labour, money and finance. For Durkheim, the emphasis is on the moral conditions and institutional structures required for the market economy to function. Polanyi's masterwork is a major twentieth century update of this genre, in that it theorizes the central role of liberal states in establishing the conditions of existence of capitalist society.

From one angle, then, Polanyi depicts the liberal state as the upholder of the liberal utopian project, as "market maker".[46] Conversely, the liberal state was itself "a creation of the self-regulating market".[47] The ascendancy of the self-regulating market is best explained, Polanyi maintained, with reference to two processes, both of which were centred in early nineteenth-century Britain. One was the occurrence of an industrial revolution within a commercial society. Commercial viability depended increasingly on the profitable introduction of machinery, and this, in turn, required a stable supply of the various factors of production (land, labour, money), a supply that could be ensured by their wholesale commodification. The other was a cultural sea-change that led to human beings being seen as, and expected to behave as, self-interest maximizers. This revolution in economic perceptions was spearheaded by liberal and conservative political economists, notably David Ricardo and Robert Malthus. It rapidly gained influence within the governing class.

Some hesitation is evident at this point in Polanyi's argument. At times he writes as if, at least in Britain, the liberal market economy and liberal state did come into being. Indeed, he suggests that in many countries such states existed, in full-fledged form, until the 1930s, at which point some were "replaced by totalitarian dictatorships".[48] At other times he suggests the "self-regulating" market economy and liberal state were utopian aspirations, goals that, however zealously pursued, could never be attained. Viewed from this angle, their elusiveness is inescapable because the full commodification of land, nature and money would spell the disintegration and ruin of human society. In Polanyi's schema, a "countermovement" inevitably arises to resist that destructive course, preventing both economy and state from becoming fully liberal.[49] Whereas Ricardo had postulated that, if a state were to seek to intrude arbitrarily into the market mechanism, spontaneous social forces will resist, Polanyi proposed the reverse. The imposition of unrestricted market competition upon society spontaneously provokes a protective response, or "countermovement", expressed in some countries through a "vast extension of government functions" and in others through "Trade Unions, Cooperatives, the Churches".[50] The "countermovement" presses for state intervention, in the form of factory laws, social legislation, tariffs, central banking and the management of the monetary system, through which the market's destructive effects may be checked. Its signal achievement was to empower the state in its roles as regulator of the economy and guarantor of basic social welfare and a modicum of equality. "The chief organ of social self-protection", in Polanyi's words, "was the state".[51]

Polanyi's description of state power in market society runs in two distinct directions. In one, we see the indispensable role of the liberal state in creating and maintaining the market economy and constructing forms of social policy tailored to managing the population in conformity with the requirements of the commercial system. Exemplifying the liberal state was nineteenth-century Britain, where state managers, in creating and servicing the market economy, also authorized social policies that managed the population in the interests of market actors. The British state was "determined"[52] and "shaped"[53] by the market in the sense that it had from the beginning supported market liberalism, with the aims of checking social resistance and removing obstacles to marketization. In the other direction, we see its attempts to protect "society" against the market system's harmful effects. Even market liberals advocate a range of "protective" measures of public policy. Commenting on the establishment of a fire service in London and compulsory vaccinations for children, Polanyi notes that these were supported by "convinced supporters of laissez-faire".[54]

Another way of putting this is that, through the British example, Polanyi provides us with an account of the contradictory nature of the welfare state – and authors who draw on him speak accordingly of a "dual state"[55] and a "conflicted state"[56]. The state facilitates social reproduction, serves to develop the material well-being and social powers of individuals, and exerts social control over the blind play of market forces, while also repressing and manipulating people, and moulding them to the requirements of capital. In an evolution from his earlier pluralism, he encased this analysis in a thesis on the separation of economic and political spheres. In the nineteenth century, the economic sphere, supported by the liberal state, had demanded autonomy and gained dominance over society. Society resisted its encroachments, forcing the liberal state to partially regulate economic affairs, in contravention of its laissez-faire principles. The outcome was a mal-integration of the economic and political spheres.

The mal-integration thesis forms the core of Polanyi's explanation for the systemic chaos of the early twentieth century. But he adds to it a class-analytic argument. In the age of democracy, liberal states come under pressure from rival social classes. The working class, exerting pressure through the ballot box, pulls in one direction while capital pulls in another – ultimately towards fascism. With this, as discussed below, Polanyi's argument exhibits parallels with instrumentalist theories of the capitalist state.

INSTRUMENTALISM AND DEMOCRACY

By and large, Polanyi rejected conceptions of the state as an instrument for the fulfilment of the interests of a specific social class. He focused instead on its functions vis-à-vis "society" and "economy". Nevertheless, in his treatment of certain states, notably those headed by fascist regimes, this is not the case. Here, his approach closely resembles that of class instrumentalism – for example that of Ernest Mandel. According to Mandel "the capitalist state is and remains, like all other political states before it, an instrument for the preservation of the rule of a definite class".[57] If crucial decisions of the twentieth century are scrutinized, Mandel argues, such as:

> the decision to appoint Hitler as imperial chancellor […]; the green light for the start of World War II in Germany and Britain; the decision to orient the USA towards participation in the war; […] then we find that these decisions were taken not in parliaments […] but directly by the captains of industry themselves. When the very survival of capitalism is at stake, then the big capitalists suddenly govern in the most literal sense of the word. At that point, every semblance of "autonomy" of the capitalist state vis-à-vis business disappears completely.[58]

There is more than a passing resemblance between this and Polanyi's view. Discussing Nazi Germany, Polanyi argues: "In such a situation the leaders of industry become hostile to popular government and try to undermine the authority of the democratic party system; as an alternative, big business offers *its own government*, the direct administration of social affairs by the captains of industry – that is the owners of capital and their appointed managers".[59]

The crux of the matter, in Polanyi's rendition of the instrumentalist thesis, is that when the maintenance of a liberal market economy was no longer feasible in the interwar period, the transformation of states into tools of big business was capitalism's last resort and the defining moment of the crisis. At that moment of emergency, a series of European states were directly instrumentalized by capital, an outcome that required the crushing of parliamentary democracy. Democracy had frustrated the instrumentalization of said states by economic forces. Universal suffrage, Polanyi believed, "made the state the organ of the ruling million – the identical million who, in the economic realm, had often to carry in bitterness the burden of the ruled".[60] Thus the modern state could be instrumentalized by different classes. The capitalist class steered it towards fascism while the working class sought to use the vote to pursue its antithetical interests: for regulation, social protection and onward towards socialism. As Polanyi saw matters in the 1930s, there were fundamentally only two solutions to the crisis of the interwar period:

> the extension of the democratic principle from politics to econom-
> ics, or the abolition of the democratic "political sphere" altogether.
> After the abolition of the democratic political sphere only economic
> life remains; capitalism as organized in the different branches of
> industry becomes the whole of society. This is the fascist solution.
> The extension of the democratic principle to economics implies
> the abolition of the private property of the means of production,
> and hence the disappearance of a separate autonomous economic
> sphere: the democratic political sphere becomes the whole of soci-
> ety. This, essentially, is socialism.[61]

It is apparent from passages such as this that Polanyi conceived of the cap-italist state as riven between two basic forces. One represented the economic interests of business, the other represented the interests of society as a whole, as expressed most visibly at the ballot box. These correspond to the two thrusts of the "double movement": one towards marketization, the other toward social protection. The latter, the counter-movement, arose in reaction against the mar-ket order and was tightly bound up with democratization, in that the economi-cally dispossessed classes were using their newly won vote to demand protection from the social dislocation occasioned by market forces.

In this position, the Polanyian anthropologist Geoff Goodwin has noted, some ambiguity exists. It concerns the relationships between the countermove-ment and the state and the political process behind social protection.[62] Polanyi portrays states as vehicles through which the countermovement channelled its demands:

> yet precisely how this was achieved is unclear. Polanyi depicted a
> [...] political process in which social pressure was converted into
> laws and policies through representative democratic institutions.
> The possibility of democratic states weakening, neutralizing or
> destroying organized sectors of society that demand protection is
> therefore overlooked. The limits of representative democracies and
> the complexity of the political and bureaucratic process behind the

design and implementation of laws and policies are also absent from his analysis.[63]

Goodwin's suggestion here, that Polanyi overlooked the possibility of democratic states supervising the dismantling of social protection, is somewhat misleading. Polanyi was a sharp-eyed observer of the pressures that international capital brought to bear on democratically elected governments. Consider his discussion of the downfall of Ramsay MacDonald's Labour government in Britain in 1931 and the slashing of unemployment benefits under its successor National Government (also led by MacDonald). That crisis, Polanyi believed, bore the hallmark of a society riven between workers and capital, between politics and economics. It highlighted the inner connection between "democracy and currency", in that the socially protective policies promised by an elected government provoked a response by wealthy elites in the form of capital flight and pressure on sterling that compelled government ministers to abandon progressive reforms and enter an alliance with bourgeois parties.[64]

Or take another example from the interwar period: the intervention of the League of Nations in Austria in 1922. Ostensibly, the motivation behind the League's intervention was strictly "technical": the provision of loans to help Austria cope with hyperinflation and to refinance its banks.[65] But the move, fatefully, wrongfooted Austria's Social Democratic Party (SDAP). It was the main opposition party at national level and ran the municipality of Vienna. Although the League pretended to political neutrality, its staffers were conscious that the interests they represented – international financial capital and the British and French empires – were implacably opposed to social democracy. A predictable outcome of the League-imposed austerity programme was the sapping of the working-class strength and morale on which social democracy depended. Worse, the SDAP, despite rhetorical denunciations of the austerity measures, refused to use its parliamentary veto to disrupt them,[66] for, as Polanyi noted, its leaders (notably Otto Bauer) supported the monetary principles that underlay the austerity programme.[67] The League of Nations, in Polanyi's pithy summary of the episode, "acted as the sponsor of a process of rehabilitation in which the combined pressure of the City of London and of the neoclassical monetary purists of Vienna was put into the service of the gold standard".[68] International capital, acting through an international organization and in concert with a democratically elected government, had successfully outfoxed the forces of Austria's left. As Polanyi stressed, international liberalism and the gold standard, had been restored, at the cost of democracy.

Goodwin is nonetheless right to identify a looseness in Polanyi's theoretical construction. Polanyi saw the liberal state as "merely the counterpart of the market economy which permitted no interference on the part of the government",[69] yet as soon as it granted suffrage he theorized it as a transformed institution: the chief organ of social self-protection. This looseness pivots on Polanyi's accept-ance of a pervasive but questionable idea: that the state is fully under the control of elected governments in democratic conditions.

With the granting of suffrage, Polanyi, alongside social democratic theorists (Otto Bauer, Eduard Bernstein, Emil Lederer and John Strachey, for example), believed the trends in the political and economic fields had begun to point in antithetical directions. As the trade unions waxed in strength, and with the extension of the vote, political power was coming under the direct control of the working classes through social-democratic parties even as economic might was increasingly vested in giant industrial and financial corporations. From a social-democratic viewpoint, the contradiction would be solved on the stage of "actually existing democracy" in the political sphere. It provided the platform on which a socialist democracy could be constructed. To elucidate this point, Hannes Lacher proposes that Polanyi was theorizing "the interpenetration of two competing forms of society: capitalism and socialism." It was in this inter-penetration that he located the essence of the interwar crisis: "Neither was viable in the partial form they had assumed, and their coexistence produced institu-tional deadlock. Popular democracy had led the state to become a beach-head for an incompletely realized socialist system, while industry remained the stronghold of a disorganized capitalism. Each of them strove to reconstitute society as a totality".[70]

Lacher's interpretation is fair and accurate. Polanyi did hold that liberal dem-ocratic structures had enabled elected governments to become beachheads of a socialist system. (In this, we can perhaps hear echoes of the young Polanyi's pluralism, in the notion that state sovereignty need not be monolithic, it can be amicably divided.) But is this position coherent? If socialism and capitalism represent irreconcilably antagonistic forms of social organization, and if mod-ern states are, as Polanyi maintained, territories with economies ordered along capitalist lines, the occupation of a beachhead by socialist forces implies intense intra-state conflict, even war. Yet when one scours the terrain for evidence of battle what one finds instead is that the elected parties of "popular democracy" have by and large been co-opted as compliant state managers of the capitalist system. It is a co-optation process that occurs in myriad ways, including (on this we are following Fred Block) direct pressure by capitalists through cam-paign contributions and lobbying, the revolving door between businesses and government, bourgeois cultural hegemony (including the acceptance of "certain unwritten rules about what is and what is not legitimate state activity"), and above all the state's dependence on revenue, the streams of which are largely in capitalist hands.[71]

If Polanyi's thesis on the clash of capitalism and democracy at a general level makes perfect sense (the former with its steep hierarchies and inequalities of reward; the latter with its principles of equal citizenship and collective decision-making), in maintaining that parliamentary government provides the deliberative arena in which "the common people" exercise real control over the state, he underestimated the potential for coexistence between parliamentary democracy and the market economy. Many of the laws and regulations that he supposed had been undermining the market system from the late nineteenth century onward either involved the provision of public goods or the correction of market failures, and did not seriously or ultimately impair the functioning of capitalism. State managers, in alliance with capitalist interests and intergovernmental organizations (from the League of Nations to the IMF), have repeatedly sought to *insulate* key economic levers of power from popular influence. This was a phenomenon that Polanyi was alert to, but which he did not assimilate into his state theory.

CONCLUSION

Polanyi did not develop a theory of the "capitalist state" (the form taken by state power in capitalist society) and did not present any systematic scrutiny of state power. Nor did he deal with the role of states in maintaining social order, their mechanisms of surveillance and social discipline, or their oppressive functions. His contribution to state theory, rather, lies in his critique of market-liberal utopianism, an approach that conceptualizes the economic sphere as separated from the political, a "stateless" zone. In this, his most celebrated formulation is that the laissez-faire (self-regulating) economy was "the product of deliberate state action".[72]

In Polanyi's era, the illusion of self-regulation at the global level was strongly associated with, and pivoted on, the gold standard – an institution that was itself engineered by states. To what extent might his analysis shed light on political affairs today? The gold standard no longer exists, but monetary regimes with a clear resemblance to it do, notably the European Monetary Union (EMU). Just as the gold standard required that national economies experiencing an outflow of gold be obliged to adopt deflationary policies, and displaced responsibility for those policies by linking the domestic currency to an international fixed rate regime, so the eurozone's neoliberal straightjacket constrains the powers of sovereign governments and imposes the burden of adjustment disproportionately upon weaker economies.[73] Euroland's exclusion of the possibility of devaluation, Wolfgang Streeck has remarked, "is akin to the nineteenth-century gold standard, whose devastating impact on the capacity of the then-emerging nation-states to defend their peoples from the unpredictability of free markets, together with its ramifications for the stability of international relations, was analysed so impressively in Polanyi's *The Great Transformation.*" The EU, Streeck continues, is designed to ensure "that democracy is tamed by markets instead of markets by democracy": that the economy is depoliticized while politics is de-democratized. This is exemplified in the operation of EMU, representing as it does the EU's central aim of liberating "the capitalist economy from democratic distortion".[74] This was nowhere clearer than in 2011, when, at the bidding of eurozone officials, elected governments in Greece (and Italy) were removed and replaced by technocrats. As in the case of the economic intervention of the League of Nations in 1920s Austria, which Polanyi criticized, the Greek government was subjected to intensive control by a (state-constructed) international institution representing creditors, who imposed an unprecedented austerity and attacked labour and the institutions of labour protection.

Polanyi's main contribution to state theory is that he shows economic liberalism to be a state project. As Claus Offe, drawing on Polanyi, remarks, "market-liberal utopians" tend to forget "that the market is itself unleashed and nurtured by political power, for instance through the adoption and enforcement of the gold standard for international trade or draconian 'structural adjustment policies' imposed by the IMF. Getting rid of politics, first of all democratic politics, is the politics of the prospective winners of market society".[75] Illustrative of this is the EU's politically coordinated efforts to make the economy immune from social demands – to remove mass influence on the state, as Werner Bonefeld has put it, thereby enabling the economy to be "envisaged as a state-less sphere".[76] In Europe and notably in Greece, countermovements (whether in the form of hundreds of strikes and protests or new social movements and political parties), attempted to challenge this, but they were ultimately unsuccessful. This is where Polanyi, his separation thesis, and his critique of liberal understandings of the state become important: they shed light on today's endeavours to impose a neoliberal regime, to the detriment of democracy.

Notes for Chapter 3

1. On the quandaries of formulating state theory in terms of a singular ideal type ("the state"), see C. Barker, "A note on the theory of capitalist states", *Capital and Class* 2:1 (1978), 118–26.

2. M. Burawoy, "For a sociological Marxism: the contemporary convergence of Antonio Gramsci and Karl Polanyi", *Politics and Society* 31:2 (2003), 217.

3. *Ibid.* (emphasis added).

4. They are a parasitic organization with no central role in economic reproduction; an epiphenomenon of the property relations system; a factor of social cohesion; an instrument of class rule; a set of institutions in the sphere of public power; and a system of

political domination with effects on class struggle; see B. Jessop, *State Theory: Putting the Capitalist State in Its Place* (Cambridge: Polity, 1990), 25–8.

5. K. Polanyi, "Sein und denken", (n.d.) KPA-2-1; K. Polanyi (1936–40) Morley College lectures, KPA-15-4.

6. N. Fraser, "Why two Karls are better than one: integrating Polanyi and Marx in a critical theory of the current crisis", Working Paper der DFG-Kolleg "Post-Growth Societies" (1/2017), 4.

7. K. Polanyi, *The Great Transformation: The Political and Economic Origins of Our Time* (Boston, MA: Beacon Press, 2001), 146.

8. K. Polanyi, "A gildszocializmus" (1922), KPA-1-52.

9. N. Carpenter, *Guild Socialism: An Historical and Critical Analysis* (New York: Appleton, 1922), 147–8.

10. K. Polanyi, "Guild and the state" [1923], in G. Dale (ed.), *Karl Polanyi: The Hungarian Writings* (Manchester: Manchester University Press, 2016), 121.

11. H. Krüger, *Allgemeine Staatslehre* (Stuttgart: Kolhammer Verlag, 1966), 153; A. Sălăvastru, "The discourse of body politic in Thomas Hobbes' *Leviathan*", *Les Cahiers Psychologie Politique* 24 (2014).

12. Polanyi, "Guild and the state", 122 (emphasis in original).

13. B. Silver & G. Arrighi, "Polanyi's 'double movement': the *belle époques* of British and US hegemony compared", *Politics and Society* 31:2 (2003), 327.

14. K. Polanyi, draft manuscript (untitled), Part 2 (1920–22), KPA-2-1.

15. *Ibid.*

16. K. Polanyi, "Gild es allam", *Bécsi Magyar Ujság*, KPA-1-52.

17. Polanyi, "Guild and the state", 122 (emphasis in original).

18. K. Polanyi, "Socialist accounting" [1922], trans. A. Fischer, D. Woodruff & J. Bockman, LSE Research Online (October 2016), 26; available at: http://eprints.lse.ac.uk/68105/1/Woodruff_Socialist%20accounting_2016.pdf (accessed 7 May 2019).

19. J. Bockman, "Socialism and the embedded society: preface to Karl Polanyi's 'Socialist Accounting'", *Theory and Society* 45:5 (2016), 395.

20. Polanyi, "Socialist accounting", 26.

21. L. von Mises, "Neue Beiträge zum Problem der sozialistischen Wirtschaftsrechnung" [1925], *Archiv für Sozialwissenschaft und Sozialpolitik* 51:2. See also Mises, *Die Gemeinwirtschaft: Untersuchungen über den Sozialismus*, second edition (Jena: Gustav Fischer, 1932), 481.

22. K. Polanyi, "Sozialistische Rechnungslegung" in M. Cangiani, K.-P. Levitt & C. Thomasberger (eds), *Chronik der großen Transformation, Band 3* (Marburg: Metropolis, 2005).

23. K. Polanyi, "Über die Freiheit", in Cangiani *et al.*, *Chronik der großen Transformation*, 141.

24. *Ibid.*, 149–50.

25. K. Polanyi, "The meaning of peace" (1938), KPA-20-13.

26. Polanyi, *Great Transformation*, 266.

27. K. Polanyi, "The nature of international understanding" (n.d.), KPA-17-29.

28. K. Polanyi, "Jean Jacques Rousseau, or, is a free society possible?" (1943), KPA-18-24.

29. Polanyi, *Great Transformation*, 193.

30. *Ibid.*

31. K. Polanyi, "Nature of international understanding".

32. *Ibid.*

33. K. Polanyi, "Russia in the world", Christian Left Group, *Bulletins for Socialists* 4 (1939), KPA-20-14.

34. Polanyi, Morley College lectures, KPA-15-4.

35. K. Polanyi, "Why make Russia run amok?" (1943), 406, KPA-18-23.

36. K. Polanyi, "The new ABC of foreign policy" (mid-1940s), KPA-8-7.

37. Polanyi, *Great Transformation*, 138.

38. K. Polanyi, "Public opinion and statesmanship", in G. Resta & M. Catanzariti (eds), *Karl Polanyi: For a New West, Essays 1919–1958* (Cambridge: Polity, 2014), 132.

39. Polanyi, *Great Transformation*, 31.

40. K. Polanyi, "Coercion and defence" (1939), KPA-20-16.

41. *Ibid.*

42. Polanyi, *Great Transformation*, 147.

43. *Ibid.*, 258. See also G. Dale, "'Our world was made by nature': constructions of spontaneous order", *Globalizations* 15:7 (2018).

44. Polanyi, *Great Transformation*, 156.

45. K. Marx, *Grundrisse* [1857] (Harmondsworth: Penguin, 1993), 507.

46. A. Palumbo & A. Scott, *Remaking Market Society: A Critique of Social Theory and Political Economy in Neoliberal Times* (Abingdon: Routledge, 2017), 25.

47. Polanyi, *Great Transformation*, 3.

48. *Ibid.*, 29.

49. *Ibid.*, 136.

50. K. Polanyi, "Conflicting philosophies in modern society" (1937–8), KPA-15-2; K. Polanyi, "Rise and decline" (1945), KPA-8-7; K. Polanyi, "Lectures on modern European history" (1937–40), KPA-16-15.

51. K. Polanyi, Lecture syllabus, "Social and Political Theory" (1939–40), KPA-17-03.

52. K. Polanyi, "Our obsolete market economy: 'civilization must find a new thought pattern'", *Commentary* 3:2 (1947), 115, KPA-35-6.

53. *Ibid.*, 31.

54. Polanyi, *Great Transformation*, 146–8, 177.

55. Dennis Searcy speaks of a "dual state" emerging from Polanyi's approach, with tasks lying "in promoting a market economy while simultaneously serving as a conduit to regulate it"; see D. Searcy, "Beyond the self-regulating market in market society: a critique of Polanyi's theory of the state", *Review of Social Economy* 51:2 (1993), 127.

56. Tim Jackson, with reference to Polanyi, speaks of a "conflicted state" and "institutional schizophrenia". On the one hand, according to Jackson, the state is committed to the pursuit of economic growth and on the other, it intervenes to protect some common goods, for example, through climate change legislation. See T. Jackson, *Prosperity without Growth: Economics for a Finite Planet* (London: Earthscan, 2009), 166.

57. E. Mandel, "Historical materialism and the capitalist state" (1980), Marxist Internet Archive; available at: www.marxists.org/archive/mandel/1980/xx/hismatstate.htm (accessed 7 May 2019).

58. *Ibid.*

59. K. Polanyi, "Conflicting philosophies in modern society" (emphasis in original).

60. Polanyi, *Great Transformation*, 216.

61. K. Polanyi, "The essence of fascism", in K. Polanyi *et al.* (eds), *Christianity and the Social Revolution* (London: Gollancz, 1935), KPA-13-6.

62. G. Goodwin, "Rethinking the double movement: expanding the frontiers of Polanyian analysis in the global south", *Development and Change* 49:5 (2018), 1268–90.

63. *Ibid.*, 6.

64 K. Polanyi, "Demokratie und Währung in England" [1931], in M. Cangiani & C. Thomasberger (eds), *Chronik der großen Transformation*, Band 1 (Marburg: Metropolis, 2002), 125.

65 B. Warnock "The First Bailout: The Financial Reconstruction of Austria, 1922–1926", unpublished PhD dissertation, Birkbeck College, University of London, 2015.

66 P. Berger, *Im Schatten der Diktatur. Die Finanzdiplomatie des Vertreters des Völkerbundes in Österreich. Meinoud Marinus Rost van Tonningen, 1931–1936* (Vienna: Böhlau Verlag, 2000).

67 Polanyi, *Great Transformation*, 26.

68 *Ibid.*, 28.

69 K. Polanyi, "Democracy vs total crisis" (n.d.), KPA 20-06.

70 Lacher, "Karl Polanyi, the 'always-embedded market economy'".

71 F. Block, *Revising State Theory: Essays in Politics and Postindustrialism* (Philadelphia, PA: Temple University Press, 1987), 56–62.

72 Polanyi, *Great Transformation*, 141.

73 P. Burnham, "Towards a political theory of crisis: policy and resistance across Europe", *New Political Science* 33:4 (2011).

74 W. Streeck, "Das Ende der Nachkriegsdemokratie", *Süddeutsche Zeitung* (2012), available at: www.sueddeutsche.de/wirtschaft/ein-neuer-kapitalismus-das-ende-der-nachkriegsdemokratie-1.1427141 (accessed 7 May 2019); W. Streeck, *Buying Time: The Delayed Crisis of Democratic Capitalism* (London: Verso, 2014), 106, 116, 175.

75 C. Offe, "Review of 'The Power of Market Fundamentalism: Karl Polanyi's Critique'", *Thesis Eleven* 125:1 (2014).

76 W. Bonefeld, "Authoritarian liberalism: from Schmitt via ordoliberalism to the euro", *Critical Sociology* 43:4/5 (Aug 2016), 16.

4

CLASS

Sandra Halperin

Many scholars see the account of Europe's nineteenth-century market system in Karl Polanyi's *The Great Transformation* as offering key insights into contemporary trends of change. That account, however, differs substantially from much of the vast contemporaneous record of nineteenth-century Europe. What the analyses of countless social theorists; the speeches, official documents, reports and other writings of European reformers and statesmen; and the work of the century's greatest literary figures emphasized were the features Europeans considered to be the most characteristic of that time: domination, exploitation, inequality, and the recurring class conflicts which these generated. But, while Polanyi is unsparing in depicting the horrors of industrialization, his account ignores the exploitation, monopoly, and political repression that created and sustained those horrors for over a century; and while contemporaneous accounts treated class conflicts as a fundamental dimension of Europe's industrial development, in *The Great Transformation*, class interests and conflicts play a decidedly secondary or subsidiary role in the rise and demise of Europe's nineteenth-century market system.

The Great Transformation focuses on the rise of Europe's nineteenth-century market system, its disastrous impact on society, and the countermovement that it triggered and that, by interfering with the logic of the market mechanism, ultimately brought about its demise. Its central claim is that the basic dynamic shaping industrial capitalism during the nineteenth century and its transformation in the course of the world wars was the antagonism that emerged, not among groups, sectors, or classes, but between "society as a whole" and the "blind action" of the self-regulating market system's "soulless institutions".[1] Polanyi argued that the rise of this system triggered a "spontaneous social protective reaction that came from all sectors of society";[2] and that all sectors or classes were successful in securing protection for themselves because their efforts served to protect the essential substances of human society (land, labour and money) and thus served the general interest of society as a whole.[3] In sum, the self-regulating market threatened, and met with resistance from, "society as a whole", and when different sectors or classes endeavored to secure protection for themselves (the "protectionist countermove"), their efforts redounded to the benefit of society as a whole.

The Great Transformation is an account of two transformations: the first occurred at the end of the eighteenth century with the rise of Europe's unregulated market system; the second occurred with the collapse of the system in the world wars of the twentieth century. Polanyi offers what might be called a "top down" analysis of these transformations. He assumes that changes at the "top" – in the organization of the international economy – provide particular kinds of opportunities for states to act which, in turn, shapes the extent to which social forces will be able to influence state policy. His account consequently focuses first on the establishment of a new liberal international order and its key institutions. It was this overarching institutional order that enabled states to institute other changes that formed the basis of Europe's unregulated market system.[4] Based on these same analytic assumptions, Polanyi predicted that, with the failure of international institutions and the collapse of the market system, a global opportunity structure would emerge that would lay the basis for a new political and economic order in Europe. However, soon after the publication of *The Great Transformation*, it became clear that, although the free market and the laissez-faire state had given way, in varying degrees, to regulated markets and interventionist states, the liberal international order had survived.[5] So, while the market system had been transformed in important ways, it was not, as Polanyi had assumed, as a result of changes at "the top".[6]

Polanyi also assumed that the rise of Europe's nineteenth-century system was an unprecedented and once-and-for-all occurrence, and that its demise and the consequent emergence of a new political and economic order would represent a permanent change. But this assumption also proved erroneous. Contrary to Polanyi's expectations, "globalizing" trends began to re-emerge in the 1970s and to reverse post-Second World War changes that Polanyi had assumed would be permanent. It was in this context that there occurred a phenomenal resurgence of interest in Polanyi's book. Polanyi's insistence that unregulated markets threatened society as a whole has resonated with those concerned with the potential ecological impacts and threats to social cohesion associated with globalization. Much of the interest in *The Great Transformation* has focused on Polanyi's claim that the rise of the unregulated market system triggered a countermovement on the part of the whole of society. However, the rise of neoliberal globalization began some 40 years ago; and while it has engendered resistance and mobilized new social groups, it has yet to trigger a protectionist countermove by "society as a whole". While Polanyi's claim speaks to the hopes, and appeals to the idealism of opponents of globalization, it provides little insight into where and how it can be effectively resisted. By focusing on "society as a whole" as the unit of analysis in describing resistance to the unregulated market, and characterizing the emergence of that resistance as "spontaneous", he offers few, if any, lessons for scholars and activists concerned to reverse, or shape in less destructive ways, the rise once again of a global market. Consequently, while Polanyi concludes *The Great Transformation* with the hope that, following the war, an international order would be established that would make "peace and freedom secure",[7] his account provides little insight into the mechanisms and possibilities that might exist for bringing about progressive change.

The Great Transformation highlights the importance of understanding the interaction and fundamental interdependencies among international structures, states, and social forces in analyzing social change. But in emphasizing how the overarching institutional structure of Europe's market system enabled and constrained states and social actors, it tends to minimize the role of human agency. In particular, it fails to consider how class-specific interests and recurring class conflicts shaped international and state structures, or whether and how they shaped the way in which these structures were transformed following the Second World War. For Polanyi, the most important way in which groups, sectors, and classes act and are acted upon are as an organic whole; and the way in which groups, sectors, and classes interrelate with state and international structures is as an organic whole, as well. Thus, while we learn a great deal about the nineteenth-century system within which human agents acted, his analysis offers few if any lessons regarding the role human agents can play in bringing about institutional change. The next section discusses what Polanyi tells us about the forces that drive the historical events and institutional changes that are the focus of *The Great Transformation*.

POLANYI'S TWO TRANSFORMATIONS

The rise of the market system

Much of Polanyi's account of the rise of Europe's unregulated market system is devoted to a detailed discussion of the intellectual foundations and development of economic liberalism's free market ideology. But while the development of economic liberalism as "the organizing principle of society engaged in creating a market system"[8] seems to play the central role in the rise of the unregulated market, often "capitalism" or the "mechanism of the market" appears to be driving this change. Private property comes about because of the "*need*" of "*agricultural capitalism*" for "an individualized treatment of the land"; the surface of the planet was subjugated to "the *needs* of an *industrial society*"; similarly, "*industrial capitalism needed* sites for its mills and laborers' settlements"[9] and it was "*the growth of towns* [that] *induced* landlords to produce primarily for sale on the market". While Polanyi rightly points out that "[t]he road to the free market was opened and kept open by an enormous increase in continuous, centrally organized and controlled [state] interventionism",[10] he also says that, in England "*the growth of the metropolis compelled* the authorities" to loosen restrictions on the corn trade.[11]

In addition to the development of economic liberalism's free market ideology, and the needs of both capitalism and the market, Polanyi suggests that the "transformation of society into a market economy" was "the job" that "a new class entering on the historical scene -- the middle classes of England" -- was "destined to perform". This new middle class "forced its way to power" in Britain in 1832 "partly in order to remove [the] obstacle" standing in the way of "the new capitalistic economy":[12] the Speenhamland Law. The Representation of the People Act passed that year "put an end to the *ancien regime*";[13] two years later, the repeal of Speenhamland by the Poor Law Amendment Act of 1834 gave birth both to the working class and to the market economy. It was with the creation of a labour market in England that the self-regulating market began to operate fully.[14] But, whether these classes are the primary agents driving this change is ambiguous. Polanyi says that the extension of the market mechanism to labour (as well as to land and money) was "*an inevitable consequence* of the introduction *of the factory system* in a commercial society".[15] He also says that "[h]uman labor *had to be made into a commodity*" because "*the mechanism of the market was asserting itself and clamouring for its completion*".[16] His discussion of the countermovement that arises in reaction to the system seems to suggest that classes are *not* the primary agents of change.

Once the system has fully emerged, Polanyi's account focuses on the clash that then ensues between the "*principle of economic liberalism*, aiming at the establishment of a self-regulating market" and the "*principle of protection*". While classes appear to play a part in this clash, Polanyi seems to relegate them to a subsidiary role: each of these principles "relies" on the support of different classes. So, for instance, economic liberalism relied "on the support of the trading classes"; while the principle of protection relied primarily on "the working and the landed classes".[17] In his elaboration of the protectionist countermove, he argues that the existence of classes and their *possibility* of exercising agency are "given" by the requirements of the market system and the needs of society as a whole. Their very existence, as well as the success or failure of their actions is determined by the system.[18] In sum, in his account of the rise of the market system, it is not clear who or what Polanyi assumes drives institutional change: what is clear, however, is that he assigns no role to the actions and interests of classes, sectors, or groups in shaping the institutional transformation that he expects will emerge following the collapse of the market system in the Second World War. This suggests that, for him, something else drives social change.

The protectionist countermovement and the demise of the system

Polanyi observes that "[i]mprovements ... are, as a rule, bought at the price of social dislocation; and that if the dislocation is too great, the community must succumb in the process". He argues, therefore that, but "for protective counter-moves which blunted the action" of the "self-destructive" market mechanism, "human society would have been annihilated".[19] It was because such an institution as the self-regulating market system "could not exist for any length of time without annihilating the human and natural substance of society" that, "*inevitably*, society took measures to protect itself".[20] As previously noted, while the argument that protective countermoves emerged in reaction to Europe's market system and ultimately brought about its demise is a compelling one for those concerned with how today's globalization can be effectively resisted, Polanyi doesn't provide a clear account of where and how, and through what agency, these countermoves emerged.

A central premise of sociological investigation is that any social or political system is created to advance a particular set of political, economic, or other types of interests; and that the interests most favoured will reflect the relative power of the actors involved, i.e. those of the most powerful members of the social system. The actors that appear in Polanyi's account, although they are not identified with much precision, are the trading classes (also *haute finance*, bourgeoisie, or middle, commercial, or entrepreneurial classes); the landed class (also landed aristocracy, landed conservatism, reaction, or feudalism – to which is attached the "peasantry"); and the working classes (or labouring people). While he frequently uses the term "class" in discussing them, he does not give sustained consideration to their relative power. He does, however, address the role of class *interests*. "Mere class interest", he argues, "cannot offer ... a satisfactory explanation for any long-run social process". This "too narrow conception of interests", he argues, leads "to a warped vision of social and political history".[21] The "true sources of class influence, he argues, lie in the services they render "to the general interest of the community".[22]

He then goes on to argue that each of the three classes he identifies "stood, even if unconsciously, for interests wider than their own", providing "services to society" by playing roles which were "cut out for them by their availability for the discharge of various functions that derived from the total situation of society".[23] The interests of the trading or middle classes "ran parallel to the general interest" because "if business was flourishing there was a chance of jobs for all and of rents for owners". But "fulfil[ing] this function" made them unable to perform the task of safeguarding other interests and, thus, provided "the chance" for other classes. So, for instance, feudalism and landed conservatism, or "reaction" survived because it was available to serve the function of "restricting the disastrous effects of the mobilization of land"[24] and could promote themselves "as the guardians of man's natural habitat, the soil. Had the danger not been genuine, the stratagem could not have worked."[25] Polanyi seems to insist that only general, and never sectional, interests can be effective: he argues that neither the aims of classes "nor the degree to which they attain them … can be understood apart" from "the situation of society as a whole".[26] Thus, in the protectionist countermovement, although their defence "fell to one section of the population in preference to another … [u]ltimately, what made things happen were the interests of society".[27]

Polanyi argues that, neither economic interests (increasing monetary income) or resisting exploitation motivates class action. He argues that "the motives of human individual are only exceptionally determined by the needs of material want-satisfaction";[28] that the "emphasis put on exploitation tends to hide from our view the even greater issue of cultural degradation",[29] and that, since it was "not the economic but the social interests of different cross sections of the population [that] were threatened by the market, persons belonging to various economic strata unconsciously joined forces to meet the danger".[30]

According to Polanyi's account, during the interwar period the "clash of principles" generated by the protectionist countermove produced "deep institutional strain" and, as a result, "tensions between the social classes" developed. It was then (and only then) that the political and the economic "functions of society" were "used and abused as weapons" in a "struggle for sectional interests". This deadlock produced the "fascist crisis", and the interaction of this conflict of classes with the clash of organizing principles "turned crisis into catastrophe".[31] But while Polanyi acknowledges that class struggles during the interwar years play a role in the catastrophe (the collapse of the system), its "proximate cause", he argues, was the failure of the gold standard, and its larger cause was the failure of the international system: for "[b]y the time the gold standard failed, most of the other institutions had been sacrificed in a vain effort to save it".[32]

Polanyi's analytic approach might be seen as a reflection of the time and place in which he wrote, which was in the United States in 1944.[33] At that time and for ideological reasons (specifically because of its association with Marxism), class analysis was rejected in the US as doctrinaire (and thus irrelevant to the purposes and aims of social scientific research and good historical practice).[34] It was perhaps for this reason that Polanyi eschewed the language of class that emerged to express and shape the struggles of Europe's industrial development and that provided the principle categories of social analysis employed by Europeans themselves to describe their own society during the nineteenth century.[35] Moreover, while *The Great Transformation* is in large part a passionate critique of economic liberalism's free market ideology; Polanyi nonetheless bases his analysis on a number of key liberal assumptions. Thus, while rejecting the notion that markets arise spontaneously and operate to satisfy human needs, he also asserts that the market operates according to its own internal logic.[36] In claiming that the unregulated market threatened all sectors of society, he seems to assume that markets are politically neutral; and his assertion that, in the protectionist countermovement, the actions of classes redounded to the benefit of society as a whole, recalls Adam Smith's argument in *The Wealth of Nations* that the pursuit of self-interest results in the achievement of the general, public interest. While Polanyi recognizes the transformative force of the industrial revolution, inconsistent with this (and perhaps for the purpose of distancing himself from Marx), he rejects the notion that the development of productive forces is the major element in historical change. He rightly points out the key role of the state in facilitating the establishment of the free market, but then, consistent with classic liberal assumptions, treats the state as largely autonomous from social forces.[37]

In contrast to Polanyi's analysis, a class approach assumes that groups within society are endowed with different power resources, and that this influences the way social institutions develop, operate, and are transformed. It is concerned, therefore, with how economic and social change differentially impacts various groups in society. But Polanyi's analysis takes no account of specific social relations or interests, or the existence of differential capacities, limitations and potentialities. It consequently gives no consideration to the class-specific nature of protectionism in nineteenth-century Europe, or the existence and role of relations of power and authority, and of human will, skill, or freedom. Instead, he treats societies as organic unities in which all are more-or-less equally victimized by the "soulless institutions" of the self-regulating market system, and the countermove against it "possesse[s] all the unmistakable characteristics of a spontaneous reaction".[38] It is difficult to see what lessons this account might offer for those concerned to better understand the mechanisms and possibilities of progressive change in this current age of globalization.

The next section revisits the two periods analysed in *The Great Transformation*, focusing on the class interests that shaped and were served by the institutional complex underlying Europe's nineteenth-century market economy. In contrast to Polanyi's analysis, it assumes that states and interstate systems reflect the interests of powerful social forces. It consequently works from the "bottom up", focusing, first, on the configuration of class power and interests that produced the system, and then reconceiving, in terms of class interests, the nature of the state and its role in nineteenth-century European industrial expansion. By recasting the protectionist countermove in terms of sectoral, rather than societal, interests, the account which follows brings into focus a quite different "double movement": one, not of market expansion and a protective countermove on the part of "society as a whole", but of dominant classes attempting to monopolize opportunities for economic gain through externally-oriented economic expansion, and a rising "red tide" of radicals and socialists of various sorts, trade unionists, and suppressed national minorities. It will endeavour to show that it was the stresses and strains generated by *this* double movement that culminated in the world wars and shaped the changes that ensued as a result of it.

RE-READING EUROPE'S NINETEENTH-CENTURY INSTITUTIONS

The first transformation

Polanyi's account of the first transformation emphasizes the role of ideas and ideology in the rise of the unregulated market system. However, because it tends to relegate to the sidelines class interests and politics in the rise of Europe's nineteenth-century market system, it misses what is perhaps the most crucial chapter in modern history for understanding contemporary globalization: the successful campaign to dismantle Europe's "moral economy".[39] The end of regulated markets and national welfare systems[40] paved the way for the rise of the unregulated market system; and it consolidated the dominance, not of new liberal commercial interests, but of rural, pre-industrial, and autocratic structures of power and authority.

Europe emerged into its first century of industrial capitalism from the crucible of the Great War. A quarter century of war and revolutionary turmoil had made clear the central dilemma for dominant groups tempted by the possibilities of great profits to reorganize production along the lines of industrial capitalism: how to mobilize – train, educate and, in other ways, empower – labour while, at the same time, maintaining the basic relation of capitalism, i.e. the subordination of labour to capital. The war had revealed the dangers of a trained and compact mass army: many analogies, in fact, were drawn between the mass army of soldiers created in the war and the mass industrial army of workers needed for industrial capitalist production. At the same time socialism had been born in the French Revolution and its focus, in particular, on eradicating private property – something dominant classes had achieved through a century or more of struggle – seemed, in combination with the revolutionary ferment unleashed by the war, to threaten an anti-capitalist revolt of the masses.

This was the context within which elites throughout Europe undertook to mobilize labour for industrial production. Mass mobilization for industry (as for war) creates, out of the relatively disadvantaged majority of the population, a compact and potentially dangerous force; thus, elites showed little interest in the expansion of industry at home. In the eighteenth century, Britain's industrial growth had been fuelled by the production of mass consumption goods and the expansion of the domestic market. However, had this expansion continued, along with the democratization of consumption and mass purchasing power needed to support it, the class, land, and income structures on which the existing hierarchy of social power in Europe rested would have been destroyed. Thus, despite the fact that at the end of the Great War abundant opportunities remained for domestic investment and the expansion of production for home consumption, the gradual expansion of local markets and production for local mass consumption that had taken place, not only in Britain but throughout Europe in the eighteenth century, was halted and put into reverse. Instead, Europeans launched a brutal expansion of production-for-export that became a model for elites and ruling groups throughout the world.

The revolutionary currents unleashed by the Great War and the overall pattern of economic expansion that emerged in its aftermath, worked to increasingly polarize European societies along class lines until it effectively generated a two-class structure. There was, first, an aggregate of those who produced surplus value from a subordinate position in terms of production functions, income, and status, and who were represented by the institutions of the working class;[41] and, second, an aggregate of people who occupied the upper rungs of the economic ladder, a dominant class that controlled the operations of capitalist enterprise (as well as some of those whose status and position was directly dependent on them, e.g. household servants).

In Britain, as elsewhere in Europe, the industrial revolution had advantaged the older and more conservative sectors of the British wealth structure (the great landowners and the bankers and merchants of the City of London) rather than manufacturers and industrialists.[42] In most European countries rising commercial classes demanded a bigger share of power but they did not, nor did they want to, overthrow and replace the old ruling class. Instead, there was a fusion of Europe's commercial/industrial and landowning classes in which Europe's "traditional" landowning and aristocratic elite remained dominant.[43]

While there were many different elements or "fractions" within this class,[44] the social conflicts that persisted following the Great War and became endemic throughout Europe brought about a unity among them. Thus, while landed and industrial capital in Britain clashed over the Corn Laws, they remained united in a struggle to prevent labour from achieving any significant political and economic power. Despite the varied circumstances of its formation and characteristics of its organization, the working class constituted the only significant challenge to the power of capital. Consequently, its demands, whether for an eight-hour day, a living wage, universal and equal suffrage, or the overthrow of capitalist property relations, evoked a swift, absolute, and uncompromising response from dominant classes. While conflict between labour and capital was not the only conflict within nineteenth-century European society, it was the most far-reaching and important; and the nature of Europe's economic expansion, and of its state and international institutions, were fundamentally shaped by it.

The "liberal" state

Polanyi claimed that, after 1834, the "middle-class state"[45] emerged in Britain as the state of the "ruling middle class".[46] But as the previous section argued, throughout the nineteenth century, the dominant element in Britain's fusion of commercial/industrial and landowning classes, was landowning and aristocratic elites. The fraction of the bourgeoisie that dominates is the fraction that actually makes the laws and rules and determines the pattern of capitalist development. Throughout the nineteenth century, European states were aligned with the dominant landed and industrial class in Europe.[47] Until 1905, every British cabinet, whether Conservative or Liberal, was dominated by the traditional landed elite.[48] Consequently, landowners did not experience significant political setbacks with respect to tariffs, labour legislation, land reform, state allocations, tax policy, or internal terms of trade, until after 1945.

Polanyi wrote that European societies in the nineteenth century were being destroyed by "the blind action of soulless institutions the only purpose of which was the automatic increase of material welfare".[49] But this increase of material wealth was neither automatic nor class neutral. States committed to monopoly and repression at home, and to the militant pursuit of markets and resources abroad,[50] enabled dominant classes to monopolize gains from industrial expansion and to exclude other classes and groups from political and economic life. Throughout the nineteenth century, states introduced laws that favoured the dominant classes, and brutally repressed those who challenged them.

According to Polanyi, it was when the passage of the New Poor Law of 1834 enabled workers in England to gain sufficient mobility to sell their labour power in the market that the "blind action" of the "soulless institutions" of the self-regulating market began to fully operate. But from the start, states enforced a variety of legal and extra-legal devices not, as Polanyi claims, to protect labour from the market, but to impede their mobility and their ability to engage in collective resistance and bargaining.[51] State legislation, as well as the wealth and power of Justices of the Peace, and the active collaboration of parish officers, enabled employers to deny workers the right to bargain, bind workers by long and inflexible contracts, and make them liable to imprisonment for breach of employment. Wage levels were determined, not by market forces or through collective bargaining, but by employers.

Polanyi argued that the market threatened society as a whole and he implies that protectionist legislation was consequently something unplanned, spontaneous, and in the interest of society as a whole. But the type and extent of protection gained by different classes differed significantly. So, for instance, while tariff policy varied throughout Europe and fluctuated throughout the nineteenth century, at no time anywhere was agriculture left without substantial protection.[52] Landowners also succeeded in blocking efforts at agrarian reform, maintaining the social and political isolation of agrarian labour, and securing favourable state tax and pricing policies.[53] By ensuring the survival of various forms of corporatism and creating new ones, states provided landowners and wealthy industrialists with privileged access to the state and to all the resources at its command. At the same time, states maintained a vast restrictive system of legal, social and land institutions. They brutally repressed labour organization and ensured that the mass of the population would be barred from any possibility of gaining significant institutionalized economic, social or political power. Consequently, while we have abundant evidence of lower-class misery, we have little evidence that the privileged classes suffered. If dominant groups sought protection it was, not from the market, but from pressures for redistribution and reform that threatened their monopoly and privilege. As Polanyi himself observed, but without drawing its implications, industrialists demanded from the state that their property be protected, not from the market, but "from the people".[54]

The concert of Europe and Europe's 100 years' peace

Polanyi begins *The Great Transformation* with an analysis of what he claims was the most striking feature of nineteenth-century Europe: its "100 years of peace". Europe enjoyed one hundred years of peace, he claims, because the Concert of Europe acted as an "international peace interest". He begins his analysis here because, for him, this "unprecedented" period of peace provides powerful evidence of the dominance in Europe of a "new" liberal bourgeoisie, and of the establishment of free markets, free trade, and the liberal state.

Polanyi claimed that this new liberal bourgeoisie dominated the Concert of Europe and, through its agency, worked to preserve liberal free market institutions.[55] But the claim that the Concert of Europe was dominated by *haute finance* overstates, again, both the power of new commercial/trading/middle/industrial classes and the waning of the ancien regime.

Throughout the nineteenth century, the Concert maintained a commitment, not to free markets and liberal states, but to protection and autocracy. Moreover, in claiming that the Concert of Europe acted as an "international peace interest",[56] Polanyi advances a popular, but erroneous, current of liberal thought which associates high finance with peace; one which is belied by the fact that European states were continually at war during the nineteenth century, and in the very areas of the world where finance capital had migrated. That is why Lenin, Hobson, and others associated finance capital, not with peace, but with war.[57] While it may be true to say that the Concert had a "peace interest", the peace it promoted was primarily concerned to serve the interest of containing class conflicts and defending the existing sociopolitical order against revolutionary threats.

After the French Revolution, it was an accepted fact in Europe that revolution in a single country would likely spread and become a European phenomenon. Eric Hobsbawm observed that "[n]ever in European history and rarely anywhere else has revolutionism been so endemic, so general, so likely to spread by spontaneous contagion as well as by deliberate propaganda".[58] It was because Europe's monarchs and aristocracies feared that such conflicts would call into use the mass armies that, during and immediately after the Napoleonic Wars, had triggered revolutionary upheavals, that multilateral great power conflicts in Europe were avoided.[59] At the conclusion of the Napoleonic Wars, Europe's royalty and aristocracies formed a "Holy Alliance" for the purpose of suppressing revolutionary uprisings throughout the region.[60] This alliance succeeded in maintaining a "reactionary peace" in Europe until 1846. But, according to Polanyi, with "the victory of the new economy", the middle classes became the "bearer of a peace interest much more powerful than that of their reactionary predecessors".[61]

Throughout the century, European domestic relations were characterized by recurring and increasingly violent class conflicts. Revolutions, insurrections, rebellions, uprisings, riots, violent strikes and demonstrations; coups, assassinations, political repression and terrorism; as well as ethnic and nationalist, religious and ideological conflicts, were characteristic of European societies up until 1945.[62] Concerned to defend their common way of life, Europe's property-owning classes of all nations joined together, fighting side by side with "foreign" class allies to suppress dissident and revolutionary elements from among their own countrymen. Concert-sponsored military interventions put down uprisings in Parma, Modena, Naples, Rome, Bologna, Ferrara, Romagna and elsewhere in Italy; in parts of German, including Saxony and Hanover, the Bavarian Palatinate and the Duchy of Baden; in Spain and Portugal, and in Hungary and Wallachia, Herzegovina and Crete. While it might be claimed that these military interventions served the interests of international finance (although the association of uprisings in these places with the interests of international finance is far from clear), they also helped to preserve the essential contours of local class structures throughout the nineteenth century.

The unraveling of Europe's nineteenth-century political economy

The global depression and agricultural decline of 1873–96 brought about a sharp escalation of imperialist expansion and accelerated the rise of a global "red tide". Thus, in the years leading up to the 1914 war in Europe, the two central features of Europe's globalizing system of production – internal repression and expansion through production for export – were rapidly coming into conflict.[63] By 1914, and the first time since 1815, European imperialist rivalries came to focus with full force on Europe itself. Confronted with an existential threat, European states were forced, once again, to mobilize the masses for war and for the expansion of industrial production needed to support it. The mobilization of increasingly politicized, radicalized, and organized masses to fight for a system that had, for decades, generated increasingly divisive social conflict, set in motion a social revolution that began in 1917 and, thereafter, swept through all of Europe.[64] As skilled and unskilled workers, workers of different occupations, anarchists and socialists, social democrats and communists, revolutionaries and reformists closed ranks.[65] There was an explosive rise of trade union membership, peasant organization, socialist parties and socialist radicalism. Attempts to block the rising "red tide" by a strategy of actively aiding and abetting the rearmament and expansion of Germany as a bulwark against Bolshevism led directly to the Second World War.[66]

After the First World War, and despite the profound dislocations that had resulted from the conflict, ruling classes in all western European countries had succeeded in re-establishing and maintaining the pre-war status quo.[67] However, the need to undertake mass mobilization for an even more destructive *second* European war, by bringing about a further shift in the balance of class power, made a restoration of the pre-war system impossible. Instead, after the war, there was a massive capitulation to social democratic reforms that had previously been strenuously and often violently resisted. As Schumpeter (and many others) observed, this explained, not only the transformation that had taken place there, but its apparent permanence:

> The business class has accepted gadgets of regulation and new fiscal burdens, a mere fraction of which it would have felt to be unbearable fifty years ago … *And it does not matter whether the business class accepts this new situation or not. The power of labor is almost strong enough in itself* – and amply so in alliance with the other groups that have in fact, if not in words, renounced allegiance to the scheme of values of the private-profit economy – *to prevent any reversal* which goes beyond an occasional scaling off of rough edges.[68]

Contrary to liberal assumptions, what the state is and what it can do shifts in response to changes in the balance of class forces, both between and within them. Thus, after the Second World War, states adopted social democratic and Keynesian goals and policy instruments that, before the war, would never have been accepted by the wealthy classes. In an historic compromise, social democrats were required to accept private ownership of the means of production and capitalists to use the profits they realised from this to increase productive capacity and to allow labour to share in productivity gains. States introduced welfare reforms, measures that partially decommodified labour, and market and industry regulation that made investment and production serve the expansion and integration of national markets. Wages rose with profits, making higher mass consumption possible for new mass consumer goods industries. This more balanced and internally oriented development brought to an end – for a time – intense social conflicts and the great movements of colonialism and imperialism. However, by the late 1970s a campaign had emerged to reverse this postwar compromise; and, since then, it has succeeded in bringing about the return of features of the globally free capitalism that had characterized nineteenth-century Europe.

CONCLUSIONS: IMPLICATIONS FOR CONTEMPORARY ISSUES

Karl Polanyi's *The Great Transformation* has been, and continues to be, a source of inspiration for political economists, international relations theorists, sociologists, and historians endeavouring to understand transformations of national, regional and global structures. However, the "top down" account that it offers is, in many ways, misleading. Polanyi's argument that the changes which took place following the Second World War were the result of a natural reaction of "society" to the ever encroaching market, gives insufficient consideration to the role of class power and interests in producing and maintaining the nineteenth-century system, or to the class tensions and struggles that the system generated and that contributed to bringing about its demise. His account of how the international economy, states, and social forces are interrelated fails to consider whether or how the interests of powerful social forces shape states and interstate systems. It thus fails to achieve its aim of clarifying the mechanisms and possibilities of progressive change.

In important respects, Polanyi's account is similar to analyses which treat technological innovations, changes in the organization of capitalist production, or the "logic" of markets or of international capital, as primary agents in processes of globalization today. These analyses have contributed to a growing consensus around the classically liberal assertion that governments can act only within the limits set by markets and the "logic" of capital.[69]

His assumption that the rise and demise of Europe's nineteenth-century system was a once-and-for-all occurrence, and his prediction of its ultimate collapse rather than its resilience and reproduction, prevents us from seeing these events as related to an on-going struggle over the distribution of costs and benefits of industrial capitalism, in which there have been periods when capital is relatively more, and relatively less, free from national state regulation. A closer reading of this struggle than that found in *The Great Transformation*, may offer important insights into the forces at work in the rise (once again) of a global market, as well as the forces of resistance that may be capable either of reversing it, or shaping it in less destructive ways.

The globalization of capital has been driven throughout its history by processes that are largely national and political.[70] The main institutional *mechanism* for resisting it is the state, and the main battle is to wrest control of states from corporate control. The strategic issue affecting the *possibilities* of effective resistance to globalism, then, is the ability to mobilize collective action in national arenas. It was through mobilizations in national arenas that the rights of citizenship, democratic governance, and economic justice were won in a few parts of the world after the Second World War. It is in those arenas that today they might be lost.

Notes for Chapter 4

1. K. Polanyi, *The Great Transformation: The Political and Economic Origins of Our Time* (Boston, MA: Beacon Press, [1944] 2001), 228.

2. *Ibid.*, 76.

3. *Ibid.*, 217.

4. A year after the publication of *The Great Transformation*, Polanyi invoked this analytical schema in an article on the transformation of liberal capitalism: K. Polanyi, "Universal capitalism or regional planning?", *London Quarterly of World Affairs* 10 (1945), 86–91; 89.

5. See K. Polanyi, "Our obsolete market mentality", *Commentary* 3 (1947), 109–17.

6. The hybrid system that this created was later characterized by John Ruggie as one of "embedded liberalism"; see J. Ruggie, "International regimes, transactions, and change: embedded liberalism in the postwar economic order", *International Organization* 36:2 (1982).

7. Polanyi, *Great Transformation*, 263.

8. *Ibid.*, 141.

9. *Ibid.*, 188 (emphases added).

10. *Ibid.*, 146.

11. *Ibid.*, 190 (emphases added).

12. *Ibid.*, 82.

13. *Ibid.*, 124.

14. *Ibid.*, 105.

15. *Ibid.*, 78 (emphases added).

16. *Ibid.*, 107 (emphases added).

17. *Ibid.*, 138.

18. "With any long-run social process, the process itself may decide about the existence of the class itself; second, because the interests of given classes determine only the aims and purposes toward which those classes are striving, not also the success or failure of their endeavours" (*Great Transformation*, 160).

19. *Ibid.*, 79.

20. *Ibid.*, 3 (emphasis added).

21. *Ibid.*, 154–5. He observes for instance that, while agrarians, manufacturers, and trade unionists all "wished to increase their incomes through protectionist action", this search for protection was primarily *non*-economic: for "even where monetary values were involved", they were secondary to other interests; "almost invariably professional status, safety and security, the form of a man's life, the breadth of his existence, the stability of his environment were in question" (*ibid.*, 154).

22. *Ibid.*, 193–4.

23. *Ibid.*, 139.

24. *Ibid.*, 193.

25. *Ibid.*, 195.

26. *Ibid.*, 160.

27. *Ibid.*, 169 (emphasis added).

28. *Ibid.*, 160.

29. *Ibid.*, 166.

30. *Ibid.*, 162.

31. *Ibid.*, 140.

32. *Ibid.*, 3.

33. While writing *The Great Transformation* in the United States, Polanyi's wife was forced to leave the country because of her communist background. It is impossible to say whether these circumstances influenced the work he was producing in the US at that time. However, its analytic orientation is fully compatible with Cold War social scientific and historical research and writing in the US at that time. Rhoda Halperin argued that, because of the political climate in the US during the time Polanyi was writing *The Great Transformation*, he had to mask his Marxism. See R. Halperin, "Polanyi, Marx, and the institutional paradigm in economic anthropology", *Research in Economic Anthropology* 6 (1984), 245–72; 249.

34. Marxism is an exploration of the role of class processes (processes of the production, appropriation and distribution of surplus value) and class struggles in human history. Thus, rejection of Marxism entailed, first and foremost, a rejection of the notion of class and of class conflict.

35. As G. E. M. de Ste. Croix argues, "it is a healthy instinct on the part of historians in the empirical tradition to feel the need at least to *begin from* the categories and the terminology in use within the society they are studying – provided, of course, they do not remain imprisoned, therein"; see G. E. M. de Ste. Croix, *The Class Struggle in the Ancient Greek World* (Ithaca, NY: Cornell University Press, 1981), 36. "The idea of class," William Reddy points out, "has been a central one in European politics ever since Sieyès wrote his pamphlet 'What Is the Third Estate?'" (*Money and Liberty*, 22). It was recognized not just by revolutionaries, but by Popes, as well (e.g., by Pope Pius XI in his 1931 encyclical, *Quadragesimo anno*). With the onset of the industrial revolution, the language of class supplanted the language of "ranks", "orders", "estates". See R. Morris, *Class and Class Consciousness in the Industrial Revolution, 1780–1850* (London: Macmillan, 1979), 9; see also 18–20, for a comparison of the eighteenth-century language of status groups and the nineteenth-century discussion of conflict groups or classes.

36. "The most startling peculiarity of the system lies in the fact that, once it is established, it must be allowed to function without outside interference" (*Great Transformation*, 44); "it is no exaggeration to say that the social history of the nineteenth century was determined by the logic of the market system proper after it was released by the Poor Law Reform Act of 1834" (*ibid.*, 87).

37. "[L]aissez-faire economy was the product of deliberate State action", but the countermove against it was "spontaneous, undirected by opinion, and actuated by a purely pragmatic spirit" (*ibid.*, 147). Weberian/institutional and liberal modernization approaches see the state as an independent institution acting in its own right. The autonomous state is also a feature of neoclassical economic and rational choice approaches and newer statist or state-centric approaches. It also came to feature, although not until the 1970s, in neo-Marxist theories of the state.

38. Polanyi, *Great Transformation*, 156 (emphasis added).

39. Europe's "moral economy" was characterized by regulations which ensured the rights of all to basic material security and protection from extreme oppression. See P. Thane, "Government and society in England and Wales, 1750–1914", in *The Cambridge Social History of Britain, 1750–1950*, vol. 3: *Social Agencies and Institutions* (Cambridge: Cambridge University Press, 1992) 1–62; 7. In the eighteenth century, England had a national welfare system, and state regulation ensured that local, face-to-face buying and selling was conducted through open transactions in the marketplace. A revolution of consumption was fuelling the expansion of a domestic market for massproduced consumer goods and, as a result, "a greater proportion of the population than in any previous society in human history" was able "to enjoy the pleasures of buying consumer goods" and "not only necessities, but decencies, and even luxuries". See N. McKendrick, J. Brewer & J. Plumb, *The Birth of a Consumer Society* (London: Europa, 1982), 29.

40. See, for a discussion, Halperin, *War and Social Change*, Chapter 2.

41. By 1832 these included "strongly based and self-conscious working-class institutions – trade unions, friendly societies, educational and religious movements, political organizations, periodicals – working-class intellectual traditions, working-class community-patterns, and a working class structure of feeling" (E. Thompson, "Standards and experiences", in A. Taylor (ed.), *The Standard of Living in Britain in the Industrial Revolution* (London: Methuen, 1975), 129–30).

42. W. Rubenstein, *Men of Property: The Very Wealthy in Britain Since the Industrial Revolution* (NewBrunswick, NJ: Rutgers University Press, 1981), 17.

43. See, for example, W. Guttsman, "Aristocracy and the middle classes in the British political elite, 1886–1916", *British Journal of Sociology* 5 (1954), 12–32; D. Spring (ed.), *European Landed Elites in the Nineteenth Century* (Baltimore, MD: Johns Hopkins University Press, 1977); H. Rosenberg, *Bureaucracy, Aristocracy and Autocracy: The Prussian Experience, 1660–1815* (Cambridge, MA: Harvard University Press, 1966); R. Dahrendorf, *Society and Democracy in Germany* (New York: Doubleday, 1967); A. Mayer, *The Persistence of the Old Regime: Europe to the Great War* (New York: Pantheon, 1981); S. Halperin, *In the Mirror of the Third World: Capitalist Development in Modern Europe* (Ithaca, NY: Cornell University Press, 1997), chapter 4. Liberals like Vilfredo Pareto, Herbert Spencer and Max Weber wrote with dismay about the "persistence" of traditional landed, bureaucratic and military elites. See, for example, V. Pareto, "The circulation of elites", in *Theories of Society: Foundations of Modern Sociological Theory* edited by T. Parsons *et al.* (New York: Free Press of Glencoe, 1961 [1901]), H. Spencer *Principles of Sociology* Vol. 3. (New York: Appleton, 1898), chapters 22–4; and M. Weber, *Economy and Society* II (New York: Bedminster Press, 1968 [1922]), 974. Until 1901, agriculture remained the largest branch of Britain's economy in employment terms; and until 1914, nonindustrial Britain could easily outvote industrial Britain; see E. Hobsbawm, *Industry and Empire* (London: Weidenfeld & Nicolson, 1968), 195–6. In 1914, industrialists still "were not sufficiently organized to formulate broad policies or exert more than occasional influence over the direction of national affairs" (R. Boyce, *British Capitalism at the Crossroads, 1919–1932* (Cambridge: Cambridge University Press, 1987), 8).

44. In Britain, as elsewhere, the dominant class consisted of a landowning aristocracy and the large manufacturing, financial and commercial interests of capitalist enterprise. In addition, those who performed the professional and other functions of a middle class on their behalf, as R. Morris explains, represented "a specialized sector of the ruling class which dealt with key aspects of economic and political domination" (*Class and Class Consciousness*, 23).

45. Polanyi, *Great Transformation*, 192.

46. *Ibid.*, 195.

47. See, for example, D. Spring, *European Landed Elites*; J. Gillis, *The Development of European Society, 1770–1870* (Boston, MA: Houghton Mifflin, 1983); J. Weiss, *Conservatism in Europe 1770–1945: Traditionalism, Reaction, and Counter-Revolution* (New York: Harcourt, Brace Jovanovich, 1977); Guttsman, "Aristocracy and the middle classes"; G. Clark, "The nobility and gentry – old style" and "The new politics and the new gentry", in *The Making of Victorian England* (London: Methuen, 1966), 206–74; J. Sheehan, "Conflict and cohesion among German elites in the 19th century", in J. Sheehan (ed.), *Imperial Germany* (New York: New Viewpoints, 1976); W. Struve, *Elites Against Democracy: Leadership Ideals in Bourgeois Political Thought in Germany, 1890–1933* (Princeton, NJ: Princeton University Press, 1973); E. Weber, *Peasants into Frenchmen: The Modernization of Rural France, 1870–1914* (Stanford, CA: Stanford University Press, 1976); H. Peiter, "Institutions and attitudes: the consolidation of the business community in bourgeois France, 1880–1914", *Journal of Social History* 9:4 (1976), 510–25; T. Zeldin, *France, 1848-1945: Politics and Anger* (Oxford: Oxford University Press, 1979); Weber, *Economy and Society*, II, 974.

48. J. Thomas, *The House of Commons: 1832–1901* (Cardiff: University of Wales Press, 1939). Brief exceptions are the Liberal ministries of 1892–5.

49. Polanyi, *Great Transformation*, 219.

50. The period 1860–75 represents the only free trade interlude in an otherwise protectionist century. It was not until the 1860s that Britain repealed the Navigation Laws and Usury Laws and abolished restrictions on exports and all but a few duties on imports. Starting in the late 1870s and continuing until the end of the Second World War, there was a steady closure and constriction of markets everywhere in Europe. See, Halperin, *Mirror*, chapter 6.

51. In Britain, efforts to destroy trade unions continued after they ceased to be formally illegal in 1824. Strikes were legalized in England in 1834, but striking workers continued to be threatened with jail. Peaceful picketing was not clearly recognized as legal until 1906 (Goldstein, *Political Repression*, 60–1). Polanyi's argument that workers were afforded protection, too, recalls de Ste. Croix's description of the Roman Empire: "The rulers of the empire rarely if ever had any real concern for the poor and unprivileged as such; but they sometimes realised the necessity to give some of them some protection … either to prevent them from being utterly ruined and thus become useless as taxpayers, or to preserve them as potential recruits for the army" (*Class Conflict*, 502).

52. It is often assumed that the abolition in 1846 of the tariffs and other restrictions on imported food and grain introduced by the Corn Laws in 1815 represented a significant setback for landlords in Britain. However, these measures had been designed, not to protect a declining sector, but to retain the high profits generated during the Napoleonic war years. Consequently, wheat prices did not fall as a result of the repeal of the Corn Laws. This occurred only with the onset of the Great Depression in the 1870s (see Hobsbawm, *Industry and Empire*, 197).

53. Whenever states imposed price controls on grain and other food staples to reduce the "wage bill" for industrialists, they offset this with measures to prevent prices from dropping too low and cutting into the profits of large landowners. Price controls were also offset by low agricultural land taxes.

54. Polanyi, *Great Transformation*, 225.

55. Here he refers to the new liberal bourgeoisie as "*haute finance*", but elsewhere as "international finance", "international banking", or "capitalist internationalism". A singular human agent is identified as representing *haute finance* and acting as its chief instrument "of enforcement" (*ibid.*, 29): "a Jewish banker's dynasty", the Rothschilds (*ibid.*, 11). In the interwar years, this role shifts to J. P. Morgan (*ibid.*, 23).

56. Polanyi, *Great Transformation*, 16, 17.

57. European states were continually engaged in conflict with their own populations, with other European states and populations, and with territories and states outside of Europe. Fourteen wars were fought in Europe between and among Britain, France, Germany, Spain, Russia, Denmark, Austria, Italy, Greece and Serbia. Twelve wars were fought by Britain, France, Russia and Austria against foreign populations in Europe. During that period, European states also fought some 58 wars outside of Europe. See S. Halperin, *War and Social Change in Modern Europe: The Great Transformation Revisited* (Cambridge: Cambridge University Press, 2004), chapter 4.

58. E. Hobsbawm, *The Age of Revolution 1789–1848* (New York: Mentor, 1962), 137.

59. Castlereagh, Britain's foreign secretary (1812–22), observed that, with "revolutionary embers more or less existing in every state of Europe ... true wisdom is to keep down the petty contentions of ordinary times, and to stand together in support of the established principles of social order" (C. Vane (ed.), *Correspondence, Dispatches, and Other Papers of Viscount Castlereagh* (London: John Murray, 1853), XI, 105), quoted in Hobsbawm, *Age of Revolution*, 26. Hobsbawm notes that "all intelligent statesmen" recognized "that no major European war was henceforth tolerable, for such a war would almost certainly mean a new revolution, and consequently the destruction of the old regimes" (*ibid.*).

60. Concluded in 1815 among Britain, Russia, Austria and Prussia and later, France.

61. Polanyi, *Great Transformation*, 17.

62. See Halperin, *War and Social Change*, chapter 4.

63. Goldstein, *Political Repression*, 246. The growing land hunger in Europe was reflected, not only by agrarian agitation and protest, but by the massive emigration which began in the final decades of the century. Between 1870 and 1914, 35 million Europeans left the region; 25 million left after 1890, most of whom were displaced peasants and agricultural labourers from Prussia's eastern agricultural regions, from southern Italy, the Austro-Hungarian Empire, and the Balkans.

64. For a detailed account, see S. Halperin, "War and social revolution: World War I and the 'great transformation'", in A. Anievas (ed.), *Cataclysm 1914: The First World War in the Making of Modern World Politics* (London: Brill, 2014), 174–98.

65. J. Cronin, "Strikes and power in Britain, 1870–1920", in L. Haimson & C. Tilly (eds), *Strikes, Wars, and Revolutions in an International Perspective: Strike Waves in the Late Nineteenth and Early Twentieth Centuries* (Cambridge: Cambridge University Press, 1982), 139, 121.

66. See Haperin, *War and Social Change*, chapter 7.

67. For a detailed discussion of these changes and of the postwar restoration, see Halperin, *Mirror*, chapters 5–7.

68. J. Schumpeter, *Capitalism, Socialism and Democracy* (London: Routledge, 1976 [1950]), 419–20 (emphases added).

69. Note how this conceptualization is reflected in this statement by former British Prime Minister Tony Blair, in a radio interview: "we are going to live in a market of global finance and there will be investors that decide to move their money in and out of countries ... I'm afraid I'm someone who says look, this is a situation you live and work with and try and prepare yourselves for, but cannot really change" (*Today Programme*, BBC Radio 4, 30 September 1998).

70. This, I have argued elsewhere (Halperin 1997), is as true for the periphery as for the core: it is local dominant classes which are decisive in bringing about external reliance and in determining how the benefits of collaboration with foreign capital are distributed and used.

5

THE GOLD STANDARD

Samuel Knafo

INTRODUCTION

Considering that the gold standard stands at the heart of Polanyi's account of nineteenth-century liberal governance, there has been curiously little discussion of his conception of this institution. Beyond casual references, few scholars have enquired into Polanyi's analysis of the gold standard. Instead, most of the attention has gravitated towards his analysis of the commodification of labour. It is thus the reform of the Poor Laws in 1834 and its impact on labour that became the focal point of much writings on this author, despite Polanyi claiming that it was the gold standard which had been the supreme vehicle of the Market society.[1]

The gold standard, however, played a pivotal role in the argument of *The Great Transformation*. Polanyi develops the thesis that it was the policies implemented in the nineteenth century in the name of progress, and more specifically Market progress, which were responsible for the apparent breakdown of European civilization in the first half of the twentieth century (two world wars, the depression and the rise of fascism). By forcing people to become more and more competitive on the market, pro-market policies pushed people to make more and more sacrifices (e.g. cutting wages, working longer hours, being less attentive to the community) until these threatened the very fabric of society. In order to demonstrate this argument, Polanyi needed to link as directly as possible the tragic developments of the twentieth-century events to what he saw as the market policies of the nineteenth century. Here, the gold standard seemed well suited to bear this analytical burden as an institution that spanned the whole period covered in this book. It also appeared as a logical choice since the gold standard is often seen as the quintessential deflationary regime of governance. The term of deflation is usually associated with a regime that intensifies market pressures by limiting the amount of money in circulation.[2] When there is less money, its value increases and market actors have to compete harder to get it. In the case of the gold standard, this would have been achieved by forcing banks to back their banknotes with reserves of gold, a rare metal that made it more difficult to create new money.

What makes perfect sense at a formal and logical level, however, often proves to be misleading when looking at concrete history. For example, it is difficult to square this thesis with the fact that the gold standard, far from restricting the supply of money in the nineteenth century, witnessed instead the broad diffusion of banknotes as a form of money. As a result, Britain saw its supply of money increase more rapidly than that of other European countries in the early decades of the nineteenth century.[3] It was a trajectory that strongly contrasted the experience of the interwar period, which Polanyi knew much better and when the gold standard did have a clear deflationary impact. Yet he failed to appreciate the differences between these two eras and projected back a conception of the gold standard that had little to do with the circumstances that surrounded the creation of this institution a century earlier.

Part of the problem is that Polanyi never really delved into the historical complexities of this case. Instead, he relied on formal writings from economists that were never properly contextualized. It is striking how Polanyi shifts register when he moves from labour and land to money, the last of his three fictitious commodities. Here, his analysis of the gold standard curiously fails to go beyond the deductive templates of classical political economy. The chapter on the commodification of money is the only one of his three studies of fictitious commodities that makes virtually no historical references either to the policies surrounding the adoption and development of the gold standard in the nineteenth century, or to the writings of classical political economists about the gold standard.[4] As a result, his explanation for the creation of the gold standard, I will argue, is surprisingly shallow and rests more on deductive economic reasoning than historically rooted analysis.

This chapter explores the tensions in Polanyi's analysis of the gold standard in three steps. I begin by showing how the gold standard holds the key to Polanyi's argument in *The Great Transformation* and how he reappropriated a longstanding critique of this institution to establish his case. This led him to rely on what seemed like a logically sound viewpoint on the gold standard, but one which turned out to be flawed from a historical standpoint. In the second section, I survey the way in which Polanyi-inspired scholars have since struggled to reconcile a theoretical standpoint they wish to build upon with growing historical evidence that points in the opposite direction. The third section offers an alternative account of the gold standard to illustrate how different this regime of governance appears when we go beyond the ahistorical and generic claims of neoclassical economists to examine what was actually done in the name of these economic templates. I conclude by arguing that the problems with

Polanyi's account of the gold standard do not simply reveal limitations with his conception of liberal governance, but more fundamentally with the notion of commodification itself.

POLANYI AND THE LITERATURE ON THE GOLD STANDARD

Polanyi's book, *The Great Transformation*, presented nineteenth-century governance as a vast project of social engineering that aimed to commodify society in order to make it function like a vast self-regulated Market. This involved a sustained attempt to commodify three aspects of society (labour, land and money) that could not be fully commodified, leading to disastrous consequences for society. Polanyi refers to these aspects as "fictitious commodities" and argues that subjecting them to the imperatives of the Market placed such extreme demands on society that it undermined its very fabric.

In the case of the commodification of money, this involved pegging banknotes to gold, essentially guaranteeing that currency could be converted back into gold at a fixed rate. As a result, one could only issue money if one had enough reserves of gold to back these banknotes. According to Polanyi, this meant that money was governed by the dynamics of the market since money (more specifically banknotes) would then fluctuate according to the supply and demand of gold.[5] In the eyes of Polanyi, this posed real problems because it is difficult to adjust the supply of gold to the needs of industry. Economic development creates great needs for money to lubricate the growing amount of monetary transactions. However, it takes time to increase the amount of gold in circulation. As a result, such an arrangement could not keep up with the needs of industry.

If the gold standard was so detrimental to industry, why adopt it? According to Polanyi, "the gold standard was merely an attempt to extend the domestic market system to the international field".[6] It was believed that generalizing market rule would entrench the economic position of Britain internationally: "Stable exchange became essential to the very existence of English economy; London had become the financial centre of a growing world trade. Yet nothing else but commodity money could serve this end for the obvious reason that token money, whether bank or fiat, cannot circulate on foreign soil".[7]

From this perspective, the gold standard appeared as an international monetary regime that pegged currencies to gold in order for countries to fix their currencies in relation to one another through their common bond to gold. This was supposed to benefit economic trade by stabilizing prices and providing guarantees for financial investors that their investments in one country would not be depreciated by the fluctuations of a currency.

In making this argument, Polanyi was inspired by longstanding grievances that foreign trade had taken precedence over domestic industry with deleterious consequences for British society. Throughout the nineteenth century, the gold standard had been repeatedly attacked in Britain for serving the needs of the City of London at the detriment of the provinces. The main theme of these critiques was that the gold standard represented a straightjacket for the British economy because the commitment to guarantee the convertibility of a currency at a fixed rate in gold limited unduly the supply of money.[8] This argument would eventually lead to John Maynard Keynes' accusation that the gold standard had dramatically limited policy options.[9] It was a viewpoint that many believe was vindicated by the disastrous experience of the return to the gold standard in the 1920s when most countries had to quickly abandon this institution a few years after adopting it.

Building on this critique, Polanyi's contribution was to reframe this old idea of the gold standard as an economic straightjacket into a broader argument about liberal governance. He essentially presented this institution as the epitome of nineteenth-century liberal governance and the main institutional channel through which society had become commodified. However, extending the traditional critique of the gold standard as a deflationary institution into an argument about the making of the Market society required that Polanyi specify how the gold standard was intended to produce a market logic. Or to put it differently, his argument entailed not only that the gold standard had a deflationary *effect* (at least by the late nineteenth century), as the critical literature on the gold standard had argued, but that it served as a key vehicle for a political project: that of implementing the Market society. This is where Polanyi's argument became less convincing.

The main difficulty he confronted was to determine what a self-regulated Market would entail so that he could specify what was the role of the gold standard in its making. This was not as obvious as he seemed to assume. As I have pointed out, the argument rested on the idea that the gold standard was a monetary regime that was *inherently* deflationary and which necessarily intensified market pressures. Yet the trajectory of the British monetary system does not bear this out for the early period of the gold standard. The decades that followed the adoption of the gold standard witnessed a cycle of booms and busts as speculative bubbles seemed to build on the back of liberal discounting and banknote issuing.[10]

In raising these doubts, my goal is not to deny the hardship that the gold standard may have caused, far from it. For example, it is clear that the British government mostly ignored the concerns of workers, which often had more to do with token money than banknote issuing. Instead, I want to highlight the blind spot that comes from using the Market as a concept to frame the analysis.

Polanyi's argument is that the self-regulated Market represented an ideal that the various institutions of the nineteenth century, such as the gold standard, were trying to institute. Yet this notion was a logical construct of classical political economy. It offered a *framework for analysis* that invited people to think about social issues in logical terms using the ideas of supply and demand and the notion of economic equilibrium. There was no model of the Market to implement. As Mirowski points out, there is not even a theory or a definition of the Market in economics. It is only a logical framework for analysing reality.[11] When classical political economists made the case that money was a commodity, they were essentially bidding for the idea that money can be analysed according to this logical scheme. This does not mean, however, that classical political economists shared a clear programme for turning money into a commodity, or that they even agreed about what this would mean, because one can apply economic reasoning in many different ways.

One can illustrate this by taking a simple example that played a big role during the nineteenth century: the issue of determining the commodity we use to analyse a given problem. It makes a big difference how one conceives of the commodity involved in the "self-regulating mechanisms" that govern the monetary system. Do we take gold or the actual banknotes as the key reference point? If it is banknotes then there is no need for any gold reserve (and the gold standard), because the Market would already be operating its "self-regulating magic" on the banknotes themselves. As I later point out, this is indeed what some writers at the time argued in order to oppose the gold standard. Of course, those pushing for the gold standard rejected this argument and countered that only a "real" commodity not paper money (i.e. something that people actually needed), could be governed by a logic of supply and demand. This meant that banknotes had to be backed by gold in their eyes. As this example illustrates, tinkering with the parameters of the logic of the Market can produce dramatically different accounts of the "logic of the market" and lead to widely divergent policy prescriptions. It is a good illustration that the Market has never been the substantive ideal that Polanyi needs for his argument to hold.[12]

We would do well here to heed the critique articulated by heterodox economists who have long challenged the very idea that money can be conceived as a commodity. Since it is constitutive of market exchange, it makes little sense to think about it as something that could be itself subjected to the "Market".[13] Money not only formats social relations in terms of abstract values allowing us to represent the value of commodities in quantitative terms (as a price), but it also shapes the workings of the economy because of its singular status as a means of payment. The amount of money in circulation and how it circulates affects the economy as a whole. This is why governing money is not simply a matter of affecting one of the commodities in the economy. Since money is a condition of possibility for market exchange, it cannot emerge from the spontaneous workings of markets. Instead, it requires obligations to be set politically to establish and systematically enforce the privileged status of money. For this reason, reducing money to a simple commodity would be a contradiction in terms. When neoclassical economists extend their reasoning about commodities in order to think about money as a purely economic phenomenon they become trapped in circular forms of reasoning. For example, critics often mention the problem of determining from this perspective whether money has value because it can be used to make payments or whether people accept it for payments because it has value.[14] The only way out of such logical conundrums is to recognize that money is anchored in social and political institutions that lend money a distinct quality as a social object. Without this, neoclassical economists struggle to move from their logical propositions to concrete historical analysis or policies. It is only after these issues have been settled outside of the frame of economics that one can deploy the economic logic of reasoning and try to determine what the logic of the Market would look like given these parameters.

Polanyi was aware of these conceptual problems, but treated them as proof that liberals could not achieve their goal of reducing money to a commodity. Instead, he should have realized that the politics of liberals cannot be derived from this idea. For what matters politically, the substantive issues that surround money, cannot be settled at the formal level of the templates of liberal economics. Does the market logic apply to the issuing of banknotes, to what guarantees them, to how many different forms of money one should have, to the numbers of agents that are able to issue money, or to the disparity in monetary governance between different countries? While one may apply the logic of economics once the parameters are known, for example to justify rhetorically a political option, it is impossible to start from the basic logical proposition that money is a commodity in order to determine what should be these parameters to begin with.

LOOKING FOR THE MARKET AT THE INTERNATIONAL LEVEL

As I argued, Polanyi struggled to connect an ideal of the Market to the gold standard. Part of the reason for this is that he largely projected a conception of the gold standard that reflected the reality of the interwar period onto the nineteenth century. It is striking for example that one will find very little in *The Great Transformation* about the arguments put forward by classical political economists to motivate the adoption of the gold standard. Instead, he relied on an internationalist interpretation that emphasized the role of the gold standard in stabilizing currencies at an international level. This view only emerged in the early decades of the twentieth century. It was first fleshed out at the end of the First World War by the Cunliffe Committee, which had been mandated to determine what monetary governance Britain should adopt after the war. The committee was led by the governor of the Bank of England, which was still a semi-private institution at the time. Unsurprisingly, the Bank was again keen to minimize its "public" responsibilities, wary of the growing demands that were placed on it to act as a public central bank at the time.[15] The best way to do so was to argue that the international monetary system could self-regulate through the operations of the market. Building on the legacy of British dominance in the nineteenth century, the Cunliffe Committee thus called for a return to the gold standard, which it portrayed as a smooth monetary system that allowed currencies to adjust seamlessly through the logic of the market.[16]

The views of the Cunliffe Committee, however, have been repeatedly de-bunked as a myth.[17] Historians have shown that the track record of central banks under the gold standard largely contradicted the image cultivated by the Bank of England.[18] Numerous scholars have demonstrated, for example, that central banks had in fact intervened in systematic ways to counter the effects of gold outflows on their own economies.[19] Instead of enforcing market trends, they compensated through policies meant to buffer the domestic economy and pro-tect central banks. In short, there was no automatic (or self-regulated) system nor were central banks trying to enforce the pressures of the international mar-ket onto their domestic monetary system.

The tension between the liberal image of the gold standard as articulated by the Cunliffe Committee and the reality of its practice poses significant problems for Polanyi's account of the gold standard based on this international perspec-tive. Polanyi tried to circumvent these by casting the evidence about central banking as a symptom of the failures of liberalism. It became representative in his eyes of the contradictions between the gold standard focused on inter-national trade and the demands of industry for more money to lubricate its activities. He thus presented central banking as part of a reaction, or a dou-ble movement, on the part of society to counter the debilitating effects of the Market. In response to the constraints of the gold standard, which tightened the supply of money, countries were thus forced to relieve the pressure by issuing fiat money (i.e. banknotes). But why read central banking activism as a correc-tion for the abuses of liberal governance rather than a more central aspect in the making of liberal governance? It is hard to avoid the impression that this is a cop out Polanyi uses to deal with counter historical evidence.

This decision to separate central banking from the gold standard, as if they were two completely different things, has become a recurrent feature of the Polanyi-inspired literature. Barry Eichengreen, for example, develops Polanyi's central point that the gold standard generated a double movement.[20] The orig-inal twist of his argument is the idea that it was democratization that made it impossible to sustain the gold standard.[21] As the competitive pressures entrenched by the gold standard placed more and more pressures on people to make sacrifices, social discontent increased. This naturally became a problem once democratization provided a channel for this resentment to be voiced. In this context, currency markets became increasingly doubtful that countries on the gold standard would have the political will to maintain the gold standard and this led currency traders to speculate against what they perceived as weak currencies.

From this perspective, the evidence about active central banking does not really matter because the focus is on currency markets. As long as traders *perceived* central banks to be committed to gold convertibility then they would themselves speculate on weak currencies and prop these currencies back up in the expectations that central banks would soon intervene. According to Eichengreen, central banks could thus have significant leeway to intervene because it was secondary to the workings of the gold standard which relied more on the operations of currency markets and the work of currency speculators. Such an interpretation, however, again seems a bit too convenient. It upholds assumptions about the gold standard as a Market-led regime by relying once more on a logical template, that is a reformulated logic of the Market seen to be the product of speculation by currency traders. As a result, the historical evidence about the actual practices of central banks is once more conveniently dismissed.[22]

A more nuanced Polanyian account of the gold standard has been put forward by Christopher Holmes who is well aware of the limitations in Polanyi's reading of the gold standard.[23] In opposition to Eichengreen, Holmes takes the position that the gold standard was not what liberals claimed it was. From this perspective, the discretionary interventions of central banks are a portent of the myopia of liberals rather than a signal of the double movement per se. According to Holmes, the problem of market fundamentalism was the inability of liberals to appreciate the departures from liberal ideology that had taken place under the gold standard. This was particularly significant in the 1920s when time came to deal with the re-establishment of the gold standard. In trying to go back to a mythical age, which had never existed, central bankers would have implemented a disastrous regime that soon collapsed with the Great Depression. In that respect, it is the dogmatism and monological nature of the market fundamentalism of the 1920s that can then be seen as partly responsible for the collapse of the world order.[24]

Holmes offers a more nuanced discussion of the gold standard and an innovative attempt to recast Polanyi's work, but it remains unclear how this can salvage Polanyi's framework. For while it may account for the narrow and blind commitment of policy-makers to the gold standard during the interwar period, it tells us little about the purpose of this institution. Yet this is precisely what Polanyi's argument hinges upon. Without an account of the adoption of the gold standard, it is no longer clear what makes the gold standard "a supreme vehicle for the Market society" rather than simply an institution that could no longer be upheld in the 1920s. Again, the problem here lies in trying to specify the politics of the gold standard. Holmes thus loses the main thread of the argument when recognizing that the gold standard had not conformed to Polanyi's perspective during the nineteenth century. For it is no longer clear what made the gold standard a product *of market fundamentalism*. While we may accept that the rigidity of officials in holding on to the gold standard had disastrous effects, this does not mean that the idea of the Market, as a frame, is any more substantive during this time than it had been a century earlier. In short, pointing to market fundamentalism once more abstracts from the issues that matter politically.

Holmes seems well aware that something is amiss, because he feels the need to bring back a "market-like" instance that could justify that this is still about the construction of the "Market". He references notably the growing interdependencies between monetary systems that took form in the late nineteenth century and which Holmes uses to show that constraints on governance were building at this level. However, being careful, his references to these interdependencies are strikingly tentative. Are they akin to some sort of logic of the Market? Holmes is mostly ambiguous about this and fails to address what these interdependencies represent.

We too often take interdependencies in markets as a sign of the growing importance of the Market, as a logic. Yet these are rooted in institutions. In the case of the gold standard, international interdependencies were a direct product of domestic developments. If one considers that the convertibility of banknotes into gold was a means to allow the issue of paper money in the first place, then we get a very different view of the gold standard. From this perspective, the gold standard essentially leveraged precious metal to produce more money in the form of banknotes. This had profound effects at the international level. In previous monetary systems where the supply of money depended mostly on coins of precious metal, the effect of an outflow of gold or silver was limited to the precious metal going out of a country. By contrast, banknote issuing offered greater flexibility at a domestic level but the downside to this new flexibility was that it also accentuated international interdependencies. With gold serving as a small reserve for a much larger supply of money dependent on banknotes and bank deposits, a small outflow of gold could now produce a much greater contraction of the supply of money. In short, it was the growing flexibility gained at the national level that made the international pressures problematic.[25] This is why we cannot think of central banking, or the rise of national monetary systems dependent on banknotes (i.e. what later became fiat money) as something disconnected from the growing interdependencies of the gold standard. For the dynamics of the gold standard were predicated on the way in which domestic monetary systems were leveraged through this institution.

WHAT IS WRONG WITH THE LIBERAL INTERNATIONALIST INTERPRETATION OF THE GOLD STANDARD?

I have shown how Polanyi and his followers have struggled to reconcile the rise of central banking with the gold standard.[26] In this section, I show that much of the confusion regarding the gold standard disappears when we analyse the gold standard as a domestic institution, which had international ramifications, rather than the opposite as Polanyi and his followers do. It is a telling fact that the gold standard was adopted in Britain in 1821, 33 years before any other country. This suggests that the intentions behind its adoption have more to do with domestic concerns than the internationalist story that was written about it a century later. Based on a historical argument that I have developed elsewhere,[27] I argue here that the trajectory of this institution is foremost the story of how the British state was forced, through experimentations, to develop a radically new paradigm of governance in order to deal with the rise of banknotes as a form of money.

To understand this, it is necessary to start by looking at the problem that the gold standard was meant to address when it was initially adopted. Early nineteenth-century Britain was in the midst of one of the most spectacular monetary developments of the modern era. By the 1810s, there were more than 700 banks spread across the country that all issued their own banknotes. This posed profound problems for monetary governance, especially at a time when there was no central bank and limited knowledge about how to govern such a suddenly decentralized monetary system. Unsurprisingly, most political interventions related to the gold standard in the early nineteenth century were directly focused on banks and their practice of issuing banknotes.[28] This was the source of great concerns since it effectively privatized the control of money. It was a prevailing sentiment at the time that the state needed to recapture the "monetary power" that banks had seized. Politicians campaigning for the gold standard saw it as a means to reclaim a prerogative that they believed belonged to the state. Robert Peel, who chaired the committee that was responsible for setting up the gold standard, thus justified the gold standard as a means for Parliament to "recover the authority which it had too long abdicated".[29] This enduring belief shaped the content of numerous Bank Acts adopted between 1819 and 1844 that defined the evolving structure of the gold standard. It was reiterated in 1832, in the build up to another important Banking Act, by the Whig leader in the House of Commons, Lord Grey who argued that "the issuing of money was a prerogative of the state, and, therefore, the Legislature had the right to say on what conditions individuals should be allowed to issue money".[30]

Policy-makers, however, faced a real predicament. Previously, monetary governance had largely been limited to the politics of the Royal Mint. This institution produced coins based on precious metal and regulated their circulation. However, with the dramatic emergence of banknotes in circulation, it became necessary to rethink the very nature of monetary governance. How to conceive of governance when there were so many banks issuing their own banknotes and when the biggest of them all, the Bank of England was still privately owned? Frustrations directed at the Bank of England bubbled up throughout the first decades of the nineteenth century. Influential ministers denounced the lack of transparency and the manipulations of the bank, while parliamentary leaders accused the bank of subverting its public duties to favour its own interests. The bank was thus repeatedly attacked for unduly accommodating demands for liquidity and stoking speculation. Critiques, however, struggled to address this situation and to find a coherent strategy of governance for this radically new monetary landscape.

This takes us to the heart of Polanyi's concerns: the legacy of classical political economy.[31] For, of course, the answers to this problem were largely crafted with the help of ideas and notions borrowed from the discourse that dominated at the time. According to Polanyi, classical political economists believed money to be simply a commodity and thus set out to turn it into one. As he points out, in a rare reference to the classical political economy literature when discussing the adoption of the gold standard, David Ricardo claimed that banknotes were a mere matter of convenience in that they were "easier to handle than gold".[32] From this, Polanyi deduced that the proponents of the gold standard believed that "it was … injudicious to imagine that the nationally different tokens were of any relevance to the welfare and prosperity of the countries concerned". He takes this as evidence that political economists were happy to let the Market govern the monetary system and that the state should do little about money because it was a "simply" commodity that could be taken care of by the Market.

As I have pointed out, however, we need to be careful here not to assume that, since classical political economists worked from the same discursive axioms, they shared in fact a common view or political project. More often than not, these discursive axioms concealed profoundly divergent views or politics. Recognizing the gap between the theoretical tools writers used and the political positions they articulated is particularly important in matters related to money. For if many wrote about money as if it was a commodity, the policies they promoted prove that they considered money to be anything but a simple commodity. It is no coincidence that Britain witnessed some of the most influential debates on money and banking in the early nineteenth century: people knew full well that much was at stake.[33] The idea that money was a mere commodity became particularly important precisely because debates over what to do with banknotes issuing were politically charged. With so much at stake, it became a common rhetorical move to present one's own monetary preferences as the natural expression of the workings of the market. In short, classical political economists had to go to great length to present money as something apolitical precisely because everyone was quick to accuse others of favouring their own interests. Usually, the idea of money as a commodity was thus used as a defensive strategy to dismiss the concerns of others by stating that the Market would surely counter any imbalance created either voluntarily or not. However, this was always only half of the story; one which was used to address the political concerns of *others* that one wanted to dismiss. When shifting to what someone wanted to be done, then the logic of the Market was conveniently forgotten or said not to be operating properly.

Take the case of Adam Smith who famously used the idea of money as a commodity to defend free banknote issuing. Smith argued that banknotes were a mere substitute for gold and did not create new wealth. Against those who attacked banknote issuing as an arbitrary expedient to create money, he countered that it was the actual commodity (gold) that stood behind banknotes (i.e. the thing with value) that mattered. It was thus impossible to arbitrarily create money. If a bank put a large amount of banknotes into circulation, Smith argued, it would see the value of these banknotes go down thus encouraging those holding them to replace them with gold. The logic of the Market would thus make sure that it was not possible to over issue banknotes beyond what was needed precisely because money was a commodity. However, Smith did not blindly commit to free banking and the Market. He looked in a different direction, for example, when discussing interest rates. Here he campaigned in favour of capping how much banks could charge with usury rates, basically regulating what should be the "price" for money.

This example suggests that there is more to learn about the politics involved at the time by looking at the *irregular* application of the logic of supply and demand, instead of assuming that there was some sort of overarching project to institute a self-regulated Market. For we need to think about politics by looking at the substantive differences that opposed authors rather than the logical axioms they shared. David Ricardo, for example, used the idea of money as a commodity to make the opposite case to Smith. Ricardo campaigned for state intervention that would discipline issuing banks, particularly the Bank of England which he accused of producing inflation by over-issuing banknotes. Whereas Smith used the rhetorical ploy of positing money as a commodity to argue that regulation was not needed in the case of issuing banks, Ricardo employed it to justify regulating banknote issuing on the grounds that this would not have the problematic outcome that some predicted.

This illustrates why it makes little sense to think of governance and the gold standard as an attempt to commodify money. For the idea of money as a commodity was used as a means to both deny and justify the need for intervention. Those who pushed for new policies and state intervention to govern banknote issuing claimed that a regulation was needed so that the monetary system could finally self-regulate itself, while those who were opposed to it responded that nothing was needed because the market was *already* correcting any imbalance.

We thus need to look elsewhere to grasp the legacy of classical political economy. As I have mentioned, the problem at the time was to conceive of a coherent framework for governing more than 700 banks issuing their own banknotes. The key here was the concept of the "lender of last resort" (LLR). We now speak of the LLR to refer to a central bank that is committed to lend in times of crisis when no one else wishes to. It is usually considered a good thing since it brings stability to the financial system by providing public backing for financial institutions. However, when the concept was first developed in the 1800s, it was perceived as a source of instability. One of its main architects, Henry Thornton, was a London banker who used the LLR to highlight the problematic responsibility of the Bank of England in stoking financial markets.[34] In his formulation, the LLR referred to the lender "who stands" behind the banking system. The Bank of England, he argued, was fueling speculation and inflation by over-issuing banknotes and providing liquidity to other financial agents. Imposing gold convertibility on the bank was then a means to tightly limit its ability to stoke speculation/inflation. In this context, the LLR was perceived more as a problem to be resolved through governance, rather than as a formula for governance. Thornton's interest was to *limit* the bank so that it would *only* support the monetary system in times of crisis when things were getting difficult.

If classical political economy had a performative effect in monetary matters, it was mostly through the impact of the idea of the LLR. The concept of the LLR became a strategic tool to conceive of state interventions in this new monetary landscape. Its significance was to highlight that the monetary system was not in fact as decentralized as it looked because the whole structure depended ultimately on the most important bank at the centre of it: the Bank of England. Since other banks depended on it for liquidity, it was believed that one could exert control over the whole banking system by regulating the bank at its centre. Unfortunately, it rapidly became clear that the banking system was not in fact as centralized as initially believed. The first half of the nineteenth century thus witnessed a series of attempts to make banks dependent on the Bank of England and progressively centralize the banking system so that one could finally control it through the Bank of England. In that respect, the gold standard did not simply involve ensuring the convertibility of all banknotes into gold. It was associated with a much broader set of initiatives to curb the issuing power of country banks, to force the Bank of England so that it would have a greater presence in the countryside and to make it more transparent about its policies. In short, the gold standard became a tool for government to gain agency over monetary matters and laid the infrastructure for central banking.

Showing that the gold standard differed profoundly from what Polanyi wrote about it does not mean that developments of the nineteenth century, and more specifically liberal governance, were not responsible for the tragedies of the twentieth century. However, they were not implicated in the way we often assume. One of Polanyi's most interesting insights which unfortunately remains somewhat marginal in his account is the observation that "the great institutional significance of central banking lay in the fact that monetary policy was thereby drawn into the sphere of politics".[35] As he correctly highlights, the evolving practices of the Bank of England politicized monetary governance in new ways. However, in neglecting the role of the gold standard here, which he sees as opposed to central banking, he misses how it was the gold standard that set the vital stepping stone for the idea that money could be politically managed.

In the early nineteenth century the conception of monetary governance was limited as I have said because there was no obvious institution that could carry it out. Regulating the banking system seemed like the only option available. However, the constraints imposed by the gold standard forced the Bank of England to evolve in dramatic ways which were to lay the foundation for modern central banking practices later in this century. Indeed, being unable to act as a lender of last resort because of the constraints of the gold standard, the bank had to experiment with new strategies to regain some form of control over financial markets. Central banking was thus developed by the Bank of England as a set of practices which were meant to ensure the bank would not be placed in the position of having to serve as a lender of last resort. The modern practices of open market operations, the dynamic use of the discount window, the so called "gold devices" which were a set of practices to control gold markets, and the various colonial monetary practices of the time were all developed in this context. They were meant to control the financial system rather than simply support it in times of crisis and this was done to address a vulnerability of the Bank of England created by the gold standard. Once these tools were developed, however, it became an increasingly important issue to determine who would use them and for what purpose and this would ultimately lead to the nationalization of the Bank of England and Keynesianism.

In this process, the international concerns related to the gold standard did become increasingly important in the late nineteenth century. However, this was not of Britain's own making. There was never a commitment in the nineteenth century to an international monetary regime. Rather, the problem started when the gold standard was adopted by a large number of countries in the 1870s, partly as a means to borrow elements from the framework of monetary governance that had emerged in Britain.[36] From this point onwards, the gold standard became an international regime of governance with increasingly problematic implications because many countries began to chase limited reserves of gold. Ironically, it was the success of Britain in creating a modern form of monetary governance that led to the problematic international dynamics of the twentieth century as other countries followed on Britain's tracks. Britain did little initially to encourage this turn of events. It was unreceptive to the overtures made by European countries, especially France, in the 1860s to create an international monetary system such as one based on the gold standard.[37] During the nineteenth century, Britain was much more concerned with the threat of losing its reserves of gold, than it was interested in securing an international gold standard. This was reflected in Britain's colonial policies[38], which sought to dissuade its colonies from joining the gold standard.[39] While Britain was struggling to adjust to changing circumstances by the 1920s, this does not mean that we should interpret the gold standard as an attempt to commodify money. Much more important was the radical transformation of the monetary landscape it ushered with the rise of modern monetary governance.

CONCLUSION

As I have argued, Polanyi may have set up a promising social constructivist agenda by insisting on the need to analyse the economy as being social constructed, but, in his analysis of the gold standard, he never lived up to his own commitment. Abstracting from the complex politics of the gold standard, he ended up construing this institution in largely deductive and misleading ways. One may respond that Polanyi may have gotten this history wrong, partly because money was not really his focus in *The Great Transformation*, but that his framework still holds. A much stronger case, for example, could then be made for Polanyi's analysis of the commodification of labour. But I want to conclude by emphasizing instead that money, because of its specific nature, helps bring out inherent problems with the very concept of commodification. In that respect, the case of the gold standard does not simply show the limits of Polanyi's specific argumentation about one of the three fictitious commodities. It also demonstrates the limitations of commodification as a concept that is ill suited for the social constructivism promoted by Polanyi.

The notion of commodification tells us much less than what scholars often realize. It only appears significant because it suggests that something is becoming dependent on the Market. Yet Polanyi tells us that markets are socially constructed through institutions and discourses and that they can take widely different forms. This should imply that commodification is limited as a concept and somewhat meaningless on its own as a form of characterization of social processes. For after all, saying that something is dependent on markets is nothing more than saying that it is dependent on a social field that is itself socially constructed. In other words, it says very little until we can specify what kind of market we are dealing with. As the case of the gold standard shows, the politics of commodification are only revealed by the institutions that frame this process, not by the appeals to the Market or by the idea that something is being "commodified". Yet this is precisely the corollary that Polanyi and his followers refuse to accept when writing as if there was such a thing as a logic of commodification that could be used to understand what liberals were trying to do in the nineteenth century.[40]

Money brings out these inconsistencies in the concept of commodification by highlighting how this notion depends on a linear understanding of markets. It can only be significant if we assume that commodification brings us closer to some sort of ideal of the Market or a purer form of the logic of supply and demand. Yet the point about the social construction of markets is that market pressures themselves are the product of institutions, not of some amorphous "Market" logic. They involve constraints and regulations. Saying that more and more things are bought and sold on the market cannot capture what commodification really is about because the very act of commodifying requires limitations that stop other things from being determined by market processes. In other words, to commodify is also to place something else beyond commodification.

This is well reflected by the case of the gold standard. Polanyi assumed that money had become commodified under this institution because it was tied to an actual commodity: gold. However, this was only possible because the British state no longer allowed banks to issue banknotes according to the logic of supply and demand for banknotes. In its attempt to keep a strict relationship of banknotes to gold, the British state had to stop banknotes from fluctuating in response to market demand. For this reason, references to an abstract pursuit of the Market are ultimately empty because there simply cannot be commodification all the way down. The problem here is not that society cannot take it, but more basically that it is logically impossible. Not everything can be the object of market competition at the same time. By definition one needs to close off all sorts of possible adjustments for competition to have any bite. There are countless trade-offs in the myriad ways that market competition can play out. That is partly what liberal (and now neoliberal) regulations are all about. They illustrate that political economy is in large part a matter of setting the terms for competition. In that respect, intensifying competition is as much a matter of restricting *what competition is about*, as it is a matter of increasing the level of competition.

We often underestimate the significance of these trade-offs for our understanding of liberal governance as if these were nothing more than variations on a common theme. Polanyi mostly uses the Market as the main reference point and then thinks of institutions as variations on this theme, as different cases or forms of the Market. His attempt to hold onto the idea that the self-regulated Market represents a substantive ideal, or political project, necessarily implies a problematic linearity that undermines his own claim to analyse markets as being socially constructed. The only way to overcome this is to stop relying on the concept of the Market and place the focus squarely on institutions and the way in which they mediate social relations.[41]

Notes for Chapter 5

1. K. Polanyi, *The Great Transformation: The Political and Economic Origins of Our Time* (Boston, MA: Beacon, 1957, 2001), 214. I use "Market" with a capital letter here to refer to the concept of self-regulated Market and differentiate it from markets as social fields that are structured by institutions.

2. Deflation means more specifically that the value of commodities is diminishing in relation to money because it is difficult to get money.

3. S. Knafo, "The gold standard and the creation of a modern international monetary system", *Review of International Political Economy* 13:1 (2006), 78–102.

4. Polanyi, *Great Transformation*, 192–200.

5. *Ibid.*, 132.

6. *Ibid.*, 3.

7. *Ibid.*, 193.

8. P. Cain, "J. A. Hobson, financial capitalism and imperialism in late Victorian and Edwardian England", *Journal of Imperial and Commonwealth History* XIII:3 (1985), 1–27.

9. J. Flanders, *International Monetary Economics, 1870–1960* (Cambridge: Cambridge University Press, 1989).

10. J. Marchal & M.-O. Picquet-Marchal, "Essai sur la nature de l'évolution du billet de banque", *Revue Internationale d'Histoire de la Banque* 14 (1977), 1–87.

11. P. Mirowski, "Markets come to bits: evolution, computation and markomata in economic science", *Journal of Economic Behavior & Organization* 63:2 (2007), 210.

12. J. Lie, "Embedding Polanyi's market society", *Sociological Perspectives* 34:2 (1991), 219–35.

13. R. Bellofiore, "Endogenous money, financial Keynesianism and beyond", *Review of Keynesian Economics* 1:2 (2013), 153–70; P. Tcherneva, "Chartalism and the tax-driven approach to money", in P. Arestis & M. Sawyer (eds), *A Handbook of Alternative Monetary Economics* (Cheltenham: Elgar, 2006), 69–87.

14. G. Ingham, *The Nature of Money* (Cambridge: Polity, 2004), 23.

15. W. Bagehot, *Lombard Street: A Description of the Money Market* (London: Kegan Paul, 1906).

16. By then the Bank of England had come to see the gold standard as preferable to more direct intervention on the part of government.

17. R. Triffin, *The Evolution of the International Monetary System: Historical Appraisal and Future Perspectives* (Princeton, NJ: Princeton University Press, 1964).

18. B. Eichengreen, *Golden Fetters: The Gold Standard and the Great Depression 1919–1939* (New York: Oxford University Press, 1992).

19. R. Nurske, "L'expérience monétaire internationale. Enseignements de la période d'entre les deux guerres" (Geneva: Société des Nations, 1944); A. Bloomfield, *Monetary Policy Under the International Gold Standard* (New York: Federal Reserve Bank of New York, 1959).

20. B. Eichengreen, *Globalizing Capital: A History of the International Monetary System* (Princeton, NJ: Princeton University Press, 1996).

21. See also A. Harmes, "Institutional investors and Polanyi's double movement: a model of contemporary currency crises", *Review of International Political Economy* 8:3 (2001), 389–437.

22. For a more systematic critique of this argument see Knafo, "The gold standard and the creation of a modern international monetary system" and S. Knafo, *The Making of Modern Finance: Liberal Governance and the Gold Standard* (Abingdon: Routledge, 2013).

23. C. Holmes, *Polanyi in Times of Populism: Vision and Contradiction in the History of Economic Ideas* (Abingdon: Routledge, 2018).

24. C. Holmes, "'Whatever it takes': Polanyian perspectives on the eurozone crisis and the gold standard", *Economy and Society* 43:4 (2014), 582–602.

25. Knafo, "The gold standard and the creation of a modern international monetary system".

26. See also F. Block & M. Somers, *The Power of Market Fundamentalism: Karl Polanyi's Critique* (Cambridge, MA: Harvard University Press, 2014); K. Hart, "Money in the making of world society", in C. Hahn & K. Hart (eds), *Market and Society: The Transformation Today* (Cambridge: Cambridge University Press, 2009), 91–105.

27. Knafo, *Making of Modern Finance*.

28. J. de Boyer, "Les débats monétaires et le développement de la théorie monétaire en Grande-Bretagne dans la première moitié du XIXe siècle", in A. Béraud & G. Faccarello (eds), *Nouvelle histoire de la pensée économique: Tome 1. Des scholastiques aux classiques* (Paris: Éditions de la découverte, 1992), 554–77.

29. Quoted in E. Evans, *Sir Robert Peel: Statesmanship, Power, and Party* (London: Routledge, 1991), 12.

30. F. Fetter, "Commentary", in F. Fetter & D. Gregory (eds), *Monetary and Financial Policy* (London: Irish University Press, 1973), 144.

31. In this short essay, I cannot do justice to the complex constellations of social interests involved in the making of the gold standard. For a close analysis, see Knafo, *Making of Modern Finance*.

32. Polanyi, *Great Transformation*, 196.

33. It is unfortunate that Polanyi who astutely pointed out elsewhere that economics was based on a segmented form of logic that could only work if it abstracted a specific causal relationship from everything else, never capitalized on this insight in his study of nineteenth-century liberalism. See K. Polanyi, "The economy as instituted process", in K. Polanyi, C. Arensberg & H. Pearson (eds), *Trade and Market in the Early Empires: Economies in History and Theory* (Glencoe, IL: Free Press, 1957), 243–70. What Polanyi correctly grasped here was that one could uphold what were tautologies that were established on problematic abstractions as science on the grounds that somehow all these segments of logics could be pieced back together. What this meant is that anyone could construct a version of the workings of the Market that would justify their own preferences. But unfortunately, Polanyi never drew the logical conclusion of these insights for the way he analysed nineteenth-century governance.

34. A. Murphy, "Paper credit and the multi-personae Mr Henry Thornton", *European Journal of the History of Economic Thought* 10:3 (2003), 429–53.

35. Polanyi, "Economy as instituted process", 198.

36. Knafo, "The gold standard and the creation of a modern international monetary system".

37. G. Gallarotti, "The scramble for gold: monetary regime transformation in the 1870s", in M. Bordo & F. Capie (eds), *Monetary Regimes in Transition* (Cambridge: Cambridge University Press, 1994), 15–67.

38. M. de Cecco, *Money and Empire: The International Gold Standard, 1890–1914* (Oxford: Basil Blackwell, 1974).

39. See Knafo, *Making of Modern Finance*, 160–74.

40. This is not to deny that the process of commodification can be studied as a social phenomenon, just like markets can be the object of social enquiries, but it is not something that we should use as a means to characterize what is at stake.

41. See S. Knafo & B. Teschke "The rules of reproduction of capitalism: a historicist critique", Working Paper series no. 12, University of Sussex, Centre for Global Political Economy, 2017.

6

MONEY

Kurtuluş Gemici

Polanyi begins his masterpiece, *The Great Transformation* (TGT), with the stark observation that "Nineteenth-century civilization has collapsed".[1] The nineteenth-century civilization was a bold attempt to establish a self-regulating market encompassing the entire globe. Polanyi believed that the self-regulating market, which he called a "gargantuan automaton" once it reached the entire globe, was perilous to society and that its full realization was impossible.[2] According to him, money – commodity-money under the international gold standard, to be precise – was, simultaneously, what held the nineteenth-century civilization together and what played the biggest role in its demise.[3]

Given the importance Polanyi attributes to money and given that money is one of the three fictitious commodities that he discusses at great length, one should expect that the vast secondary literature on Polanyi pays sufficient attention to the place of money in Polanyi's thought. Unfortunately, that is not entirely the case. Although there are excellent discussions of Polanyi's writings on international finance,[4] the nature of money,[5] and the functions of money in different economic systems in history,[6] Polanyi's theoretical framework on money remains elusive. This chapter fills this gap by outlining the analytical connections between Polanyi's theory of money, commodity fiction, and embeddedness. It will be shown that Polanyi's theory of money is an integral part of his criticism of the market system and that Polanyi corroborates this criticism through historical analyses of the international gold standard as well as special-purpose money in different allocation systems. This chapter also suggests that Polanyi's theory of money offers rich avenues for examining money and finance in contemporary capitalism.

The basic argument of the chapter can be summarized as follows. Polanyi's theory of money rests on a thorough criticism of orthodox perspectives on money. These conventional accounts of money, which harken back to Aristotle[7] and are reproduced without critical reflection in economics textbooks,[8] portray money primarily as a medium of exchange that serves as a measure of value and unit of account. The orthodox theories find the origins of money in the evolution of market society, which replaced the inefficiency of barter and truck with the genesis of a generalized medium of exchange. The core argument in orthodox theories of money, applicable to commodity money based on precious metals as well as fiduciary money such as fiat currencies, is that money – despite its function as medium of exchange – is also subject to the laws of demand and supply.[9] Money's capacity as medium of exchange is simply a consequence of its maximum saleability, which, according to orthodox theories, explains its evolution from precious materials as commerce and market exchange were "perfected".[10]

Polanyi suggests otherwise. For him, in line with Knapp,[11] money is primarily a means of payment and treating it as a commodity subject to the market mechanism is a dangerous fiction. The "general-purpose money" that serves as a measure of value and unit of account is not a universal phenomenon, as evidenced by the prevalence of "special-purpose money" in economic systems other than the market exchange in history.[12] As a corollary, Polanyi argues that "general-purpose money", like land and labour in a market economy, is also a fictitious commodity. Furthermore, similar to the other fictitious commodities that lie at the heart of Polanyi's critique of market society, the commodity fiction applied to money inevitably leads to pernicious consequences. Polanyi illustrates these negative consequences through the history of the international gold standard in the nineteenth century. This critical history of the gold standard is, in turn, the key to understanding how Polanyi's theory of money is related to the notion of embeddedness. For Polanyi, the commodity fiction applied to money entails treating it as primarily a medium of exchange subject to the market mechanism, which was the case under the gold standard. However, this ideational and political project to "disembed" money necessarily leads to the subordination of money as a means of payment and a unit of account to its function as a medium of exchange. Polanyi views such subordination as perilous because it makes the purchasing power of individuals vulnerable to the vagaries of the market mechanism.

MONEY AND THE COMMODITY FICTION

"Money" is mentioned 168 times in TGT; these numerous uses of "money" follow a handful of patterns. First, Polanyi discusses money in relation to the international financial system and the central actors of the nineteenth-century *haute finance*.[13] Second, he examines the role of money in different allocation systems in history – namely, householding, reciprocity, redistribution, and market exchange.[14] In particular, Polanyi devotes a considerable amount of attention to how money played a role in the rise of the market system and how it was essential to the operation of market mechanism.[15] Third, he investigates how the institutionalization of money in the international arena through the gold standard was a key factor in creating strains in various national economies.[16] As is well-known, Polanyi argues that these strains were intimately linked to the countermovement against the market and the ensuing cataclysm in the first half of the twentieth century.[17]

These distinct patterns in TGT reveal a sophisticated account of money that is woven into a sweeping historical narrative. Polanyi does not theorize about money in a vacuum. In contrast, he develops his theoretical arguments through a historical analysis that is simultaneously comparative, diachronic, and multi-scalar. The comparative dimension has to do with Polanyi's contrast with regard to the institutionalization of money in different allocation systems. Here, Polanyi suggests that, although money was used in different allocation systems, such use was peripheral and did not necessarily transform householding, reciprocity, and redistribution to the market system.[18] The diachronic dimension emerges from the evolving role of money as the market became the dominant mode of allocation in society. Namely, Polanyi stresses that money was transformed from an accessory to a central element of the economy as the motive of gain replaced motive of subsistence. Thus, the increasing preponderance of the price-supply-demand mechanism developed in tandem with the denomination of transactions in monetary terms.[19] The multi-scalar dimension is related to Polanyi's account of how the international financial system that crystallized under the gold standard disrupted the organization of production and thus the livelihood of ordinary people in different national economies. Here, Polanyi offers a compelling account of how the rise of "one big market" at the world scale through the gold standard generated irrevocable tensions between the international economic system, national organization of production, and the maintenance of livelihood at the local economic level.[20] Building on his journalism years in Vienna and observations on the international economy during the 1930s, Polanyi links the disruptive institutional strains of the international self-regulating market to the contradictions of "commodity money" and deflationary policies under the gold standard.[21] Table 6.1 presents the analytical dimensions of Polanyi's treatment of money in TGT.

How to make sense of this complex and highly original picture of money? The thread that unifies these patterns – and the skeleton key to deciphering Polanyi's approach to money – is the notion of commodity fiction. The oft-quoted passage regarding fictitious commodities is the natural starting point in untangling the analytical connections in Polanyi's theory of money:

> [L]abor, land, and money are obviously not commodities; the postulate that anything that is bought and sold must have been produced

Table 6.1 Analysis of money in *The Great Transformation*

Analytical dimension	Argument
Comparison	Money was peripheral in all economic systems except market exchange; the proposition that the use of money was necessarily coupled with the market economy has no historical basis.
Historical evolution	Denomination of transactions in monetary terms developed in tandem with the replacement of the motive of subsistence with motive of gain.
Scale	Commodity money was at the heart of the gold standard and the operation of the self-regulating market at the international level; and commodity money led to disruptive strains between international finance and national economies.

for sale is emphatically untrue in regard to them. [...] Labour is only another name for a human activity which goes with life itself, which in its turn is not produced for sale but for entirely different reasons, nor can that activity be detached from the rest of life, be stored or mobilized; land is only another name for nature, which is not produced by man; actual money, finally, is merely a token of purchasing power which, as a rule, is not produced at all, but comes into being through the mechanism of banking or state finance. None of them is produced for sale. The commodity description of labour, land, and money is entirely fictitious.[22]

Commodity fiction, according to Polanyi, is a constitutive ideational element of the self-regulating market.[23] Its necessity emanates from the operation of the market mechanism.[24] The interplay of supply and demand requires fluctuating prices; fluctuating prices are possible only when the object circulating through market exchange is treated as "produced for sale"; the presupposition of "production for sale" assigns the market-exchanged object a value determined by market forces.[25] However, because labour, land, and money are crucial elements of the social fabric, their exchange through fluctuating prices engenders various strains arising from the clash between the market and other institutions in society. Table 6.2 offers a simplified schema of the connections between fictitious commodities and institutional strains.

Table 6.2 Commodity fiction, fictitious commodities and disruptive strains

Fictitious commodity	Object of commodification	Disruptive strain
Labour	Human beings, productive activity, and social relations	Disruption of private and public life; erosion of social fabric
Land	Natural environment and endowments	Ecological decay and ruin
Money	Purchasing power	Austerity and deflationary economic dynamics

It should be noted that the commodification of labour and land – essential aspects of capitalist markets – lend themselves to a fairly clear interpretation.[26] The same cannot be said about the conceptualization of money as "merely a token of purchasing power". Unlike productive activity and natural endowments, "purchasing power" does not have an immediate referent outside market exchange. "Purchasing power" refers to a generalized capacity to acquire objects in an exchange system,[27] and such generalized capacity sits uneasily with the non-market allocation systems that Polanyi identifies (i.e., household, reciprocity and redistribution).

Yet Polanyi's usage is consistent and formulaic. Despite such consistent use, the bulk of the secondary literature pays scant attention to why Polanyi insists on seeing money as "a token of purchasing power", and most analyses of the market's perils revolve around labour and land as fictitious commodities.[28] Such an approach to Polanyi's works is not entirely errant, since Polanyi's thought embodies considerable conceptual unity around the notion of commodity fiction. However, it misses a rich dimension of Polanyian analysis. The next section addresses this analytical lacuna by showing that Polanyi's formulation of money as "merely a token of purchasing power" derives from (1) a critical stance against the orthodox theories of money in classical political economy, and (2) the influence of heterodox theories of money – theories that pay particular attention to the state's role in institutionalizing money as a symbolic token of value, standard of accounting, and means of payment.

ORTHODOX THEORIES OF MONEY

The starting point in understanding Polanyi's approach to money is the criticism he levels against the conceptualization of money in classical political economy:

money being nothing other than a commodity that functions as a *numéraire*. In Polanyi's own words:

> Purchasing power is, in principle, here [the market system] supplied and regulated by the action of the market itself; this is meant when we say that money is a commodity the amount of which is controlled by the supply and demand of the goods which happen to function as money – the well-known classical theory of money. According to this doctrine, money is only another name for a commodity used in exchange more often than another, and which is therefore acquired mainly in order to facilitate exchange. [...] If gold happens to be used as money, its value, amount, and movements are governed by exactly the same laws that apply to other commodities.[29]

Furthermore, Polanyi's views are not different in his later writings, where he offers the same critical stance. Classical political economy errs in presupposing that all-purpose money is just a commodity that also functions as a unit of account: "Money is defined as a commodity primarily used in exchange. Money is therefore a function of barter and exchange. Monetary problems should be resolved by reducing them to commodity problems. Token money (such as paper currency) is not money proper."[30]

The target of Polanyi's criticism is the commodity theory of money, which is associated with theoretical and practical metallism in classical political economy. The distinction comes from Schumpeter,[31] who, building on Knapp,[32] suggests that theoretical metallism boils down to the proposition that money is essentially a commodity and that "the exchange value or purchasing power of money is the exchange value or purchasing power of that commodity". Practical metallism, in contrast, is the proposition that money, even when it is a symbolic token, should be linked to a commodity – a precious metal in most discussions of money in classical political economy.[33]

Polanyi is not wrong in attributing a virtual hegemony to the commodity theory of money in classical political economy. In fact, as a theory pertaining to the essential qualities of money, the commodity theory enjoyed universal acceptance.[34] Furthermore, some of the most influential figures of classical political economy fused the proposition that money is essentially just a commodity with the theoretical position that "prices move in accordance with changes in the quantity of money in circulation".[35] The latter proposition, the central tenet of the quantity theory of money, is of course one of the oldest ideas in economic thought.[36]

The combination of commodity with quantity theory of money has several implications, as can be readily observed in the writings of two influential classical political economists whom Polanyi criticised: Hume and Ricardo. For instance, Hume's analysis pertains mostly to exogenous changes in the supply of money. He proposes that an increase in the quantity of money (e.g., inflow of gold following discovery of new mines) leads to an increase in economic activity and thus production, but such an increase is temporary and national wealth remains at its normal level in the long run.[37] However, Hume argues that the new equilibrium level of prices will be higher than they were before the inflow of money.[38] As he puts it, "the greater or less plenty of money is of no consequence; since the prices of commodities are always proportioned to the plenty of money".[39]

Hume's analysis of money is not limited to his contributions to the quantity theory of money. Even more influential was his formulation of the *price-specie-flow* mechanism. Hume viewed trade between neighbouring countries, in the absence of impediments to the flow of commodity-money between them, as a self-regulating system.[40] If specie (i.e., commodity-money) gets multiplied in a country, such an increase causes an accompanying rise in the prices of all commodities including labour, which in turn makes the commodities of neighbouring nations cheaper. Equilibrium is restored as commodity-money flows out to the neighbouring countries with cheaper goods and as prices in these neighbouring countries increase.[41] As such, Hume deems the level of commodity-money in each country to be "proportionable to the art and industry of each nation".[42]

Ricardo, in contrast to Hume, considers money to be a commodity whose value and quantity were *endogenously* determined in a market economy. As with Hume, Ricardo was aware of the importance of bank notes and thus of paper money.[43] However, for Ricardo, gold constitutes the "standard of money". As he argues, "paper money conforms, or ought to conform, to the value of gold, and therefore its value is influenced by such causes only as influence the value of that metal".[44] Furthermore, for Ricardo, the labour cost of producing gold – or any commodity used as the standard of money – is a crucial factor in determining the value of commodity-money.[45] In fact, although he often considers money to be invariant in value for analytical purposes, Ricardo insists that money is subject to fluctuating prices determined by the capitalist market: "Money, from its being a commodity obtained from a foreign country, from its being the general medium of exchange ... is subject to incessant variations".[46] This analytical framework results in a two-tiered theory of money where the purchasing power of money – money being any particular instrument such as bank notes – consists of "the exchange ratio between money and gold, i.e. the value of money, and the exchange ratio between gold and other commodities".[47]

The radical innovation in Ricardo's ideas concerning money cannot be overemphasized. It was Ricardo who offered a comprehensive analytical framework where money is a produced commodity subject to the mechanisms of capitalist markets, just like any other commodity. In this framework, what makes money special is that it is a produced commodity that serves as a *numéraire*. This exceptional aspect notwithstanding, the laws of the capitalist market are equally applicable to commodity-money. Thus, the production of commodity-money is responsive to market conditions. Under circumstances where commodity-money is scarce, its price goes up and the expansion of its production presents profit opportunities. Accordingly, the commodity-money supply increases and equilibrium is restored. Similarly, should the production of commodity-money increase as a result of technological change or discoveries, its price falls, which makes the prices of other commodities increase.[48]

The combination of (1) Hume's *price-specie-flow* mechanism and (2) the Ricardian theory of money – where commodity-money is produced and its price is endogenously determined – remained remarkably influential on virtually all theoretical and practical monetary problems during the nineteenth century. As an influential economic historian remarks: "There is no more effective testament to the elegance of Hume's model of the gold standard as a homeostatic system nor to the ability of elegant theory to hypnotize the minds of economists than the continued dominance of the price-specie-flow model 150 years later, at the beginning of the twentieth century, despite the extent to which circumstances had changed".[49]

Polanyi directs his criticism precisely to this particular combination of Hume and Ricardo – a combination that successfully merged the commodity-description of money, quantity theory of money, and *price-specie-flow* mechanism to the effect of a self-regulating system at the international level. Polanyi castigates Hume, whom he credits with the notion of "balance of power" in other places,[50] for not realizing the disastrous effects of commodity fiction applied to money: "Hume became the founder of the quantity theory of money with his discovery that business remains unaffected if the amount of money is halved since prices will simply adjust to half their former level. He forgot that business might be destroyed in the process."[51] Polanyi argues that Ricardo was the chief architect in "the institutional separation of the political and economic spheres" simply because his theories achieved considerable hegemony:

> Ricardo indoctrinated nineteenth-century England with the conviction that the term "money" meant a medium of exchange, that bank notes were a mere matter of convenience, their utility consisting in their being easier to handle than gold, but that their value derived from the certainty that their possession provided us with the means of possessing ourselves at any time of the commodity itself, gold.[52]

The above paragraph reveals the gist of Polanyi's objection to the conceptualization of money found in classical political economy. According to Polanyi, conceptualizing money as a commodity is a fiction because it loses sight of the fact that money is primarily a symbolic token and means of payment. The orthodox approach to money postulates that money is a means of payment and standard of accounting because it is a means of exchange. Polanyi suggests that the opposite is the case; money is primarily a means of payment and standard of accounting.

MONEY AS MEANS OF PAYMENT AND STANDARD
OF ACCOUNTING

At a theoretical level, Polanyi's formulation of money as a "token of purchasing power" is closely related to Knapp's theory of money, Chartalism, which had a lasting influence on several heterodox theories of money.[53] The main proposition of Chartalism is that "money ... is a unit of account, designated by a public authority for the codification of social debt obligations".[54] This proposition rests, of course, on rejecting the idea that money is a medium of exchange "deriving its value from its metallic content".[55]

The family resemblance between Polanyi's approach to money and Knapp's Chartalism is not surprising, given that Knapp's book followed in the footsteps of the German historical school and commanded a considerable degree of authority in the German literature on money and monetary history.[56] His primary work, *The State Theory of Money*, was first published in 1905 and went through multiple revisions.[57] In this book, Knapp stresses that money as means of payment and unit of value is independent of the actual object that underpins commodity-money.[58] The crucial quality of money is that debts and obligations are payable by using the particular object chosen as money, be it a metal or paper ticket. It is the political authority that lends "a use independent of its material" to this object.[59]

Overall, an unmistakeable element of Knapp's state theory of money is that it offers a sustained criticism of orthodox theories of money and in particular of both theoretical and practical metallism. Knapp's work offers a detailed account, both historical and theoretical, of how the acceptance by the public authority is the necessary factor in turning an object used as a means of payment into a generalized medium of exchange. Thus, Knapp upends the conventional causal account of money being primarily a medium of exchange that naturally evolved as commerce and market society developed in history.

The implications of such an argument can best be understood by contrasting it with the orthodox theories of money. In a classic theoretical article that influenced both Austrian and neoclassical economics, Menger[60] captures the line of reasoning emblematic of orthodox theories of money:

> Money has not been generated by law. In its origin it is a social, and not a state-institution. Sanction by the authority of the state is a notion alien to it. On the other hand, however, by state recognition and state regulation, this social institution of money has been perfected and adjusted to the manifold and varying needs of an evolving commerce, just as customary rights have been perfected and adjusted by statute law. Treated originally by weight, like other commodities, the precious metals have by degrees attained as coins a shape by which their intrinsically high saleableness has experienced a material increase. The fixing of a coinage so as to include all grades of value (*Wertstufen*), and the establishment and maintenance of coined pieces so as to win public confidence and, as far as is possible, to forestall risk concerning their genuineness, weight, and fineness, and above all the ensuring their circulation in general, have been everywhere recognised as important functions of state administration.

In Menger's account, money is a *sui generis* social institution; it is demanded and supplied as a function of its utility, which derives from its high saleability. Knapp reverses the causality in this line of reasoning. Money becomes a social institution when state acceptance turns an ordinary means of payment, which could theoretically be any object, into a generalized medium of exchange that serves as a measure of value and unit of account.[61]

Knapp's propositions and insistence on money's function as means of payment and unit of account have clear affinities to the model of a socialist economy that Polanyi proposed in the early 1920s, and thus to the main theoretical problems that preoccupied Polanyi at that time.[62] In an article published in the prestigious academic journal *Archiv für Sozialwissenschaft und Sozialpolitik*,[63] Polanyi offered a model of a socialist economy heavily influenced by guild socialism. In this model, certain prices such as wages are fixed – after taking into account both social justice and technical productivity requirements – through agreement between a political community[64] and organizations of producers and consumers. Thus, money-income in Polanyi's model is a type of endowment that is allocated to different members of society according to social justice and technical requirements of production.[65] In this model, only a limited range of goods[66] are valued through the market mechanism, and money is definitely not one of them. In other words, Polanyi treats money as a means of payment and a standard of accounting used to establish the equivalencies between different goods. However, and this should be emphasized, money in this system of a socialist economy is not envisioned as a means of exchange whose value is determined in the marketplace. This is also what Polanyi proposes in TGT as the replacement of commodity-money: "Let us try to imagine a 'society' in which every individual is endowed with a definite amount of purchasing power, enabling him to claim goods each item of which is provided with a price tag. Money in such an economy is not a commodity; it has no usefulness in itself; its only use is to purchase goods to which price tags are attached, very much as they are in our shops today."[67]

In a footnote, Polanyi notes that the "underlying theory" of this *purchasing power economy* "has been elaborated by F. Schafer [sic]", whose thesis Polanyi supervised in 1920s Vienna.[68] Beyond this, Polanyi's notes and correspondences do not provide a direct link between Knapp and Polanyi's proposal for a *purchasing power economy*. However, Felix Schaffer himself offers strong evidence on the connection.[69] Schaffer notes that two contrasting theories of money were taught at the University of Vienna in the 1920s. On the one hand, according to Schaffer, Ludwig von Mises offered a picture of money akin to commodity-money or theoretical metallism.[70] On the other hand, Othmar Spann, whose fascist theories Polanyi dissected in his "Essence of Facism" a decade later,[71] presented a view much closer to Knapp's theory of money.[72] Schaffer explains Polanyi's views on money with respect to these contrasting positions:

> In connection with talks on these two money theories Polanyi determined the position of the "purchasing power" in his model. He felt that the "purchasing power" was in the essence a kind of "chartal money". For the community, i.e. the State, could be thought to have instituted the purchasing power as the means of payment. The confidence of the consumers in the purchasing power was based upon their trust that they could buy commodities with it, which was confirmed by the practice.

This passage highlights the crucial link between commodity fiction and money in Polanyi's thought. Money as means of exchange – money as commodity – contradicts, according to Polanyi, the most important aspects of money in economic life, its functions as means of payment and unit of account. As such, any monetary system that turns money into a commodity – the value of which is determined by supply and demand – subjects the purchasing power of consumers and producers to the vagaries of the market economy. In line with his model of a socialist economy, Polanyi finds this objectionable not only on grounds of social justice, but also on the basis of the technical requirements of production.

Thus, the commodity fiction applied to money is self-destructive, since it jeopardizes economic production and the social fabric.

IMPLICATIONS: EMBEDDEDNESS OF MONEY

The contrast that Polanyi establishes between money as means of exchange and as means of payment is related to another crucial aspect of his thought: embeddedness.[73] At the expense of simplification, we can stipulate that Polanyi operates with an analytical schema that focuses on the embeddedness of money in different economic systems and periods that he examines. On the one hand, money conceived as a commodity was at the heart of an ideational-political project – backed by a powerful class alliance[74] – to subject the purchasing power of consumers and the organization of production to the automatic self-regulation of the market system, without much regard for political and social factors. This project reached maturity in Britain in the first half of the nineteenth century; it attained its zenith under the gold standard during the second half of the twentieth century. Hence, Polanyi calls the gold standard "the faith of the age".[75] On the other hand, money in economic systems other than the market was not primarily a means of exchange. To the contrary, it was a means of payment and standard of value that was tightly integrated with other social institutions. In these capacities, money strengthened social cohesion. Thus, under the international market system accomplished through the gold standard, money was at the core of the project to institutionally separate market from society. Money as means of payment was, in contrast, enmeshed with and submerged in other social institutions in economic systems other than market.[76]

Seen in this light, Polanyi's blistering verdict on the gold standard is a logical conclusion of his approach to money. As Block remarks, for Polanyi the gold standard "was an institutional innovation that put the theory of self-regulating markets into practice, and once in place it had the power to make self-regulating markets to be natural".[77] Furthermore, the gold standard extended the destructive logic of the self-regulating market to the global scale.[78] The perils of the gold standard lay in its frequent tendency to cause "deadly deflation" or "fatal monetary stringency" in cases of financial meltdown.[79] Deflation was necessary, since the gold standard had exchange rate stability as its ultimate objective. That objective was achieved by "the lowering of domestic prices whenever the exchange rate was threatened by depreciation".[80] These measures had to be used frequently because the gold standard operated *as if* money was a means of exchange and thus a commodity with a fluctuating price. Stability in exchange rates could be obtained by repeatedly sacrificing productive organization and employment. The repeated bouts of deflation presented mortal threats to "productive organizations" – threats that too frequently materialized in "a complete disorganization of business and consequent mass unemployment".[81] Accordingly, for Polanyi the collapse of the gold standard was the culmination of a civilization that put an automaton, the self-regulating market, into the driver seat: "final failure of the gold standard was the final failure of market economy".[82]

For Polanyi, the gold standard was the embodiment of the institutional separation of politics and economy at the international scale.[83] And such separation stood in contrast to the institutionalization of money in societies where the market exchange was not the dominant allocation system. Thus, Polanyi's scholarly work on money after the Second World War, which includes remarkable examinations of the uses and functions of money in different economic systems in history, is closely related to his theoretical approach that differentiates money as means of exchange – which overlapped with commodity-money under the gold standard – from money as means of payment and standard of value.

The key analytical axis of this body of work following the publication of TGT is the distinction between all-purpose and special-purpose money. Polanyi, with a clear reference to the Austrian school's view of money as a means of exchange,[84] defines all-purpose money in the following manner: "The catallactic definition of money is that of means of indirect exchange. Modern money is used for payment and as a 'standard' precisely because it is a means of exchange. Thus our money is 'all-purpose' money. Other uses of money are merely unimportant variants of its exchange use, and all money uses are dependent upon the existence of markets."[85]

Polanyi deems this view ahistorical and derivative of market mentality.[86] As opposed to such a view of money, Polanyi offers a "substantive definition of money", where the use of money for "the discharge of obligations" and as unit of accounting are closely tied to particular social institutions such as redistributive systems of religious organizations. Polanyi argues that money is a "system of symbols" with numerous forms and uses. Money does not have a single origin. Nor does it have a definite "nature and essence", contrary to the claims of neoclassical theories that locate the origins and essence of money in barter and exchange.[87]

The substantive meaning of money, which examines money in a particular constellation of social institutions such as kinship and religion, leads Polanyi to the definition of special-purpose money: "Early money is ... special-purpose money. Different kinds of objects are employed in the different money uses; moreover, the uses are instituted independently of another".[88] Polanyi emphatically argues that such special-purpose money is not prone to the perils and contradictions of all-purpose money: "There is ... no contradiction involved in 'paying' with a means with which one cannot buy, nor in employing objects as a 'standard' which are not used as a means of exchange. In Hammurabi's

Babylonia barley was the means of payment; silver was the universal standard; in exchange, of which there was very little, both were used alongside of oil, wool, and some other staples."[89]

In line with such an argument, Polanyi's well-known analysis of cowrie money in West Africa has a firm focus on how its "societal effects" contributed to "the near-perfect regional currency system of the eighteenth-century Guinea coast".[90] Polanyi suggests that cowrie money reinforced existing status structures. He also highlights how the establishment of cowrie money was linked to political centralization, which Polanyi examines through the case of the Kingdom of Dahomey.[91] Again, the parallels to Knapp's theory of money are evident: "Cowrie … gained the status of a currency by virtue of state policy, which regulated its use and guarded against its proliferation by preventing shiploads from being freely imported".[92] In other words, "archaic money" for Polanyi was firmly embedded in particular political and social institutions; and, such institutionalization of money eliminated problems such as "excessive fluidity" associated with commodity-money of the market system.[93] Table 6.3 presents the analytical relationship of special and all-purpose money to embeddedness.

Table 6.3 Embeddedness, special-purpose money and all-purpose money

	Special-purpose money	All-purpose money
Functions	Distinct functions (payment, accounting, exchange) are autonomous.	Distinct functions (payment, accounting, exchange) are dominated by money as means of exchange.
Institutionalization	Distinct functions of money correspond to distinct forms and usages.	Distinct functions of money disappear through isomorphism under money as means of exchange.
Social integration	Distinct functions of money are submerged in and thus reinforce particular social institutions.	Money as means of exchange is the locus of efforts to disembed the market.

CONCLUSION

Polanyi's writings on money span an impressive range of theoretical and empirical issues. Polanyi examines the international financial system, the nature of money, the functions of money in different economic systems, and the place of money in society. In this chapter, I have argued that the notion of commodity fiction applied to money is the thread that unifies these seemingly disjointed investigations. For Polanyi, money – a symbolic system without a singular function, a polymorphous token with distinct usages – has a crucial place in both non-market and market societies. In non-market societies, money is a special-purpose token where the distinct functions of money – payment, accounting, and exchange – maintain a certain degree of autonomy from each other. Under the market system, in contrast, money is conceived as a commodity whose value is endogenously determined by market forces. Polanyi puts the blame on classical political economy, in particular Hume and Ricardo, for the application of commodity fiction to money. He also shows that money as a fictitious commodity played the central role in establishing the self-regulating market on a global scale. For him, the commodity fiction on a global scale sealed the fate of the market system and of the nineteenth-century civilization that revolved around the market system.

Thus, once we take into account his criticism of commodity fiction applied to money, Polanyi's theoretical and empirical investigations on money show considerable continuity. The "purchasing power economy" that Polanyi envisioned as early as 1922 finds its counterpart in his criticism of the gold standard. Similarly, Polanyi's analyses of "archaic money" revisit the same theoretical issue – the tensions and contradictions engendered by the preponderance of means of exchange function of money under the market system. For Polanyi, the institutional separation of money from political and social institutions is a dangerous folly – a folly that he attacked on both theoretical and empirical levels.

Given that central bank independence, unfettered international capital mobility, and the separation of monetary management from fiscal issues are still the reigning orthodoxies of today, Polanyi's theoretical framework on money remains relevant in today's world. The mainstream of economic thought portrays money in a manner that is not very different from the orthodox theories that Polanyi attacked vehemently. In neoclassical economics, money and finance are autonomous economic institutions that are thinly connected to other social institutions.[94] Polanyi offers a sustained criticism of such accounts. He also offers ideas concerning the embeddedness of money in political and social institutions. If these ideas are followed, they will entail profound changes in monetary and fiscal policies. Polanyi's thought on money implies that monetary and fiscal policies as well as the institutionalization of money in contemporary capitalism are long overdue for fundamental changes – changes that should prioritize employment and income stability as opposed to prioritizing the profits and health of financial institutions. Although there are proposals and ideas that show considerable affinity with Polanyi's theory of money,[95] there is much to be done to explore the full potential of Polanyi's theory of money.

Notes for Chapter 6

1. K. Polanyi, *The Great Transformation: The Political and Economic Origins of Our Time* (Boston, MA: Beacon Press, 2001), 3.

2. *Ibid.*, 226.

3. *Ibid.*, 209.

4. F. Block, "Introduction," in K. Polanyi, *The Great Transformation: The Political and Economic Origins of Our Time*, xviii–xxxviii; E. Helleiner, "Globalization and haute finance: déja vu?" in K. McRobbie & K. Polanyi-Levitt (eds), *Karl Polanyi in Vienna: The Contemporary Significance of the Great Transformation* (New York: Black Rose Books, 2000), 12–31; C. Holmes, "'Whatever it takes': Polanyian perspectives on the eurozone crisis and the gold standard", *Economy and Society* 43:4 (2014), 582–602.

5. J. Melitz, "The Polanyi school of anthropology on money: an economist's view", *American Anthropologist* 72:5 (1970), 1020–40; H. Saiag, "Towards a neo-Polanyian approach to money: integrating the concept of debt", *Economy and Society* 43:4 (2014), 559–81.

6. J. Blanc, "Karl Polanyi et les monnaies modernes: un réexamen," in G. Lazuech & P. Moulévrier (eds) *Contributions à Une Sociologie Des Conduites économiques* (Paris: L'Harmattan, 2005), 51–66; J.-M. Servet, "L'institution monétaire de la société selon Karl Polanyi," *Revue économique* (1993), 1127–49.

7. Aristotle, *Politics*, trans. C. D. C. Reeve (Indianapolis, IN: Hackett, 1998).

8. F. Mishkin, *The Economics of Money, Banking, and Financial Markets* (Boston, MA: Addison-Wesley, 2003), 44–6.

9. D. Ricardo, *On the Principles of Political Economy and Taxation* (London: John Murray, 1821), 101.

10. K. Menger, "On the origin of money", *Economic Journal* 2:6 (1892), 255.

11. G. Knapp, *The State Theory of Money* (London: Macmillan, 1924).

12. P. Grierson, *The Origins of Money* (London: Athlone Press, 1977); K. Polanyi, "The semantics of money uses", in G. Dalton (ed.), *Primitive, Archaic, and Modern Economies: Essays of Karl Polanyi* (New York: Anchor, 1968), 175–203.

13. Polanyi, *Great Transformation*, 11, 15, 214–15.

14. *Ibid.*, 56–7, 61–2.

15. *Ibid.*, 81, 96, 120–21, 136.

16. F. Block, "Karl Polanyi and the writing of the Great Transformation", *Theory and Society* 32:3 (2003), 275–306; Polanyi, *Great Transformation*, 204, 239, 260–2.

17. Polanyi, *Great Transformation*, 201–06.

18. *Ibid.*, 57–62.

19. G. Dale, *Karl Polanyi: The Limits of the Market* (Cambridge: Polity, 2010), 124–8; K. Gemici, "Karl Polanyi and the antinomies of embeddedness", *Socio-Economic Review* 6:1 (2008), 16; Polanyi, *Great Transformation*, 43–5.

20. F. Block, *The Origins of International Economic Disorder: A Study of United States International Monetary Policy from World War II to the Present* (Berkeley, CA: University of California Press, 1977); F. Block & M. Somers, "Beyond the economistic fallacy: the holistic science of Karl Polanyi", in T. Skocpol (ed.) *Vision and Method in Historical Sociology* (Cambridge: Cambridge University Press, 1984), 47–84; M. De Cecco, *Money and Empire: The International Gold Standard* (Oxford: Blackwell, 1974); B. Eichengreen, *Globalizing Capital: A History of the International Monetary System* (Princeton, NJ: Princeton University Press, 1996); K. Polanyi, *The Livelihood of Man* (New York: Academic Press, 1977), 10.

21. M. Cangiani, "Prelude to the Great Transformation: Karl Polanyi's articles for Der Oesterreichische Volkswirt," in *Humanity, Society, and Commitment: On Karl Polanyi* (Cheektowaga, NY: Black Rose Books, 1994), 7–24; K. Polanyi, *Essais*, eds. M. Cangiani & J. Maucourant (Paris: Éditions du Seuil, 2008); K, Polanyi, *For a New West: Essays, 1919–1958*, eds. G. Resta & M. Catanzariti (Cambridge: Polity, 2014).

22. Polanyi, *The Great Transformation*, 75–6.

23. F. Block & M. Somers, *The Power of Market Fundamentalism: Karl Polanyi's Critique* (Cambridge, MA: Harvard University Press, 2014); S. Hejeebu & D. McCloskey, "The reproving of Karl Polanyi", *Critical Review* 13:3/4 (1999), 285–314; S. Hejeebu & D. McCloskey, "Polanyi and the history of capitalism: rejoinder to Blyth", *Critical Review* 16:1 (2004), 135–42; G. Hildebrand, "Review of the Great Transformation by Karl Polanyi", *Journal of Economic Review* 36:3 (1946), 398–405; K. Gemici, "The neoclassical origins of Polanyi's self-regulating market", *Sociological Theory* 33:2 (2015), 125–47; D. Immerwahr, "Polanyi in the United States: Peter Drucker, Karl Polanyi, and the midcentury critique of economic society", *Journal of the History of Ideas* 70:3 (2009), 445–66; Polanyi, *Livelihood of Man*.

24. Gemici, "The neoclassical prigins of Polanyi's self-regulating market", 134–6; Polanyi, *Great Transformation*, 70–76.

25. There are significant conceptual problems raised by Polanyi's notion of commodity fiction, but such issues can be bracketed out for the analysis presented here. See the following for further discussion: the distinction between real and fictitious commodities in Block, "Introduction."; the examination of fictitious commodities vis-á-vis Marx and Tönnies in H. Özel, "Reclaiming humanity: the social theory of Karl Polanyi" (unpublished PhD dissertation, University of Utah, 1997); the analysis of the notion of self-regulating market in Gemici, "The neoclassical origins of Polanyi's self-regulating market"; and Chapter 4 in G. Dale, *Karl Polanyi: A Life on the Left* (New York: Columbia University Press, 2016), as well as Chapter 2 in G. Dale, *Reconstructing Karl Polanyi: Excavation and Critique* (London: Pluto, 2016).

26. In discussing commodification of labour and land, Polanyi himself readily acknowledges his intellectual debt to various authors, including Marx, although he is quick to note that the notion of fictitious commodities is different from related Marxist notions such as "fetishism of commodities" Polanyi, *Great Transformation*, 76.

27. Grierson, *The Origins of Money*; T. Parsons, "On the concept of political power", *Proceedings of the American Philosophical Society* 107:13 (1963), 232–62; D. Robertson, *Money* (London: Nisbet, 1948).

28. For exceptions, see H. Saiag, "Towards a neo-Polanyian approach to money", in Dale, *Reconstructing Karl Polanyi*, and Holmes, "'Whatever it takes'".

29. Polanyi, *Great Transformation*, 137.

30. Polanyi, "Semantics of money uses", 195.

31. J. Schumpeter, *History of Economic Analysis* (New York: Oxford University Press, 1954), 274.

32. Knapp, *State Theory of Money*.

33. *Ibid.*, 32–6.

34. T. Aspromourgos, *On the Origins of Classical Economics: Distribution and Value from William Petty to Adam Smith* (London: Routledge, 1996); R. Green, *Classical Theories of Money, Output and Inflation: A Study in Historical Economics* (New York: St Martin's Press, 1982); Schumpeter, *History of Economic Analysis*, 276; G. Vaggi & P. Groenewegen, *A Concise History of Economic Thought* (London: Palgrave Macmillan, 2006), 17–19; J. Viner, *Studies in the Theory of International Trade* (London: Allen & Unwin, 1955).

35. A. Roncaglia, *A Wealth of Ideas: A History of Economic Thought* (Cambridge: Cambridge University Press, 2006), 197–8.

36. See G. Davies, *A History of Money: From Ancient Times to the Present Day* (Cardiff: University of Wales Press, 2002), 229. Although dated, Schumpeter's *History of Economic Analysis* (in particular Ch. 6 in Part 2) is still a crucial reference on the history of the quantity theory of money. In addition, see M. Blaug, *Economic Theory in Retrospect* (Cambridge: Cambridge University Press, 1997); Green, *Classical Theories of Money, Output and Inflation*; C. Kindleberger, *A Financial History of Western Europe* (London: Allen & Unwin, 1984); and P. Vilar, *Or et monnaie dans l'histoire, 1450-1920* (Paris: Flammarion, 1974).

37. See D. Hume, "Of money" [1752], in *Essays, Moral, Political, and Literary*, ed. E. Miller (Indianapolis, IN: Liberty Classics, 1987), 281–94. Hume was fully aware of the increasing role of paper money and other types of instruments (281), which is not surprising given that the quantity of paper money well exceeded the quantity of commodity-money in England by the time Hume was writing on economic affairs. See Davies, *A History of Money*, 279. He nonetheless remained deeply sceptical and hostile to paper money all his life. For an extended discussion, see C. Caffentzis, "Fiction or counterfeit? David Hume's interpretations of paper and metallic money", in M. Schabas & C. Wennerlind (eds) *David Hume's Political Economy* (New York: Routledge, 2008), 146–67; 148.

38. Vaggi & Groenewegen, *Concise History of Economic Thought*, 78–9.

39. Hume, "Of money", 281.

40. D. Hume, "Of the balance of trade", in *Essays, Moral, Political, and Literary*, 308–26.

41. *Ibid.*, 311–12.

42. *Ibid.*, 311.

43. I. Rima, *Development of Economic Analysis* (New York: Routledge, 2001); Roncaglia, *A Wealth of Ideas*, 198.

44. Ricardo, *On the Principles of Political Economy and Taxation*, 101.

45. *Ibid.*, 42; L. Robbins, *A History of Economic Thought: The LSE Lectures*, ed. S. Medema & W. Samuels (Princeton, NJ: Princeton University Press, 1998), 194.

46. Ricardo, *On the Principles of Political Economy and Taxation*, 47–8.

47. Roncaglia, *Wealth of Ideas*, 198.

48. L. Tsoulfidis, "Quantity theory of money", in W. Darity, Jr (ed.), *International Encyclopedia of the Social Sciences* (New York: Macmillan, 2008), 659–61.

49. B. Eichengreen, *Golden Fetters: The Gold Standard and the Great Depression, 1919–1939* (New York: Oxford University Press, 1992), 32.

50. Polanyi, *Great Transformation*, 270.

51. *Ibid.*, 201–02.

52. In his criticisms concerning commodity-quantity theory of money, Polanyi is not entirely fair to Hume, who was chiefly a practical metallist. See Hume, "Of money", 284. In fact, Hume recognizes, to a certain extent, the "fictitious" character of money and the bases of money in social conventions (285). See C. Wennerlind, "An artificial virtue and the oil of commerce: a synthetic view of Hume's theory of money," in Schabas & Wennerlind, *David Hume's Political Economy*, 105–26 for an extended discussion. Nonetheless, Polanyi's criticism of Hume is apt given that it was Hume who successfully applied the notion of self-regulation to the international sphere. See Viner, *Studies in the Theory of International Trade*, 291–3. His attack on Ricardo has an equally solid basis. It was Ricardo who developed a theory of money that took the commodity description of money to its logical conclusions. Furthermore, Ricardo exercised considerable influence on the development of monetary orthodoxy in both theoretical and policy domains, as evident in the history of complex debates concerning monetary policy in the first half of the nineteenth century. See F. Fetter, *Development of British Monetary Orthodoxy, 1797–1875* (Cambridge, MA: Harvard University Press, 1965); D. Laidler, "British monetary orthodoxy in the 1870", *Oxford Economic Papers* 40:1 (1988), 74–109; M. Daugherty, "The currency-banking controversy: part 1", *Southern Economic Journal* 9:2 (1942), 140–55; N. Skaggs, "Thomas Tooke, Henry Thornton, and the development of British monetary orthodoxy", *Journal of the History of Economic Thought* 25:2 (2003), 177–97; Viner, *Studies in the Theory of International Trade*, 119. For instance, Ricardo was the dominant figure in the bullion debate following the suspension of specie payments in 1797 and his arguments shaped many of the proposals by the Currency School – proposals that greatly influenced Peel's Banking Act of 1844, which governed British banking and monetary policy during the second half of the nineteenth century.

53. G. Ingham, *The Nature of Money* (Cambridge: Polity, 2004); S. Karimzadi, *Money and Its Origins* (New York: Routledge, 2013).

54. P. Tcherneva, "Chartalism and the tax-driven approach to money," in Arestis & Sawyer, *A Handbook of Alternative Monetary Economics*, 69.

55. *Ibid.*

56. See R. Hawtrey, "Review of The State Theory of Money, by Georg Friedrich Knapp", *Economic Journal* 35:138 (1925), 251. Hawtrey, himself an authority on money and credit, remarks in his review of the English translation of *The State Theory of Money*: "Since it appeared, twenty years ago, Prof. Knapp's very remarkable book has taken

its place in economic history. Its appearance in an English translation is something of an event. The book has deeply influenced German thought on monetary theory."

57. J. Bonar, "Knapp's theory of money", *Economic Journal* 32:125 (1922), 39.

58. Knapp, *State Theory of Money*, 25–36.

59. "Chartal" is a term that derived from the Latin word "*Charta*", meaning ticket or token. See Knapp, *State Theory of Money*, 32.

60. Menger, "On the origin of money", 255.

61. L. Wray, *Understanding Modern Money: The Key to Full Employment and Price Stability* (Cheltenham: Elgar, 2003).

62. Gemici, "Neoclassical origins of Polanyi's self-regulating market."

63. J. Bockman, A. Fischer & D. Woodruff, "'Socialist accounting' by Karl Polanyi: with Preface 'Socialism and the Embedded Economy'", *Theory and Society* 45:5 (2016), 385–427; K. Polanyi, "La comptabilité socialiste", *Cahiers Monnaies et Financement* 22 (1994), 49–97; K. Polanyi, "Functionalist theory re-stated", *Cahiers Monnaies et Financement* 22 (1994), 115–26.

64. Here, "political community" corresponds to the term "commune" in Polanyi's original work. Note that Polanyi uses the term "commune" in a versatile manner. Thus, it is possible to use other terms such as "functional state" whenever Polanyi refers to "commune". See Bockman, Fischer & Woodruff, "'Socialist accounting' by Karl Polanyi", 414.

65. *Ibid.*, 413–16.

66. For a discussion of the dual-pricing mechanism in Polanyi's model, see Gemici, "Neoclassical origins of Polanyi's self-regulating market", 128–9.

67. Polanyi, *Great Transformation*, 206.

68. Further research on Schaffer's thesis and subsequent publications is necessary to substantiate Polanyi's remarks since the documents in the Karl Polanyi Archive (KPA), including various notes by Schaffer himself, do not give a hint of such theoretical elaboration.

69. KPA-29-10, 17.

70. Schaffer's account of the canonical Austrian school views on money are not entirely accurate. For instance, Mises does not just argue that money is in essence commodity-money, his theory of money and credit is more sophisticated than commodity theories of money. However, Schaffer is right to note that Polanyi was critical of the monetary economics found in Mises' work and the Austrian school in general. Mises suggests that money has its origins in barter economy and exchange, and his analysis of money is in line with Menger, "On the Origin of Money." He further advances the orthodox theory of money as means of exchange by linking the value of money itself to its subjective utility in an exchange economy. See L. Von Mises, *The Theory of Money and Credit* (Auburn, AL: Mises Institute, [1912] 2009). For an extended discussion, see A. Festré, "Money, banking and dynamics: two Wicksellian routes from Mises to Hayek and Schumpeter", *American Journal of Economics and Sociology* 61:2 (2002), 439–80.

71. K. Polanyi, "The essence of fascism", in J. Lewis, K. Polanyi & D. Kitchin (eds), *Christianity and the Social Revolution* (New York: Scribner's, 1936), 359–94.

72. Schaffer is accurate on this point, as can be seen in the discussion of Knapp and different theories of money presented in O. Spann, *Types of Economic Theory* (Hoboken, NJ: Taylor & Francis, [1929] 2013), 285–91.

73. G. Krippner, "The elusive market: embeddedness and the paradigm of economic sociology", *Theory and Society* 30 (2001), 775–810; Gemici, "Karl Polanyi and the antinomies of embeddedness"; Dale, *Reconstructing Karl Polanyi*, Chapter 1.

74. Polanyi, *Great Transformation*, 41, 132, 138, 144.

75. *Ibid.*, 26.

76. K. Polanyi, "The economy as instituted process," in C. Arensbert, H. Pearson & K. Polanyi (eds), *Trade and Market in Early Empires* (Glencoe, IL: Free Press, 1957), 243–70.

77. Block, "Introduction", xxx.

78. Polanyi, *Great Transformation*, 3.

79. *Ibid.*, 144.

80. *Ibid.*, 203.

81. *Ibid.*, 169, 204.

82. *Ibid.*, 3, 21, 31, 209.

83. In Polanyi's words (*Great Transformation*, 226): "With the international gold standard the most ambitious market scheme of all was put into effect, implying absolute independence of markets from national authorities. World trade now meant the organizing of life on the planet under a self-regulating market, comprising labor, land, and money, with the gold standard as the guardian of this gargantuan automaton."

84. Mises, *Theory of Money and Credit*, 461–3.

85. Polanyi, "Economy as instituted process", 264.

86. K. Polanyi, "Our obsolete market mentality", in *Primitive, Archaic, and Modern Economies*, 59–77.

87. Polanyi, "Semantics of money uses", 175.

88. Polanyi, "Economy as instituted process", 266.

89. *Ibid.*, 266.

90. K. Polanyi, "Archaic economic institutions: cowrie money", in *Primitive, Archaic, and Modern Economies*, 280–305.

91. *Ibid.*, 302–05.

92. *Ibid.*, 299.

93. *Ibid.*, 286, 300.

94. Ingham, *Nature of Money*; Wray, *Understanding Modern Money*.

95. H. Minsky, *Stabilizing an Unstable Economy* (New York: McGraw-Hill, 2008); Wray, *Understanding Modern Money*.

7

COMMODIFICATION

Hüseyin Özel

Karl Polanyi's analysis of the commodification process under capitalism in *The Great Transformation* (1944) provides us with a profound and perceptive understanding of how society as a whole becomes subordinate to the market, even to the degree that it faces the danger of annihilation.[1] This threat posed by the market, to make the society an "appendage"[2] to the market also represents a violation of the human essence, conceived in an Aristotelian way as the "political animal". This chapter deals with commodification as a continuous *process* within which everything, produced or not, including human beings, or more accurately their agency or transformative capacities and powers, is transformed into commodities, rather than as a state characterized by the three "fictitious commodities", labour, land and money. In other words, commodification will transform every human aspect and quality into abstract, functional units that are necessary for the working of the market institution. It is believed that the terms "extension of the market" (Polanyi), "commodity fetishism" (Marx), and "reification" (Lukács), all refer to the same process. The market system continuously extends its boundaries into every sphere of life, down to the most basic ingredients of human existence, from family to science, to "commodify" them. In other words, it is contended, Marx's conception of commodification would be a nice addition to that of Polanyi's for two reasons. First, whereas Polanyi seems to restrict commodification with the three commodity fictions even if he shows in a masterful way that this process does not stop at the creation of these fictions and it continues until it includes all aspects of human lives, Marx considers it as an inclusive social and economic process that eventually causes human existence to become "subsumed" by capital as a social relation. Second, whereas Polanyi seems comfortable with a theory of price determination emphasizing demand and supply, such as the neoclassical utility theory of value and price determination, Marx's (or the classical school's in general) labour theory of value, which forms the foundations upon which the notion of commodity fetishism is built, has the capacity to "demystify" exchange relations, and thus to show how human properties are "negated" or violated. These are the two arguments advanced in this chapter. For this, first, a critical presentation of Polanyi's narrative of commodification is given, and secondly, how these two approaches together can be used to reach a better understanding of commodification is discussed.

POLANYI'S NARRATIVE: A CRITICAL PRESENTATION

Polanyi's historical narrative of the "collapse" of the market system can be seen as relying on a powerful social theory in two respects: it presents both an institutional analysis of the market system and also a "collapse" mechanism.[3] This theory is built upon three main analytical building blocks, namely, the institutional separation between the market and the "rest of the society"; the creation of the "fictitious commodities" and the resulting "commodification" process; and the "double movement". The narrative, in a nutshell, goes something like this: firstly, capitalism is established on an institutional separation between the "economic sphere" (the "self-regulating market"), and the "political sphere" (the "rest of the society") through the creation of the three "fictitious commodities", namely, labour, land and money. The market institution, being "disembedded" from the "rest of the society", is "self-regulating" in the sense of its being subject to the "laws of supply and demand".[4] No intervention from the "political" sphere must be allowed if the market is to function "smoothly". Yet, such separation forces human beings to live through two forms of existence, one within the market, as *Homo economicus* guided by the "motive of gain and the fear of starvation"[5], the other as a "political animal", the social being proper, who is concerned with achieving a "good life" much in the Aristotelian way. Secondly, this separation, itself a result of the creation of the three "fictitious commodities", becomes the main channel through which both human "agency power" and their "habitation from nature"[6] is commodified, a process that also implies violation of sociality and connectedness. However, thirdly, against this process is a "protective countermovement"[7] that takes the form of a "self-protection of the society" as a whole against the extension of the market, which will eventually disrupt the functioning of the market. This "double movement" will give way to the tendencies for economic and social crisis, and cause the market society to be unstable.

The most significant aspect of the creation of the fictitious commodities is the separation of human beings both from their own life activities and from their natural environments within which these activities occur. First of all, according to Polanyi, what one calls "labour" is nothing but the whole human activity which cannot be separated from life. To put this activity under the rule of the market, by making it subject to the fear of hunger, then, will mean no less than the breakdown of the "totality" of life itself. As a result, human life activity comes to be broken down into specific compartments, such as economic, political, religious, etc., and only the "economic" motives, the fear of hunger and hope of gain, are allowed to govern individuals' lives. In other words, the whole life activity is now "commodified". Yet, this means the separation of human beings not only from their own life activity, but also, even more importantly, from their own "agency", human transformative power. Polanyi argues that "the alleged commodity 'labor power' cannot be shoved about, used indiscriminately, or even left unused, without affecting also the human individual who happens to be the bearer of this peculiar commodity. In disposing of a man's labor power the system would, incidentally, dispose of the physical, psychological, and moral entity 'man' attached to that tag".[8] The process of the disintegration of society through the creation of atoms, who are forced to sell their own agency power, is also a process of the separation of human life activity from the natural setting within which it takes place through "an individualized treatment of the land".[9] That is to say, land becomes a commodity that means the separation of human life from its natural surroundings. In short, commodification of labour and land represents a "dehumanization" process, for under the market system, human beings are forced to live through a "perverse" life within which they are deprived of the very qualities that make them human. In other words, the market system represents the artificial, externalized embodiment of the individual or the "blind and dark alter ego", as opposed to the moral one;[10] that is, under capitalism the "totality" of human existence breaks down, for the system forces them to live through a separate, fragmented life.

However, such a dehumanization process, according to Polanyi, could not go on indefinitely without resistance in the form of a protective counter-movement on the part of society: "the extension of the market organization in respect to genuine commodities was accompanied by its restriction in respect to fictitious ones".[11] This "double movement" represented two simultaneous tendencies that exist in the market society: the process of commodification, i.e., extension of exchange relations to the fictitious commodities, on the one hand, and society's "response", i.e., the resistance carried out by different classes and organizations within society to the extension of the market on the other. The double movement, according to Polanyi can be "personified as the action of two organizing principles in society", namely, "the principle of economic liberalism" supported by the trading classes, and "the principle of social protection aiming at the conservation of man and nature as well as productive organization", defended by "primarily, but not exclusively, the working and the landed classes".[12] In other words, the causal agents that carry out the double movement were the classes themselves: "The services to society performed by the landed, the middle, and the working classes shaped the whole social history of the nineteenth century".[13]

In fact, these two contradictory movements give the market society an unstable character: the protective countermovement as an attempt at restricting or at least slowing down the extension of the market will eventually impair the working of the self-regulating market. Since the system is organized on the basis of these commodity fictions, any intervention on the part of the social classes or state, or both, into the markets, create impairments in these three markets. These impairments will in turn intensify the tensions already inherent in society which will obstruct the working of the market as a whole. Therefore, the double movement, the extension of the market and society's "response" to it, actually signifies a circular process. Since the social classes themselves and their conflicts emanate from the economic sphere in a capitalist society and since this society is subordinate to the market, conflicts between these classes will necessarily have social dimensions even when they are purely economic in character, and this in turn will cause further disruptive effects on the economic sphere whose impairment will intensify the tensions existing in society.[14] In other words, since the protectionist countermovement is a direct intervention into the working of the self-regulating market, which inevitably has political consequences, the process of double movement will tend to break the institutional separation of the economic and the political upon which the market system is built. The result of such a process would be the disintegration of society, for the attempt to re-establish this institutional separation requires eradication of every form of social opposition against the market by any means, including the use of overt force as the fascist period has shown.

It is fair, then, to conclude that the double movement actually describes a social process within which the disruptive strains, inherent in the organization of the market system, manifest themselves in the form of class struggle and lead not only to the impairment of the self-regulating market but even to the "collapse" of the whole market system with all its institutions. Even if the double movement is a result of some institutional strains inherent in the market system, it also aggravates these strains. According to Polanyi, "these conditions themselves were set by the 'double movement'".[15] In other words, the protective movement which had immediately begun as soon as the market system was instituted, and within which class struggle played an essential role, caused these strains. The interplay between the economic and social effects, or between the market and society itself, causes the market system to be inherently unstable.

On this presentation, one might be surprised to observe that this narrative of Polanyi's has some striking similarities to Marx's overall account of human nature, history, society and capitalism. Such notions as commodity fictions, disembeddedness, the substantive definition of economics, and the idea that the market system goes against human nature and therefore provokes resistance and is prone to crises, all sound like Marxian themes, or at least can be "translated" without almost any loss of meaning.[16] However, given the breadth and richness of Polanyi's account it should not be a surprise to observe some elements from other analytical frameworks, such as neoclassical economics, mostly its Austrian version whose leading figure is Carl Menger.[17] Especially in connection to the "self-regulating" market idea, Polanyi seems to rely on a neoclassical framework. Taken together with commodification and the double movement, this element causes Polanyi's account to become a blend of two alternative traditions in the history of economic thought, namely, the "political economy" tradition, and neoclassical economics.[18] Yet, the relations between these two traditions would never be easy within the same analytical structure, because there are many significant differences between them, regarding especially determination of values and prices and working of the competition process. In this respect, it must be noted that Marx's analysis of capitalism depends on the objective, labour theory of value, whereas the neoclassical tradition adopts a subjective, utility theory of value. In this case, Polanyi seems to attempt at integrating a utility-value perspective with the process of "commodification" of labour and land. For this reason, one needs to locate the places of these distinct and incompatible traditions within Polanyi's analytical structure.

With respect to the relevance of the neoclassical economics for Polanyi, two points appear particularly important: that the "self-regulating" market cannot accept interventions emanating from the "political sphere" and that the protective countermovement eventually impairs the working of the self-regulating market, which, in turn, creates political tensions that will again further obstruct the functioning of the market. This interaction, especially interventions in the market on the part of the political sphere, if one ignores for a moment the role of the social classes, appears as a neoclassical "mechanism" for the market "is governed by laws of its own, the so-called laws of supply and demand, and motivated by fear of hunger and hope of gain".[19] The protectionist movement, being a direct, and necessarily a political, intervention into the working of the self-regulating market, makes it increasingly difficult to maintain the institutional separation of the economic and the political spheres upon which the market system is founded. Since this difficulty further intensifies the tensions already existing in society, the result would be instability, or even the "collapse" of the market society.

The use of these two incompatible traditions together in the same analytical structure may be justified by Polanyi's thesis that capitalism needs an institutional separation between the "economic" and the "political" spheres.[20] Since the market, as a disembedded institution from the rest of society, should function according to its laws, the demand-supply framework must be sufficient to understand how market prices are to be determined. In other words, neoclassical theories of competition and of price should be valid within the market sphere. In this regard, another notion of Polanyi's which can also be used to justify having two different theories is the "economistic fallacy", that is, the identification of "economic" phenomena with market phenomena,[21] or the extrapolation of the categories that are prevalent in capitalism to other societies and/or other times. Once the fictitious commodities were created, the desire of gain and the fear of hunger have automatically become the universal motives, for the subordination of the social to the economic has been completed. As a consequence of this process "the delusion of economic determinism"[22] has begun to dominate our minds. In this system, not only are the social classes identical with "supply" and "demand" for the markets for labour, land and capital[23], but all institutions existing in the society, including family, organization of science and education, and of religion and arts, in short, every aspect of life, must conform to the requirements of the market.[24] Against this extension is of course the protective countermovement that attempts at restricting or at least slowing down the extension of the market. This countermovement takes the form of political interventions (such as government interventions, or the actions of trade unions, or of working-class parties, etc.) in the market, which will hinder competition by causing monopolistic tendencies to emerge:

> Protectionism helped to transform competitive markets into monopolistic ones. Less and less could markets be described as autonomous and automatic mechanisms of competing atoms. More and more were individual replaced by associations, men and capital united to non-competing groups. Economic adjustment became slow and difficult. The self-regulation of markets was gravely hampered. Eventually, unadjusted price and cost structures prolonged depressions, unadjusted equipment retarded the liquidation of unprofitable investments, unadjusted price and income levels caused social tension. And whatever the market in question – labor, land, or money – the strain would transcend the economic zone and the balance would have to be restored by political means. Nevertheless, the institutional separation of the political from the economic sphere was constitutive to market society and had to be maintained whatever the tension involved. This was the other source of disruptive strain.[25]

The above quote suggests that the introduction of monopolistic elements into the market by social protection is the main cause for the impairment of the self-regulating market, a point that is quite consistent with a neoclassical point of view: if the markets are left to their own devices, and if they are kept separate from any political and social influence, there should be no problem in their functioning, for "the protective legislation, restrictive associations, and other instruments of intervention"[26] caused the market to lose its self-regulating character. Even though Polanyi stresses the importance of the role played by different classes and organizations, interventions themselves appear as causal mechanisms. In other words, here the political sphere and the interventions on the part of it appear as "external" to the market. As is well-known, this "externality" has become an integral part of mainstream economics' explaination for market failures. But in this interpretation, Polanyi can be taken as pointing to the institutionalization of state interventions in the late 1930s and the prevalence of monopolistic tendencies in individual markets as the sign of the collapse of the market system. This in turn may lead to another interpretation that this narrative can be seen as an instance of a neoclassical framework within which the existence of "frictions" in the markets in the form of outside intervention hampers the working of the market by destroying competition, or at best it takes Polanyi's contribution as a form of the "monopoly capitalism" argument which asserts that the phase of capitalism within which we live is drastically different from the earlier one, liberal or competitive capitalism. Of course, to be fair, it should be noted that many non-mainstream economists, from Schumpeter[27] to some Marxists such as Baran and Sweezy,[28] held that capitalism had entered in the 1940s into a new, monopolistic phase characterized by big conglomerates that destroy competition altogether. However, without going into detail, it can be shown that this conception of competition has its own problems in understanding the working of capitalism.[29] I also believe that, as will be discussed shortly, this interpretation is not the best way of understanding the commodification process, for it rests on a characterization of the human being as *Homo economicus* and this does not fit well into Polanyi's framework. The point here is not whether Polanyi's approach can be reduced to a neoclassical one, but it is whether this type of argument is really compatible with his, mostly Aristotelian, conception of human nature that emphasizes self-realization. It is obvious that the inevitability of political interventions of any kind can be seen as expressions of the political nature of man:[30] since the market violates essential human powers, political interventions representing the self-protection of society would sooner or later emerge and disrupt the working of the market. Nevertheless, if one thinks the causal mechanism at work here is some kind of "market failure" or "imperfectionist" argument, it is hard to escape from the conclusion that the neoclassical narrative about the working of the market is a correct characterization of the functioning of the market system. Unfortunately, in order for this narrative to make any sense, human beings should be understood as individuals who are concerned with their own self-interest.[31]

Here, one can think of two possibilities: either human beings are really rational in the neoclassical sense, so that markets function according to optimizing behaviour of individuals, or they are forced, against their will and nature, to behave as *Homo economicus* within the market, and this creates a contradiction with their sociality, which will lead them to resist the market in order to reclaim their humanity. Of course, it is the second possibility that Polanyi embraces; protectionism is nothing but an attempt at curbing the commodifying effects on the market through intervention. Then, a natural question is whether the emphasis on non-market interventions is really necessary to understand, first, the causes of the resistance on the part of society against the market, and, second, the disruptive effects of this resistance on the functioning of the market? The answer should be clear enough. The main point here is that Polanyi, who is very convincing in his defence that human beings are social beings in the first place, does not need an argument that relies on political interventions in order to explain the collapse of the system. That is to say, for the sake of consistency, his account needs a theory of the functioning of the market that could be integrated to the process of commodification in such a way that it could eschew such neoclassical arguments of causality. I believe a good strategy to deal with this analytical problem could be to discard whatever remains of the neoclassical tradition and supplant them with the political economy tradition, thereby avoiding the disturbing implications of the individualist rationality assumption. Such a theory would also be able to integrate the notion of human nature and the commodification process, in a clearer way. This is the topic of the next section.

COMMODIFICATION IN POLANYI AND MARX: ANALYTICAL CONNECTIONS

It is true that Polanyi's relation to Marx is, at best, ambivalent,[32] or even "tangential",[33] but still, taken as a whole, two points of connection of Polanyi's analytical structure to that of Marx's are worth mentioning. First, the idea of "commodity fictions", above all labour power's becoming a commodity as the distinguishing feature of capitalism, corresponds to Marx's analysis of commodity fetishism, and his "substantive" understanding of economics, which emphasizes the "non-economic nature of man"[34], has a certain affinity with Marx's "historical materialism". Secondly, the "dehumanizing" aspect of capitalism was noticed and made the very basis of a critique of capitalism itself by both Marx and Polanyi. In both, capitalism is a "violation" of essential powers of human beings, or human nature in general, that is, both thought that human essence is contradicted by their existence under capitalism. In Polanyi, this "violation" calls for a "protective counter-movement"[35] on the part of society, which will eventually cause the market society to disintegrate whereas Marx emphasizes class struggle, a notion that is not excluded by Polanyi as well. With respect to the commodification process too, there are important affinities and overlaps between them. For example, Kari Polanyi Levitt and Marguerite Mendell argue that Polanyi "did not agree with those who set the late Marx against the early Marx" and that "in *The Economic and Philosophic Manuscripts of 1844* Marx elaborated precisely those aspects of commodity fetishism, objectification and alienation which Polanyi had long considered to be central, and which he later explored in their historical dimension in *The Great Transformation*".[36] As is well-known, it is Marx's *1844 Manuscripts*[37] which develops the notions of the "species-being" and "alienation" that have direct conceptual links to the notion of "commodity fetishism".[38] In Marx, commodity fetishism is an overall process in which products of human labour, commodities, "appear as independent beings endowed with life, and entering into relation both with one another and the human race" and this fetishism "attaches itself to the products of labour, so soon as they are produced as commodities, and which is therefore inseparable from the production of commodities".[39] Within this process, human transformative power, i.e., labour power, which itself becomes a commodity under capitalism, together with its products, acquire thing-like character and become the controlling force over human lives. In other words, this process is not only an "economic" one within the market, but it is a pervasive social process which affects every single individual and the social sphere as a whole.

Nevertheless, Polanyi seems to disagree: he writes in *The Great Transformation* that "Marx's assertion of the fetish character of the value of commodities refers to the exchange value of genuine commodities and has nothing in common with the fictitious commodities".[40] It should be noted that Polanyi uses the term "commodity" in its "empirical" sense; that is, a commodity is something that is bought and sold on the market. Then, the term "fictitious commodity" implies that labour, land, and money are not real commodities; they are just treated as commodities, contrary to their natures. This raises doubts that Polanyi may not be very careful about commodification. He distinguishes between "genuine" commodities which are produced for the market and the "fictitious" ones which are not, but does not seem to consider the possibility of something that is not a commodity in the empirical sense, such as knowledge, could be transformed into a "real" commodity. That is to say, to use classical or Marxian language, a use-value produced to satisfy some human need will be treated as an exchange value in the market. Then, Polanyi's wish to restrict commodification with the fictitious ones is really curious, because even if he starts his narrative with the creation of the three commodity fictions, his whole conception of double movement, more specifically extension of the market, describes the process in which all aspects of human lives are transformed so as to conform to the requirements of the market. Commodification refers to a process in which everything, produced or not, material or non-material, is to become a "commodity". That is to say, for Polanyi too, commodification does not end with the creation of the fictitious commodities, and it is an overall social process affecting every social institution and human being. This transformation amounts to the blurring of the institutional separation between the economic sphere and the political one as a result of the extension of the market so as to include "marriage and the rearing of children, the organization of science and education, of religion and arts, the choice of profession, the forms of habitation, the shape of settlements down even to the aesthetics of every-day life", which all "must be moulded according to the needs of the system".[41] This, as we are about to see, is a distinguishing feature of commodification, a process that could be understood better with Marx's concept of the fetishism of commodities. Unfortunately, Polanyi did not take this route.

With respect to Polanyi's reluctance to extend commodification beyond the fictitious commodities, two comments seem relevant. First, since Polanyi engages in building a new and independent analytical structure and therefore is forced to develop new concepts he is consequently keeping Marx at arm's length. This is understandable because otherwise his account would have been considered as yet another attempt to elaborate or justify Marx from an empirical and historical point of view. Given Polanyi's dislike of the deterministic elements that exist in Marx,[42] such an attitude would not be surprising, because his critique of the market system is mostly a social and moral one, rather than an economic one based on some "tendencies working with iron necessity"[43], as in the historical materialism or crisis theory of Marx. Such a deterministic framework in which human volition is lost could not be acceptable to Polanyi.[44] The second point is related to Polanyi's dislike of the labour theory of value, as opposed to the marginalist utility theory. In Marx, commodity fetishism is an integral part of the labour theory of value, because he argues that it is this theory which unlocks the "mystery" of the market processes, within which the individual loses her "power of will" and becomes the "personification" of the reified social relations. Had Polanyi followed Marx in this respect and connected the double movement to commodity fetishism, his account would appear again as an inquiry within Marxian lines, no matter how distinct his understanding from that of Marx. Instead of pursuing this, it would be sufficient for Polanyi to have a price determination theory that emphasizes demand and supply framework, for the backbone of the argument of double movement lies in the political, and therefore moral, sphere, rather than the economic one. As argued above, the neoclassical theory of price determination that is based on the marginal utility theory can be used to explain the collapse of the market through political interventions. For this reason, one can contend, Polanyi "favoured the Vienna school over the more mechanistic labor theory of value because it introduced volition in the form of choices by consumers and producers".[45] Polanyi's endorsement of the neoclassical theory of price formation and value theory may also be justified by the idea that this theory works well in capitalism because human beings are forced to be behave "rationally" so as to maximize their gain. In other words, Polanyi's critique is directed toward capitalism itself, not to the theory which "mirrors" this very reality, for the theory seems correct. However, as Marx argues, the theory reflecting that reality may be "false" because:

> [...] in competition [...] everything appears upside down. The fin-ished configuration of economic relations, as these are visible on the surface, in their actual existence, and therefore also in the notions with which the bearers and agents of these relations seek to gain an understanding of them, is very different from the configuration of their inner core, which is essential but concealed, and the concept corresponding to it. It is in fact the very reverse and antithesis of this.[46]

If the very reality itself is "upside down" in capitalism, if the "reference cri-terion – reality –already itself a counterfeit standard" as Colletti aptly puts it, then the theory that only "reflects" this reality will be a form of "ideology".[47] If this is the case, not this form, but instead the analysis of commodity fetishism could be a better tool to use in "demystifying" this reality and to understand the very process of social disintegration caused by commodification. In fact, it can be contended, Marx's notion of commodity fetishism is exactly the same as Polanyi's fictitious commodities with respect to its effects: the dissolution of the social bond and hence the "annihilation" of society. In both, the capitalist "com-modification" process will ultimately lead to the "breakdown" of society, even though Polanyi is more explicit about this than Marx. And, following Marx, this "mystery" can only be solved through a labour theory of value perspective. In order to see this, a brief discussion of the connections between labour theory of value and commodification is necessary.

Marx does not take the labour theory of value as simply a "technical problem" of the transformation of values into prices, as in the Ricardian tradition,[48] but for him it is a most important tool to reveal the "hidden" realities of capitalism. It is mostly an "ontological" (or "metaphysical") theory, which is essential in explaining the fundamental "laws" and tendencies of the capitalist mode of pro-duction.[49] For Marx, a commodity is not simply a "thing" to be bought and sold; it is a *social relation*, a social relation that is carried through "things". That is to say, in Marx, the reduction of labour power to a commodity, to a "thing", charac-terizes the very process of fetishism through which human relations are "reified" to the extent that even human beings themselves are treated as "exchange val-ues". Labour power is never a "commodity", it is the "power" that characterizes human agency, the "aggregate of those mental and physical capabilities existing in the physical form, the living personality, of a human being".[50] If these capabilities are subject to exchange, this simply means that human beings themselves are separated from their own powers in a very real way and become only bearers of "exchange values". On the other hand, the treatment of land, or nature in general, as a commodity simply means the separation of human beings from their "inorganic bodies".[51] Last, but not the least, money is only the "alienated *capacity of mankind*" and it becomes the "true *agent of separation* and the true *cementing agent* ... the *chemical* power of society".[52] In short, Marx never considers these three as "genuine" commodities, on the contrary, it is the commodification of these which characterizes capitalism. In this regard, it should be emphasized that the concept of alienation is the direct link between commodity fetishism and Marx's labour theory of value.[53]

Under capitalism, Marx argues, not only the human's own product, but also her own labour power,[54] is reduced to a "thing" through its becoming a commodity. That is, labour power as an abstract category comes to be completely separated from its "bearer", human beings, and it becomes a "thing". Put another way, it characterizes the process of the inversion of the "subject" into its "predicate", and the "predicate" into the "subject": human labour-power, a predicate, becomes an alien entity which transforms real subjects, human beings, into "things". Therefore, we have a twofold process here: on the one hand things seem to acquire human attributes while on the other human relations take on the character of things and thus have a "phantom objectivity"; that is, they are "reified".[55] Human relations, however, appear as relations between things only when both the products of labour and labour power itself become alienated. Whereas the objects produced by man appear as the bearers of social relations, i.e. fetishism, the social relations between real people appear as the relations between things, i.e. reification. Reification refers to the act of transforming human properties, relations and actions into the properties, relations and actions which have become, or are thought as originally, independent of human activity. And these facts govern the life of human beings in accordance with the laws of the thing-world. Hence both the terms fetishism and reification refer to the same process, which is itself the result of alienation.[56] Here, it should be stressed that capitalism needs to function as though abstractions are real; in capitalism, individuals see each other as commodities, purely as means to be exchanged for the sake of continued existence.[57] Although the effects of alienation seem to be restricted to the worker, in fact it is an all-pervasive social relation in capitalism. For example, not only does the fertility of soil seem to be an attribute of the landlord,[58] but the powers of labour, of human beings, appear as the powers of capital, since "what is lost by the specialized workers is concentrated in the capital which confronts them".[59] Moreover, even the capitalist himself is "only capital personified. His soul is the soul of capital".[60] Then, in Marx's own words, the "trinity" of capital-profit (interest), land-ground rent, labour-wages completes the mystification of capitalism, i.e., a "bewitched, distorted and upside-down world haunted by Monsieur le Capital and Madame la Terre, who are at the same time social characters and mere things".[61] One of the best descriptions of this process is given by Polanyi himself, when he explains Marx's notion of commodity fetishism:

> In a developed market society distribution of labour intervenes. Human relationships become indirect; instead of immediate co-operation there is indirect co-operation by the medium of exchange of commodities. The reality of the relationships persists; the producers continue to produce for one another. But this relationship is now hidden behind the exchange of goods; it is impersonal: it expresses itself in the objective guise of the exchange value of commodities; it is objective, thing-like. Commodities, on the other hand, take on a semblance of life. They follow their own laws; rush in and out of the market; change places; seem to be masters of their own destiny. We are in a spectral world, but in a world in which *spectres are real*. For the pseudo-life of the commodity, the objective character of exchange value, are *not* illusion.[62]

It is, therefore, the basic characteristic of the labour theory of value that what the value form represents is nothing but inverted human creative abilities, or potentialities that exist in a living human being. However, under the dominance of the market, and of the associated "market mentality"[63], purposive actions of human beings, directed to realize their own potentialities, reproduce the same reified social relations. Under such conditions, while human beings on the one hand try to affirm their individuality, their uniqueness, they are also reduced to mere "atoms". And as a result of this reification, the abstraction of the "rational economic man" *Homo economicus*, becomes a reality: the individual is transformed into a functioning component of a system, and therefore as such must be equipped with essential features indispensable for running the system. Here, it is essential to understand that:

> *not theory but reality itself reduces man to an abstraction. Economics is a system and set of laws governing relations in which man is constantly being transformed into the "economic man". Entering the realm of economics, man is transformed. The moment he enters into economic relations, he is drawn, irrespective of his will and consciousness – into situations and lawlike relations in which he*

functions as the homo oeconomicus, in which he exists and realizes himself only to the extent to which he fulfils the role of the economic man. Thus economics is a sphere of life that has the tendency to transform man into the economic man and that draws him into an objective mechanism which subjugates and adapts him.[64]

Individuals are forced to behave rationally in the market against their nature. If the reality is "false" in the sense of being formed by reified relations, the theory that simply reflects this without questioning itself must also be "false". That is to say, the neoclassical theories of value and prices are a form of "reified consciousness". A theory which is itself a product of fetishism and reification processes cannot be an adequate theory to understand commodification process as a whole. Individuals, when they enter the market sphere, or "civil society",[65] are forced to be guided by "private egoism" and hence the market sphere is characterized by a state in which *"bellum omnium contra omnes".*[66] The individual lives an egoistic life, and she becomes an "isolated monad",[67] while in the political sphere, she becomes an abstract "citizen".[68] Polanyi, too, shares Marx's belief that human beings are forced to have two different forms of life in the market society, and that human beings are not by nature egoistic ones. In fact, it is this violation of their nature by the market that drives them to rebel against the extension of the market. Thus, Polanyi and Marx share the same attitude towards the market in its destructive effects on human "livelihood" and society. However, as the commodification process deepens, the egotistic and self-interested behaviour becomes a rule even in the "political sphere", and therefore the individual herself is transformed into *Homo economicus* to a degree that she treats everything according to "costs and benefits". Gradually, the very agency powers of human beings are transferred into the commodities, and as a result, the political sphere is brought under the control of the market. Such a situation characterizes loss of freedom, both at the individual and societal levels. In order to understand this contradictory aspect of social life in capitalism, then, one needs the labour theory of value, for it explains how labour power as the transformative capacity of human beings, become "alien" entities annihilating freedom.

To sum up, Marx's understanding of the commodification process and the labour theory of value as a tool for "demystifying" capitalism appears as a better candidate to explain both the commodification process, and therefore, the process of the extension of the market. Polanyi's exposition of the notion of the double movement makes one think that it is based on some kind of imperfectionist position, as we have seen, but Marx's theory of competition and price formation, arguably inherited from the classical political economy school of Smith and Ricardo, does not need such ideas.[69] In Marx, the analytical layer of values is the "deepest" one of the whole analysis of prices and competition, and it is the ultimate determinant of the other two "upper" ones, namely the market prices and the prices of production. But these upper levels are somewhat misleading in order to understand the capitalist reality, because of the "inverted" nature of this reality, whose true nature can only be understood by examining the world of values. Such a theory of value and prices, if integrated into Polanyi's narrative, will not only allow the analysis to be more perceptive, through adding a "deeper" dimension that is necessary to understand the "hidden" and "upside-down" character of the capitalist reality, but it will also cause the narrative to become richer in content and "sharper", through the interactions between social or class forces and the tendencies disrupting competitive processes.

CONCLUSION: EMBEDDING SOCIETY INTO THE MARKET

It seems possible to derive two conclusions from our discussion about the commodification process in a capitalist system. First, it needs to be emphasized again that commodification is not limited to a state characterized by the existence of the three commodities, but it should be broadened to refer to a continuous *process* within which everything, including human beings themselves, will be transformed into "spectres", some abstract, functional units that are necessary for the working of the system. The terms "extension of the market" used by Polanyi, "commodity fetishism" used by Marx, or "reification" used by Lukács, all refer to the same process. The market system continuously extends its boundaries into every sphere of life, down to the most basic ingredients of human existence, to "commodify" it.

A second conclusion, which is related to the first, is that this commodification of life is more or less reaching its climax in our new, "neoliberal" phase. The commodification process has been exacerbated by the neoliberal transformation of the past 30 years which has attempted to "embed" society in the market.[70] In this state, which represents the "limit condition" of the commodification, the objective to "annihilate all organic forms of existence and to replace them by a different type of organization, an atomistic and individualistic one"[71] has almost been achieved. Any alternative that can be conceived must consider how deep this commodification is, and humanity as a whole must try to build new form of resistance to the market in a serious way.

Notes for Chapter 7

1. I am grateful for the comments and suggestions by the editors of this volume.
2. K. Polanyi, *The Great Transformation: The Political and Economic Origins of Our Time* (Boston, MA: Beacon Press, [1944] 2001), 77.

3. H. Ozel, "Reclaiming Humanity: The Social Theory of Karl Polanyi", unpublished PhD dissertation, University of Utah, 1997.

4. C. Arensberg, K. Polanyi & H. Pearson (eds), *Trade and Markets in the Early Empires: Economies in History and Theory* (New York: Free Press, 1957), 68.

5. K. Polanyi, "Our obsolete market mentality: civilization must find a new thought pattern", *Commentary* 3 (1947), 113.

6. K. Polanyi, "On belief in economic determinism", *Sociological Review* (1947), 97.

7. Polanyi, *Great Transformation*, 144.

8. *Ibid.*, 73.

9. *Ibid.*, 179.

10. A. Rotstein, "The reality of society: Karl Polanyi's philosophical perspective" in Polanyi-Lewitt (ed.), *The Life and Work of Karl Polanyi* (Montreal: Black Rose Books, 1990), 98–110.

11. Polanyi, *Great Transformation*, 76.

12. *Ibid.*, 132.

13. *Ibid.*, 133.

14. *Ibid.*, 201.

15. *Ibid.*, 214.

16. Özel, "Reclaiming Humanity"; H. Özel & E. Yılmaz, "What can Marxists learn from Polanyi?", paper presented to the Tenth International Polanyi Conference, "Protecting Society and Nature from Commodity Fiction", October 2005, Boğaziçi University, İstanbul. Thus, Deirdre McCloskey writes: "in economic history dependent on Marx, such as … Karl Polanyi's *The Great Transformation*, the market is seen as a novelty … From this Marxist historical mistake arose the fairy tales of lost paradises for aristocrats or peasants and a reason for ignoring the bourgeois virtues" (D. McCloskey, "Bourgeois virtue", *American Scholar* 63:2 (1994), 191).

17. For Menger's views on methodology of economics, and his importance for Austrian economics, see H. Özel "Methodological individualism in Carl Menger: an evaluation," *Hacettepe University Economic and Administrative Sciences Journal* 16:1/2 (1998).

18. It should be noted that throughout this chapter the term "political economy" is used in a narrow and "technical" sense, which specifically refers to the "classical" political economy school of thought whose most prominent figures are Adam Smith, David Ricardo and Karl Marx. A distinguishing feature of this school or tradition is the labour theory of value, together with a heavy emphasis on production and capital accumulation processes. The neoclassical tradition, on the other hand, is taken to be addressing the "resource allocation" problem and adopting a utility theory of value perspective. For a detailed explanation of the analytical features of these two traditions and their differences, see M. Hollis & E. Nell, *Rational Economic Man: A Philosophical Critique of Neo-Classical Economics* (Cambridge: Cambridge University Press, 1975) and A. Shaikh, *Capitalism: Competition, Conflict, Crises* (New York: Oxford University Press, 2016).

19. Arensberg *et al.*, *Trade and Markets in the Early Empires*, 68.

20. Polanyi, *Great Transformation*, 71.

21. Arensberg *et al.*, *Trade and Markets in the Early Empires*, 270 and K. Polanyi, *The Livelihood of Man* (New York: Academic Press, 1977), 20.

22. Polanyi, "Our obsolete market mentality", 114.

23. *Ibid.*

24. Polanyi, "On belief in economic determinism", 100.

25. Polanyi, *Great Transformation*, 218.

26. *Ibid.*, 132.

27. J. Schumpeter, *Capitalism, Socialism and Democracy* (London: Allen & Unwin, 1943).

28. P. Baran & P. Sweezy, *Monopoly Capital: An Essay on the American Economic and Social Order* (New York: Monthly Review Press, 1966).

29. For a thorough critique of this position, see Shaikh, *Capitalism*, who clearly refutes the idea that Marxist (or classical) analysis of price formation depends on the assumption of "perfect" competition (333–5). For a clear exposition of the classical price and competition analyses, see also Hollis & Nell, *Rational Economic Man*.

30. "Aristotle was right: man is not an economic, but a social being. He does not aim at safeguarding his individual interest in the acquisition of material possessions, but rather at ensuring social good-will, social status, social assets" (Polanyi, "Our obsolete market mentality", 112); "Given the right institutions, such as *oikos* and *polis*, and the traditional understanding of the good life, Aristotle saw no room for the scarcity factor in the human economy" (Polanyi, *Livelihood of Man*, 30–1); "Aristotle had taught that only gods or beasts could live outside society, and man was neither" (Polanyi, *Great Transformation*, 114).

31. Frank Hahn, for example, identifies the three important tenets of neoclassical economics as follows: "(1) I am a reductionist in that I attempt to locate explanations in the actions of individual agents. (2) in theorizing about the agent, I look for some axioms of rationality. (3) I hold that some notion of equilibrium is required and that the study of equilibrium states is useful" (F. Hahn, *Equilibrium and Macroeconomics* (Oxford: Blackwell, 1984), 1–2).

32. G. Dale, *Reconstructing Karl Polanyi: Excavation and Critique* (London: Pluto, 2016), chapter 2.

33. A. Sievers, *Has Market Capitalism Collapsed? A Critique of Karl Polanyi's New Economics* (New York: Columbia University Press, 1949), 307.

34. Polanyi, *Great Transformation*, 151.

35. *Ibid.*, 144.

36. K. Polanyi Levitt & M. Mendell, "Karl Polanyi: his life and times", *Studies in Political Economy* 22 (spring 1987), 28.

37. K. Marx, *Early Writings*, trans. R. Livingstone (Harmondsworth: Penguin, 1975).

38. Özel, "Reclaiming Humanity", 94–104.

39. K. Marx, *Capital, Volume I*, trans. B. Fowkes (Harmondsworth: Penguin, 1976), 163.

40. Polanyi, *Great Transformation*, 72n. Incidentally, Polanyi's remark is consistent with Nancy Fraser's use of the term "fictitious commodification", referring to the three fictions, as a distinguishing feature of Polanyi's account. See N. Fraser, "Why two Karls are better than one: integrating Polanyi and Marx in a critical theory of the

current crisis", in M. Brie & C. Thomasberger (eds), *Karl Polanyi's Vision of a Socialist Transformation* (Montreal: Black Rose Books, 2018), 67–76 and N. Fraser, "Can society be commodities all the way down? Post-Polanyian reflections on capitalist crisis", *Economy and Society* 43:4 (2014), 541–58. I will return to this issue shortly.

41. Polanyi, "On belief in economic determinism", 100.

42. Polanyi writes that "Marx's close adherence to Ricardo and the traditions of liberal economics" (*Great Transformation*, 126), led him to a deterministic position. In a similar vein, in 1913, he rejects the "fatalism" of historical materialism on the basis of its giving no role to human purposeful activity and argues that "in order to transform society, men must establish moral goals and employ political means in the service of their attainment" (L. Congdon, "Karl Polanyi in Hungary, 1900–19", *Journal of Contemporary History* 11 (1976), 175). Also in 1919, he argues that Marxism is built on three pillars, namely, "the utilitarian ethic, the materialist conception of history, positivist epistemology and the determinist philosophy" (K. Polanyi, "Ideologies in crisis", in Brie & Thomasberger, *Karl Polanyi's Vision of a Socialist Transformation*, 267).

43. Marx, *Capital Volume I*, 91.

44. But still, Polanyi himself believes that "it was an illusion to assume a society shaped by man's will and wish alone" (*Great Transformation*, 251). This tension between free will and necessity haunts both Polanyi and Marx throughout their own works. See Özel, "Reclaiming Humanity", 85–94, for the contradictions between human free will and necessity in historical materialism.

45. K. Polanyi-Levitt, "Karl Polanyi as socialist" in K. McRobbie (ed.), *Humanity, Society and Commitment: On Karl Polanyi*, 115–34 (Montreal: Black Rose Books, 1994), 116. Polanyi believes that "Adam Smith followed Locke's false start on the labor origins of value" (*Great Transformation*, 124), whereas Ricardo, "in a mistaken theorem of tremendous scope … invested labor with the sole capacity of constituting value, thereby reducing all conceivable transactions in economic society to the principle of equal exchange in a society of free men" (*ibid.*, 126).

46. K. Marx, *Capital Volume III*, 311.

47. L. Colletti, *From Rousseau to Lenin: Studies in Ideology and Society*, trans. J. Merrington & J. White (New York: Monthly Review Press, 1972), 233.

48. P. Garegnani, "The labour theory of value: 'detour' or technical advance?", in G. Caravale (ed.), *Marx and Modern Economic Analysis*, Vol. I: *Values, Prices and Exploitation* (Aldershot: Elgar, 1991), 97–118.

49. H. Özel, "The notion of power and the 'metaphysics' of labor values", *Review of Radical Political Economies* 40:4 (2008), 445–61.

50. Marx, *Capital Volume I*, 270.

51. Marx, *Early Writings*, 328.

52. *Ibid.*, 377 (emphasis in original).

53. E. Hunt, "Philosophy and economics in the writings of Karl Marx", in S. Helburn & D. Bramhall (eds), *Marx, Schumpeter & Keynes: A Centenary of Dissent* (Armonk, NY: M. E. Sharpe, 1986).

54. Polanyi is actually aware that it is not labour, but labour power which becomes a commodity: "the price of the use of labor power is called wages …" (Polanyi, "On

belief in economic determinism", 98); "The competitive labour market hit the bearer of labor power, namely, man" (Polanyi, *Great Transformation*, 162); "They [methods of social protection] achieved what had been intended: the disruption of the market for that factor of production known as labor power" (*ibid.*, 176).

55. G. Lukács, *History and Class Consciousness: Studies in Marxist Dialectics*, trans. R. Livingstone, (Cambridge, MA: MIT Press, 1971), 83.

56. A. Schaff, *Alienation as a Social Phenomenon* (Oxford: Pergamon, 1980), 80–82.

57. E. Hunt, "Marx's theory of property and alienation", in Parel & Flanagan (eds), *Theories of Property: Aristotle to the Present* (Waterloo: ON: Wilfred Laurier University Press, 1979), 309.

58. Marx, *Early Writings*, 311.

59. Marx, *Capital Volume I*, 482.

60. *Ibid.*, 342.

61. Marx, *Capital Volume III*, 969.

62. K. Polanyi, "The Essence of Fascism" [1935] in J. Lewis, K. Polanyi & D. Hitchin (eds), *Christianity and The Social Revolution* (London: Victor Gollancz, 19XX), 375.

63. Polanyi, "Our obsolete market mentality".

64. K. Kosík, *Dialectics of the Concrete: A Study on Problems of Man and World*, Boston Studies in the Philosophy of Science, R. Cohen & M. Wartofsky (eds), vol. LII (Dordrecht: D. Reidel, 1976), 52 (emphasis in original). In this connection, Marx's distinction between "formal" and "real subsumption" seems helpful. See https://www.marxists.org/archive/marx/works/1864/economic/ch02a.htm (accessed 2 May 2019). The real subsumption of capital refers loosely to the end-state of the transformation of the whole society.

65. As is well-known, the distinction between "civil society" and "political society" has a long conceptual history, emanating from Hegel and adopted by Marx and other important social thinkers, such as Ferdinand Tönnies, whose distinction is between "community" (*Gemeinschaft*) and "society" (*Gesellschaft*), and Max Weber, whose distinction is "communal" (*Vergemeinschaftung*) versus "associative" (*Vergesellschaftung*) social organizations; see F. Tönnies, *Community and Society*, trans. C. Loomis, (New Brunswick, NJ: Transaction, 1988) and M. Weber, *The Theory of Social and Economic Organization*, ed. T. Parsons (New York: Free Press, 1947), 136.

66. Marx, *Early Writings*, 101–2.

67. *Ibid.*, 229.

68. *Ibid.*, 220.

69. Anwar Shaikh, in his recent study, *Capitalism*, clearly refutes the idea that Marx's (or the classical school's, for that matter) analysis of price formation depends on "perfect" competition assumption (Shaikh, *Capitalism*, 333–5). For a clear exposition of the classical price and competition analyses, see also Hollis & Nell, *Rational Economic Man*.

70. H. Özel, "'Neoliberal violence': an attempt to embed society into the market", in Brie & Thomasberger, *Karl Polanyi's Vision of a Socialist Transformation*, 110–24.

71. Polanyi, *Great Transformation*, 171.

8

FASCISM

Gareth Dale and Mathieu Desan

INTRODUCTION

Polanyi is not thought of as a theorist of fascism. And yet he was. A defining purpose of *The Great Transformation* ([1944] 2001), after all, was to explore the aetiology of interwar fascism. It argued that an economic-liberal policy regime – the godmother of today's neoliberalism – was a crucial determinant of the interwar crisis as a whole, including two world wars, the Great Depression and fascism. War, the depression, and fascism, Polanyi maintained, were not causally discrete phenomena that just happened to coincide in the early twentieth century. They were symptoms of a deeper interconnected social emergency, a crisis of liberal civilization. For what was fascism? It was the last throw of the dice by embattled capitalist elites as they confronted working-class revolt and a succession of crises that culminated in the Great Depression. And what was the Great Depression? It was the outcome of a series of "disruptive strains" – Polanyi's term for the tensions and imbalances that had arisen as social fall-out from the operation of the gold standard. And what was the gold standard? It was the global institutional embodiment of free market economics. And where did free market economics come from? From the pens of Robert Malthus and David Ricardo. Hence Polanyi's celebrated dictum: "In order to comprehend German fascism, we must revert to Ricardian England".[1]

Polanyi's attempts to theorize fascism were not located in a political vacuum. In the context of global economic crisis and a widespread questioning of the future of capitalism, Polanyi closely followed debates, on left as well as right, on the morphology and trajectory of fascism. By the time his first significant essay on the topic, "The Essence of Fascism", appeared in 1936, the question of fascism – its nature and how to combat it – had become a central concern for the left. In both the communist and social-democratic camps, the setbacks suffered by working-class movements across Europe during the 1930s at the hands of fascist and authoritarian rightist regimes forced a reckoning with the inadequate strategies of the past.

In this chapter we provide an exposition of Polanyi's theory of fascism as it evolved against this backdrop. We examine his understanding of the relationship between fascism and capitalism, the institutional separation of the economic and political spheres, the conflict between capitalism and democracy as it unfolded in the interwar era, and his distinction between socialist and fascist forms of corporatism. In the process we situate Polanyi's theory of fascism within the social-democratic and communist debates of his era, teasing out its elements of commonality with, and distinction from, other major contributions.

POLANYI ON FASCISM

Prior to Hitler's seizure of power, Polanyi wrote nothing on fascism, bar a few commentaries in Hungarian and Austrian periodicals on the proto-fascism of the Horthy dictatorship in Hungary and on early fascist stirrings in Germany.[2] But in 1933–6, with left-wing forces in torment over their failure to prevent the Nazi dictatorship and confronting ascendant fascism in Austria, Spain and beyond, he began his reckoning with what he called, as the speculative title of a book, *The Fascist Transformation*.[3] That book was never written, but the fact that its synopsis foreshadows most of the core theses of *The Great Transformation* is evidence, if any were needed, of the importance of fascism in the provenance of the later book.

In writings and lectures from the mid-1930s, Polanyi developed two main lines of argument. One was on the causes of the interwar crisis that had given fascism its opportunity. Simply put, society's political and economic spheres had become riven. The rift mapped onto the struggle between the two main classes, capitalists and workers. A clash of economics and politics (of "economy and democracy") ensued, to which fascism offered itself as the "totalitarian solution": it sought to unify society on the basis of absolute capitalist power.[4] Whereas socialism is "democracy made supreme over capitalism", Polanyi argued in *The Fascist Transformation*, fascism is capitalism saved through sacrificing democracy.[5] Fascism, he wrote elsewhere, "is merely the outcome of the mutual incompatibility of Democracy and Capitalism in our time".[6]

The other argument concerned the nature of fascism. Polanyi sought to identify its "essence".[7] He focused on the philosopher Othmar Spann. "The essence of a social movement," Polanyi proposed in one of his more idealist moments, "lies in its philosophy", and that had been stated most clearly by Spann.[8] An anti-semite, NSDAP member, and guru of a highly influential current of far-right Viennese intellectuals, Spann was the best-known fascist philosopher in Austria.[9] To Polanyi, his writings revealed that fascism is at bottom an anti-individualist force. Individualism was the common denominator of the full set of Spann's adversaries: "democracy, representative government, equality, and freedom", and therefore also liberalism, capitalism and socialism.[10] For Polanyi, and for Spann, liberal democracy opens the door to socialism, and socialism (including Marxism) is fundamentally an individualistic philosophy.[11] But whereas Spann found in Christianity a counter to individualism, Polanyi saw it as the source of the best forms of individualism, as borne by the liberal, democratic and socialist traditions. The essence of fascism, for Polanyi, was that it belligerently and radically opposes socialism, democracy and Christianity in order to bring about an ultra-capitalist regime; hence, a socialist-democratic–Christian coalition was required to combat it.

In a biographical sense, Spann's proximity to Polanyi must have been disconcerting. In creed, both were Christians. In war, both had fought and been injured – and they may well have met at the home in Vienna where Polanyi was convalescing. They both emerged from the First World War on a radical trajectory. Both had earlier found some inspiration in the social theory of the German Historical School, with its concern for social cohesion, but, in the new world of postwar fragmentation, both came to see such reformism as inadequate. In their search for an institutional means of fashioning a unified society, both turned to the guild idea: Polanyi to guild socialism, and Spann to the medieval world of authority and deference, in justification of a corporate-fascist order.

To guild socialists such as Polanyi, Spann represented a challenge. Drawing on the work of Adam Müller, a reactionary Romantic economist who railed against economic individualism and advocated a return to a medieval order, Spann proposed that guilds be resurrected and institutionalized as a central pillar within the Austrian *Ständestaat*. In France, meanwhile, a brief convergence between left- and right-wing corporatism developed in the 1930s, particularly around the "neo-socialist" *L'Homme nouveau*.[12] In Italy, too, the boundary between fascism and guild socialism had become very blurred – notably by Polanyi's own cousin, Odon Pór. In 1923, Pór published a book, *Guilds and Co-operatives in Italy*, that praised Mussolini for his labour policies. It also included an appendix by Britain's leading guild socialist (and a close friend and comrade of Polanyi), G. D. H. Cole.[13] Pór justified his embrace of despotism in a vocabulary familiar to the left: Mussolini's movement was a "revolutionary" project designed to construct "a functional democracy" and to unify society; Italy would be reorganized as a corporatist unit, through a revolution in which fascist trade unions would play a key role, drawing their inspiration from Italy's "mediæval guilds and Guild Republics".[14]

When Polanyi turned to write on fascism, therefore, he sought to draw the sharpest possible line between fascist and socialist guild concepts. He does note, in an essay on "Spann's Fascist Utopia", that if we "compare the sketch of a Guild

Socialist constitution with the actual constitution of a Fascist State, e.g. Austria, [we] will discover a striking similarity between the two".[15] In the guild-socialist blueprint and the fascist constitution alike, we find not a single unitary parliament but separate bodies administering the various spheres of public life. But such comparisons are formalistic. They obscure "the difference between Democracy and Socialism on the one hand and Capitalism and Fascism on the other".[16] The guild system, in short, had become "the watchword of two opposite groups: those who regard it as the utmost expression of individual liberty as well as those who make it the embodiment of a social ideal which is the very negation of individual liberty".[17]

In a raft of essays in the mid-1930s Polanyi developed a critique of Spann that carefully differentiated right- and left-wing versions of the principles of social unity (or "totality"), "function", and guild organization. In an abstract, academic sense Spann was right to suggest that "functional and corporative organization" is more adequate to the "essential nature" of society than the chaotic, atomistic and centrifugal structure of liberal capitalism, but his concept of totality went far beyond any reasonable and scientific understanding of society's organic character and his "romantic predilections turn him towards the Middle Ages", to a conception of social order that would supplant equality with hierarchy, with freedom conservatively defined as action according to preordained rules.[18] Spann's application of functional theory to modern society, with power envisaged as vested in economic and political "chambers", supposedly offered an institutional alternative to capitalism, but in reality, Polanyi argues, it does nothing of the sort. In a socialist order, "the Political Chamber", embodying and expressing "the Idea of common human Equity and Justice", would take precedence; under its sway, private property "would tend to turn into 'Socialist', i.e. public property".[19] In Spann's model, by contrast, "it is emphatically the Economic, not the Political, Chamber which dominates. And this settles the matter, whether Spann likes it or not, in favour of Capitalism".[20] Indeed, in Spann's "functionally organized" fascism, private property would govern in an "even more downright and thorough" manner than in liberal capitalism. This was clearly visible in the corporatist Austria of 1934. Whereas a genuine functional state would democratically elevate the political sphere, giving greater say to the "common man", in Austria it was the business class that had been empowered, with a "functional mask" slipped on to disguise the abolition of democracy.[21]

At the core of the fascist project, for Polanyi, was the subordination of the state to capitalist interests and the destruction of its socially protective capacities. It was, in other words, the construction of a radically capitalist regime dedicated to reducing workers to commodity-producing automata, for which their exclusion from the political sphere is a prerequisite.[22] As a regime, fascism represented the rescue of capitalism "under the aegis of the capitalist class" and by pseudo-revolutionary means, including the introduction of a planned economy. As a movement, it was "borne by those classes which are most opposed to the workers".[23] Workers are least susceptible to the "emotional epidemic" of fascism; the intelligentsia is its breeding ground (and this reminds us that "education is no safeguard against social superstition").[24] The secret of fascism's advance, however, was not the numerical strength of its support base but the tacit support it received from capitalists, the judiciary, the army and police, and, crucially, the weakening of the labour movement.[25]

Why, though, should fascism's victories have been achieved so swiftly? Here, Polanyi's explanation emphasizes not so much the support fascism received from capitalists and other elites or the strategy of the labour movement but the underlying political-economic crisis that had materialized in the late nineteenth century before being unleashed upon the world from 1914 onward. If this mega-crisis had a single root, it was the "hostility of capitalism to popular government".[26] In this sense, fascism was nothing but the latest and most virulent outbreak of the "anti-democratic virus" that had been inherent in industrial capitalism from the outset.[27] With capitalism now beholden to fascism, democracy had become aligned with socialism.

At the end of the 1930s, Polanyi elaborated this thesis in an essay, "The Fascist Virus". Using materials from Britain it surveyed the fears of nineteenth-century elites that enfranchising the working classes would spell the end of capitalism. "Only if the poor bore their lot patiently", they argued with reference to the economic "laws" established by Robert Malthus and David Ricardo, "would they be safe from starvation, only if they resigned themselves to their misery could they survive at all. They must therefore be kept away from the levers of government, which they would otherwise try to use to wreck the property system on which the community depended for their subsistence".[28]

In different ways, the axiom that democracy and capitalism were incompatible was defended by conservatives (Edmund Burke, Robert Peel), liberals (Thomas Babington Macaulay) and socialists (Robert Owen) alike. Peel opposed the Chartist demand for universal suffrage on the grounds that it would "impeach the constitution of the country". Macaulay, the historian of Rome and Member of Parliament, warned that "institutions purely democratic must sooner or later destroy liberty or civilisation, or both".[29] The danger was plainly visible in the United States, too, where "the majority is the government and has the rich, which are always a minority, absolutely at its mercy". That unfortunate nation, Macaulay lamented in 1857, had entered a downward spiral that would culminate in the destruction of liberty or civilization. "Either some Caesar or Napoleon will seize the reins of government with a strong hand" or the US "will be as fearfully plundered and laid waste by barbarians in the twentieth century as the Roman Empire was in the fifth".[30]

For Polanyi, Macaulay's words anticipate fascism. Given that the destructive effects of the market mechanism oblige workers to defend themselves by pressing for political and industrial democracy, which would inevitably be deployed in their interests and against civilization, capitalism will have to be rescued by Caesarist methods (in the modern vernacular: fascism). The same era in which Macaulay expressed his fears of latter-day Huns and Vandals had also witnessed early presentiments of fascism in literature: in Dostoevsky we see the demands for an "impossible freedom" of the people deflected by spiritual despotism into a condition of permanent dependence, joyfully accepted by the masses; later examples included the dystopias of H. G. Wells, in which a labouring population is reduced to a sub-human condition, and Jack London's apparition of a people crushed under the iron heel of big business.[31] Such premonitions were based on a valid intuition: capitalist elites would deploy extreme measures to counter the democratic aspirations of the uprising working class.

Despite such portents, Polanyi continued, liberals in the age of Dostoevsky and London were able blithely to assume that universal suffrage would mesh harmoniously with a flourishing market economy. They could point to the fact that several countries had broadened the franchise, and without much ado. Was this not robust evidence that the conflict between democracy and capitalism was abating? No, he insists; their sense of security was a fantasy. It had been facilitated by a series of contingent and transitory phenomena, such as the expansion of the world market and "the false impression created by the prosperous American scene".[32] Following the First World War all such illusions were dispelled, in the course of a dual transformation: the extension of the franchise, and capitalism's lurch from laissez-faire to an organized, regulated form, which enabled political power to immediately and effectively steer the economy. The concession of universal suffrage, it was plain to see, would lead to the working class exerting a "decisive influence upon the state" but this, in turn, would induce market panic and the "imminent danger of a complete stoppage of the productive apparatus", for parliaments "weaken, discredit and disorganise" market capitalism by meddling with its self-regulating mechanisms.[33] Democracy, in consequence, had become dysfunctional. It depressed the profitability of the economic system, which was grinding to a halt.[34] While the workers sought to deploy their electoral power to protective ends, capitalist elites sought to squash popular influences, either through suborning democracy and pressing leftist governments to accede to their will, or, when that failed, by the forcible suppression of democracy.

The "fascist era", in this perspective, heralded the "total crisis of a market organized industrial society", with fascism conceived of as a high-stakes gamble by beleaguered capitalist elites (or, as Polanyi conceived it later, as the "reaction of the middle classes" to the workers' revolts in Russia and elsewhere).[35]

Fascism, in short, was the pathological symptom of the fact that, as Hitler put it in his Düsseldorf speech of 1932, economic inequality and political equality are incompatible.[36] Democracy and capitalism, in Polanyi's framing of the point, "have reached a deadlock, because they have become the instruments of two different classes of opposing interests" – and this was the clue as to why the social upheavals of the age were characterized by such "cataclysmic vehemence".[37]

There were only two ways out of the impasse. Its underlying cause was the liberal quest for a utopia: the self-regulating market. This had generated an unsustainable acceleration of change and the "disembedding" of the economy from the social fabric.[38] The consequence had been civilizational collapse. A solution could only come about if society were to unify once again, with the scission between politics and economics sutured. Fascism offered a reunification of society on an inegalitarian, undemocratic basis; socialism its reunification on the basis of equality and the extension of democratic principles throughout society. A modern industrial society, Polanyi concluded, can in the long run be either fascist or democratic and socialist.

The above theses are in many respects distinctive to Polanyi. This is the case in his emphasis on the need for a socialist–Christian coalition, and in his account of the relationship of fascism to capitalism – including of course the tracing of fascism's roots to Ricardo's Britain. But his theses on fascism were not scribbled in an ivory tower. They were developed in conversation with, and in response to, attempts by social democrats and communists to analyse the fascist threat.

FASCISM AND THE SOCIALIST LEFT

Polanyi was a socialist and an anti-fascist, and as such he was caught up in the self-reflection on the international left about its failure to effectively resist the rise of fascism. Like a growing number of leftists, he was alarmed at the rise of fascism and recognized that it had to be confronted – and theorized – more effectively. He saw fascism as a monstrous threat. Indeed, in the 1930s he held that it was at the heart of *all* the "social wars and the civil wars of our time".[39] But how did his diagnosis of fascism relate to those of others on the left? Let us first survey the evolution of socialist theories of fascism.

The arrival of fascism on the political scene in 1922 initially provoked little serious reflection within socialist circles. The social-democratic left tended to see Italian fascism as an aberrant development that was limited to Italian conditions and in any case likely to pass. As such, there was little reason to rethink social-democratic presuppositions of a peaceful and steady path to socialism. The communist left, on the other hand, tended not to recognize the special character of Mussolini's movement, seeing in it merely an instance of capitalist reaction and refusing any meaningful distinction between fascist dictatorship and a parliamentary regime which it already saw as the dictatorship of capital.[40] In different ways, the immediate communist and social-democratic reactions to the emergence of fascism were to deny that it constituted a special problem.

As fascist power in Italy consolidated and as authoritarian movements made gains elsewhere in Europe, this initial indifference became untenable. Nonetheless, the basic contours of left-wing analysis and strategy with regard to fascism remained largely unchanged until the early 1930s. Social democrats responded to the new political conjuncture with complacency. Emile Vandervelde, who would become president of the social-democratic Labour and Socialist International (LSI) from 1929–36, could still pronounce in 1928 that it was "exclusively … in this second-rate Europe, economically and politically backward, that dictatorships proliferate".[41] Nazi advances in Germany of course belied this notion, but even so, many social democrats were slow in coming to terms with the threat.

The absence of any original social-democratic theorizing about fascism in the 1920s was a function of the general doctrinal incoherence of the LSI, which was badly split between a frankly reformist wing represented by the German SPD and the British Labour Party, and more orthodox parties like the French SFIO and the Austrian SDAP. Despite this split – or, rather, precisely because the need to maintain an uneasy unity militated against the development of any fresh thinking on strategic questions – the leading figures of the LSI, both reformist and revolutionary, broadly continued to see fascism as an anomalous and historically anachronistic detour on the democratic road to socialism.

To the extent that there was any substantial theoretical ferment within 1920s social democracy, it was around the ideas of "organized capitalism", a concept associated in particular with Rudolf Hilferding, and "capitalist rationalization".[42] These, however, tended merely to reinforce social-democratic quietism with regard to fascism. The basic idea was that postwar trends of economic rationalization had stabilized capitalism and made possible an ordered development of the productive forces. It was thus the task of socialists to democratically direct this process toward explicitly socialist ends. The strategic implication of all of this was clear and harmonized with the reformist practice of 1920s social democracy: socialism simply entailed the extension of democracy from the political to the economic sphere, and could thus be achieved within the framework of bourgeois legality. Fascism in this view was still considered a deviation from an ineluctable movement toward socialist democracy.

Whether out of opportunistic reflex or theoretical conviction, the social-democratic response to fascism was thus to get history back on track, so to speak, by privileging the defence and, in cases where it had already been lost, restoration of bourgeois democracy above all else. From this followed the SPD's disastrous policy of "toleration", which saw the party throw its tacit support behind increasingly reactionary and undemocratic governments in the name of preserving the Republic. Elsewhere in Europe, social democrats were less craven in their appeasement of bourgeois parties, but the basic pattern of seeing the struggle against fascism as a defensive one in which most of society, including the bourgeoisie, had a common interest was repeated.

If the social-democratic theory of fascism called for a defensive alliance with the progressive bourgeoisie, the official communist theory of fascism in the 1920s led to the opposite policy of revolutionary isolation. The communist world was not lacking for original thinking about fascism – especially compared to the social-democratic world.[43] Despite its initial flat-footedness, the Italian Communist Party (PCI), under the impulsion of Antonio Gramsci and Palmiro Togliatti, began to elaborate a theory of fascism that recognized its distinctive character. The main thrust of their analysis – parts of which were also echoed by Clara Zetkin – differed from the official Comintern line in two significant ways. First, as opposed to a conspiratorial view which saw fascism as the simple instrument of big capital, they underlined the mass character of fascism as a political expression of the petit bourgeoisie. This meant that fascism in power was a contradictory and unstable phenomenon. Second, they saw fascism as the consequence, not the cause, of socialism's political failure during the postwar revolutionary wave. It was the inability of socialists to seize the revolutionary initiative in the immediate postwar period that created the conditions for their brutal suppression by the fascist offensive.

But such nuance in communist thinking was quickly drowned out by the consolidation of the official Comintern line around an ultra-left denial of any fundamental distinction between capitalism and fascism. According to the infamous "third period" line laid down at the Sixth Congress of the Comintern in 1928, the decaying capitalist order had entered into another revolutionary period following the stabilization of the 1920s. All non-revolutionary forces were now thus objectively counter-revolutionary and constituted a single "reactionary mass".[44] This led to the notorious identification of social democracy with fascism, given expression in the epithet of "social fascism". If capitalism was already fascism, and if the social democrats were reformists, then it followed that social democracy was simply the moderate wing of fascism. Practically, the consequences of this sectarian line were ruinous, particularly in Germany, where it led the communist party (KPD) to fatally underestimate Hitler and to train its hostility on the SPD instead. The stakes were of course highest in Germany, but throughout Europe communist parties turned their sights on their social-democratic counterparts, whom they denounced as the primary obstacle in the fight against a fascism.

On the eve of the 1933 Nazi conquest of power and the ensuing destruction of the KPD and SPD, the European socialist response to fascism was thus basically divided between the social-democratic defence of bourgeois democracy at all costs and the communists' ultra-left conflation of this defence with fascism. Both in their own ways underestimated the specificity and strength of fascism. The German debacle, however, forced a reckoning among social democrats and communists, many of whom now openly criticized the role of the failed policies of the past in demobilizing, disorienting, and dividing the working-class movement in the face of an existential threat. The newfound sense of urgency was further reinforced by events like the 1934 suppression of the SDAP and subsequent establishment of an "Austrofascist" regime in Austria.[45] Furthermore, the spectre of fascism seemed now also to threaten societies in which democratic institutions were entrenched, like France, where a February 1934 riot by right-wing paramilitary leagues was widely interpreted by the left as an abortive fascist coup.[46] The combined effect of these events, against a backdrop of deepening economic crisis, was to upend the existing coordinates of socialist thinking about fascism.

After 1933, the struggle against fascism became an overriding imperative for the European left. The most significant development in this direction was the constitution of the Popular Front. In its essence, the Popular Front was a continuation of the social-democratic policy of defending bourgeois democracy against fascism, albeit this time endowed with a more coherent and dynamic "anti-fascist" mythos.[47] Paradoxically, however, it was the communists who became the animating force of this coalition uniting the communist, social-democratic, and liberal left. Evident failure and geopolitical considerations compelled the Comintern to pivot away from its "third period" line. Thus in 1934 it initiated a proletarian "united front" with social-democratic parties, which it then extended in 1935 into a "popular front" including bourgeois-democratic parties. The new strategy, justified on an explicitly "anti-fascist" basis, proved an immediate success, with Popular Front governments forming in 1936 in France and Spain, and communist prestige and influence reaching new heights.

This turnabout in communist strategy entailed a significant shift in communist discourse on fascism. Instead of the old capacious definition, fascism was now defined as the "open terrorist dictatorship of the most reactionary, most chauvinist and most imperialist elements of finance capital" – a narrow formulation providing the theoretical basis for a broad anti-fascist front.[48] This definition also had the effect of foreclosing any serious consideration of the relationship between capitalism and fascism, appearing to endorse the earlier social-democratic view of fascism as a minoritarian conspiracy. Ironically, then, just as the Comintern began to take fascism more seriously politically, it downgraded it theoretically. Official communist discourse on fascism during the

Popular Front era became more and more adapted to immediate political exigencies.[49] Indeed, in its effort to accommodate its centre-left coalition partners, communist discourse took a dramatic popular-democratic and social-patriotic turn and, like its erstwhile social-democratic rival, subordinated revolution to the defence of bourgeois democracy.

The vagaries of Comintern strategy elicited limited criticism within the communist orbit, but it was among these dissenters that one finds the most original communist theorizing about fascism in this era. The most prominent of these was Leon Trotsky.[50] Trotsky had criticized the "third period" line for underestimating the gravity of the fascist danger, and advocated a united front between the social democrats and communists. But with the Comintern's pivot to the Popular Front, Trotsky also mercilessly denounced what he considered to be an opportunistic disavowal of revolutionary socialism. He elaborated his own theory of fascism, which emphasized fascism's character as a mass movement of the disaffected middle classes. According to Trotsky, fascism represented a mobilization of petit-bourgeois despair in the service of monopoly and finance capital. However, the inevitable contradiction between the reactionary goals of the latter and the aspirations of the former meant that fascist regimes were bound to lose their mass base and degenerate into an unstable form of Bonapartism. This in turn provided an opportunity for the workers' movement to turn the defensive struggle against fascism into an offensive struggle to defeat capitalism.[51]

For social democrats, the Popular Front era was a fractious one and coincided with the decomposition of the LSI. Some resisted the call to form popular fronts out of suspicion of communist motives. Such was the case, for example, with the British Labour Party, which rejected communist overtures despite the enthusiasm of figures like G. D. H. Cole for a broad anti-fascist coalition. Others, notably the majority of the French Socialist Party, SFIO, eagerly embraced the Popular Front, which they tended to interpret as a validation of social-democratic positions. In neither case was a fundamental rethinking of the defensive premises of social-democratic anti-fascism involved. The reasons for opposing and joining the Popular Front were essentially the same: to give absolute priority to the defence of democracy in the struggle against fascist dictatorship. As head of the French Popular Front government in 1936, Léon Blum repeatedly reminded his impatient supporters that he had come to power on a Popular Front, and not a socialist, programme.

The Popular Front represented a convergence of social democrats and communists around a vision of anti-fascism that was republican in character, national in content, and defensive in posture. Although this basically represented an affirmation of the classic social-democratic position, at the same time many social democrats, embittered by experience, began to question such received wisdom. German and Austrian social democrats in particular effected a sharp left turn while in exile. Hilferding and Otto Bauer,[52] for example, no longer saw fascism as an anomaly, but as the symptom of a structural capitalist crisis. Because fascism was ultimately rooted in the objective conditions of capitalism, the struggle against it would have to go beyond the defence or restoration of democracy and take the form of revolutionary struggle against capitalism.[53] This position, echoed by social democrats elsewhere who were frustrated by the self-imposed limits of the Popular Front, was not unlike that taken by communist oppositionists like Thalheimer and Trotsky.

The Popular Front effectively repolarized the anti-fascist field around the question of democracy and revolution in a way that scrambled the old divide between social democracy and communism. Fitting imperfectly into this reclassification, however, was another influential social-democratic alternative to the Popular Front: planism. Planism was in large part the brainchild of Hendrik de Man, a Belgian social democrat who developed a reputation in the 1920s as a leading revisionist theorist with his attempts to reorient the workers' movement toward an ethical conception of socialism grounded in the Christian values of equality, dignity and justice.[54] De Man was the author of the "Plan du Travail", whose official adoption by the Belgian Labour Party (POB/BWP) in 1933 caused a sensation and inspired a proliferation of "plans" across the continent. A distinctive feature of planism was its appeal among both right- and left-wing social democrats, and indeed it claimed to transcend the traditional antinomy between reformism and revolution. Nonetheless, planism represented an important element in the radicalization of social democracy following the victory of Nazism in 1933.[55]

In de Man's conception, the "Plan" was a socialist response to the twin crises of economic depression and fascism. Combatting the latter required eliminating its roots in the former, but this in turn required abandoning social democracy's traditional *attentisme*. The urgency of the fascist threat meant that social democrats could no longer hold out for a distant revolution, but neither were reformist measures that left the basic framework of liberal capitalism intact sufficient. Moreover, the working class had to make common cause with the middle classes, who would otherwise be seduced by fascism. The idea behind the "Plan" was therefore to present a program of structural – as opposed to redistributive – reforms capable of addressing the fundamental causes of the crisis but limited enough in scope that a broad economic majority could be won over to it. To this end, the "Plan" prescribed the step-wise construction of a mixed economy allowing the state to consciously regulate economic life. Although such an "intermediary regime" – a concept looked upon with suspicion by socialist orthodoxy – stopped short of socialism, de Man argued that it was the only feasible alternative to a fascist solution to the terminal crisis of liberal capitalism. If planism shared certain affinities with fascism, as its critics never tired of pointing out, these were nevertheless given an anti-fascist inflection. As Cole remarked, the "Plan" represented "an attempt to steal for Socialism the thunder which will otherwise be appropriated by Fascist demagogues".[56]

The logic of planism differed from that of the Popular Front in that it saw the anti-fascist struggle as an offensive one, although it was not revolutionary in that it conceived the construction of a planned economy as a limited and orderly affair. The "Plan" was only a transitional measure on the road to social-ism, albeit one urgently imposed by the conjuncture. But the point of planism as an anti-fascist strategy, ultimately, was not simply to rescue the economy and democracy, but to consolidate the material and moral foundation for an even-tual socialist transformation.[57]

The heyday of planism, however, was short-lived. By 1936, the enthusiasm for planism had waned, as the Popular Front proved to be a more potent mobilizing myth for the anti-fascist left. After 1936, anti-fascist theory and practice was dominated by the defensive logic of the Popular Front, and with few exceptions critical thinking about fascism withered within both social-democratic and communist circles until it became completely subsumed under the problem of national defence on the eve of the Second World War.

POLANYIAN THEORY IN CONTEXT

How did Polanyi's approach relate to the currents discussed above? Like Trotsky, Polanyi saw fascism as a product of capitalism. Both saw the post-First World War era as one of systemic crisis in which social tensions grew inflamed, and both predicted that it marked the death agonies of capitalism – albeit for Polanyi the emphasis was on the demise of the liberal market economy. Trotsky how-ever, far more than Polanyi, emphasized the mass character of fascism as a petit-bourgeois movement. Methodologically too, the differences are apparent. Trotsky sought to grasp fascism as (in his words) "a living political phenomenon … a dialectical and changing phenomenon" and was dismissive of those who sought to identify its "essence".[58]

What of planism? Whereas Polanyi's close associate G. D. H. Cole was plainly attracted to planism, and introduced the English translation of de Man's planist writings (in words that, as Fleming[59] has pointed out, resemble parts of *The Great Transformation*), there is little evidence of Polanyi's own attitude. This is perhaps surprising. De Man wrote in German (Polanyi's first language) and there are clear affinities between the two thinkers. Both Polanyi and de Man emphasized the Christian foundations of socialism, both were influenced by the guild social-ists and Austro-Marxists, both tended to focus on the general social will rather than that of the proletariat, and both saw a theory of fascism as indispensable for effective socialist strategy. Like de Man and the planists, Polanyi believed that the crisis of liberal capitalism had imposed a decisive choice between socialism and fascism. Moreover, the way in which he conceived socialism – less about property relations and more about the political and social reintegration of the economy – echoed that of de Man and the planists. Polanyi would likely have sympathized, too, with the planist advocacy of a planned economy as a third way (between communism and fascism) out of the crisis of capitalism. Both also took pains to distinguish between socialist and fascist corporatism, although de Man's quasi-technocratic conception of the "new economic State" was more ambiguous than Polanyi's understanding of socialist corporatism, which, *contra* fascist corporatism, Polanyi saw as a form of society-economy integration in which politics dominates economics.[60]

There is rather more evidence on Polanyi's view of the Popular Front than on his view of planism. We can be confident in stating he gave it at least qualified support, approving of the strategy of "republican defence" on the grounds that liberal democracy is a waystation toward socialism. In the 1930s he championed the role of the Soviet Union in working for a "union of the forces of democracy" (to borrow Cole's paraphrase of Polanyi), "an international democratic front" that would unite Moscow with what Polanyi called the "democratic great powers" – Britain and other liberal-capitalist states – in opposition to the "war-mongering and aggressive" fascist camp.[61] Together with Labour Party radicals such as Cole and Harold Laski, Polanyi warmed to the Communist Party. Although never a member or even (quite) a fellow-traveller, he did advocate unity in anti-fascist action of Christians and leftists of all hues, and commended the CP as a vital ally in that fight.

Polanyi's affinities with planism can be stated only provisionally and speculatively, and his support for the Popular Front was contingent and strategic. How, then, can his position on fascism best be characterized? A useful place to begin is with his essay on "The Christian and the World Economic Crisis". In it he postulates two transhistorical tendencies that traverse and define modern history: one to freedom, the other to social unity. Their conjoint telos consists in the extension of democracy into the economy, a prospect that, however, was "prevented by the class structure of society due to the capitalist system".[62] In the 1910s and early 1920s Polanyi's emphasis was, with mainstream social democracy, on the positive part: history was steering humanity to socialism. This was far from being a simple or pacific development. War, the white terror in Hungary, and Italian fascism were reminders of that. However, history's arc was clear enough: toward democratic socialism. As he asserted in an essay from 1922, "Historical progress driven by genuine ideals cannot be derailed for long … The idea of democracy is being reborn, with redoubled potency, in the minds of the masses, and no power will be able to halt its victorious march".[63]

That victorious march was, in Polanyi's view, nowhere more evident than in Austria – or at least Vienna. There, the social democrats, led by Bauer, had entered office. In Bauer's understanding, Austria in the early 1920s exhibited a balance of class power: the bourgeoisie owned the means of production while the workers had made substantial inroads into political power. This resulted in a hybrid of bourgeois and proletarian power, of political and "functional" democracy. "The conflicting classes hold each other in equilibrium", Bauer concluded, and this necessitated compromise.[64] In the 1930s, Bauer developed this "equilibrium" thesis into an explanation of fascism: its rise was the outcome of a stalemate of class forces that resulted from democratization. Workers used the vote to demand concessions; capitalists reacted to the ensuing profits squeeze by fostering fascism.

Polanyi developed his perspective contemporaneously with, and partly inspired by, Bauer. In Polanyi's analysis, the rise of capitalism had summoned a "countermovement", or "protective interventions". These "helped to create a strong popular demand for political influence of the masses", but "the use of the power so gained was greatly restricted by the nature of the market mechanism".[65] The result, Polanyi argued, was social impasse and "disruptive strains". Workers, armed with trade-union strength and political representation, defended themselves against the depredations of the market by electing parties to parliament that "continuously interfered with the working of the market mechanism".[66] This in turn – in Polanyi's view, echoing orthodox Austrian economics – prevented market forces from functioning properly, and their beneficiaries, above all business leaders, reacted by seeking to subordinate democracy to their interests or to abolish it.

In fleshing out this argument, Polanyi's eye was trained on the political events of the day, viewed through a social-democratic lens. In brief, capitalist development expanded the working masses; their instincts are socialist; ergo, capitalism leads via democracy to socialism. The mechanism that "maintained the working class in power was universal suffrage and representative government. In short, it was democracy".[67] This posed a challenge to capitalist elites, whose every effort to restore the pre-war system was countered by workers and peasants, their grievances and demands now strengthened by their institutionalized political voice. Where economic elites felt threatened by democracy they pressed for its outright abolition, a tendency that reached its acme with the elevation of fascist governments to power.

Polanyi's conclusion was that democracy did not display an elective affinity with capitalism, as some supposed. In opposition to Marxist views, which he believed, in a rather caricatured formulation, required that democracy be seen as "*the* political superstructure of capitalism",[68] he held that capitalism and democracy exist as separate systems. These systems were, at least in the contemporary conjuncture, increasingly and irreconcilably antagonistic. Their incompatibility had led inexorably to an impasse, manifested in the interwar cataclysm. As capitalism entered a crisis-ridden period following the war, workers and peasants, empowered by the vote, demanded that parliamentary parties shield them from the worst effects. This prevented markets from clearing, intensifying the crisis. At that moment a sharp alternative was posed: society would be integrated either through political power under the hegemony of the working class and in the form of socialism, or under the leadership of the propertied classes in the form of a recharged capitalism, purged, with fascist assistance, of all democratic elements. In the long run, as Polanyi put it in *Europe To-day*, a modern industrial society: "is either democratic or Fascist. It is either based on the ideal of common human equality and responsibility or on their negation. But democracy cannot be maintained under the conditions of present-day life unless the principles of democracy are extended to the whole of society, including the economic system. This is commonly called Socialism".[69]

CONCLUSION

Karl Polanyi, this chapter has proposed, was a significant theorist of fascism. This may not have been apparent from his initial efforts. His first major excursion, "The Essence of Fascism" (1936), made a negligible contribution. Its goal, to distil fascism's philosophical "essence," was scholastic, and its central thesis, that European fascism's fundamental enemy is Europe's *dominant* religion (Christianity), with no mention of fascism's scapegoating of minorities, was unhelpful, to put it mildly. Its thesis that fascism represents the primacy of economics over politics veers too close to the sort of crude instrumentalist analysis of fascism that held it to be driven overwhelmingly by economic imperatives. Relatedly, Polanyi also tended to understate the role of fascist movements. In this, his approach was aligned with a number of Austro-Marxists who held the conviction that fascism "could establish itself solely by means of the instruments of state power".[70]

But there is more to Polanyi's theory than this. In *The Great Transformation* he dug deeply into the question of the relationship between fascism and capitalism. The context was a rethinking by leftists of that relationship, in the wake of Hitler's seizure of power. Capitalism appeared to be collapsing, fascism was ascendant. But it was not enough to simply claim that "capitalism produces fascism". What were the mediations? For Gramsci and Trotsky – and one could add for de Man – fascism was a politically overdetermined phenomenon: what gave fascism its specificity was its character as a mass movement of the disaffected petit bourgeoisie over whom socialists had failed to exercise hegemonic leadership. For Polanyi the emphasis was socio-economic. He sought to trace the roots of fascism to the rise of the liberal market economy in Britain and the "disruptive strains" to which it led.[71]

Where 1920s social democracy had generally seen fascism as an aberration, understating its historical importance and threat, Polanyi flipped to the opposite pole, seeing fascism as a "phase", one of only two ways through which the fundamental problem of modernity – the separation of economics and politics – could be resolved in the current period. In this, his conception was close to de Man and the planists (although in their cases the belief that fascism represented a historical solution to this problem could blur into an indulgence of fascist regimes). The problem here is that fascism comes to stand for all forms of non-communist dictatorship, thus evacuating the concept of specificity and substance.

Why did Polanyi hold that there are only two ways to solve the basic problem of modernity? Because "the crisis of modern society", as he maintained in "Fascism and Socialism", stems fundamentally from the division of politics and economics. The crises generated by this division naturally throw up the "idea of the totality of society" as the solution.[72] In this perspective there are echoes of Spann, for whom social "totality" is the "master-key".[73] For Spann, social totality should be restored through fascism, entailing a national rebirth of Germany, the *Führerprinzip*, authoritarianism and the crushing of democracy, anti-semitism and racism. For Polanyi, social totality required restoration through socialism, understood as the extension of democratic norms and institutions throughout the social whole. Polanyi sees socialism as the ineluctable extension of democracy from the political to the economic sphere, and fascism as a movement to prevent economic democracy by suppressing political democracy. Hence, the anti-fascist struggle for democracy is also necessarily a struggle for socialism.

In all this, what remains somewhat ambiguous in Polanyi is his position vis-à-vis the central axis of interwar socialist debates on fascism: is the restoration of political democracy a necessary precondition for reopening the road to socialism, or can political democracy only be saved through the immediate conquest of economic democracy? Polanyi argued that in capitalism "the influence of the working class both in politics and industrial life are insolubly linked with the liberal and democratic organisation of society".[74] One wonders, however, if socialism indeed stands in a relation of continuity with liberalism, or if the historical challenge posed by the crisis of liberal democracy is instead the necessity of articulating the specificity of socialist democracy.

Notes for Chapter 8

1. K. Polanyi, *The Great Transformation: The Political and Economic Origins of Our Time* (Boston, MA: Beacon, 2001), 32.

2. For example, K. Polanyi, "The defenders of race in Berlin", in G. Dale (ed.), *Karl Polanyi: The Hungarian Writings* (Manchester: Manchester University Press, 2016).

3. K. Polanyi (1934–5) book synopsis for "The fascist transformation", KPA-20-8.

4. K. Polanyi (1933) lecture, "Die wirtschaft ist für den faschismus", KPA-2-21; cf. K. Polanyi (1934–46) notes, "The theory of fascism: the deadlock of politics and economics", KPA-11-1.

5. Polanyi, book synopsis, "The fascist transformation".

6. K. Polanyi (1934) "Fascism and Marxian terminology", *New Britain* 3:57, 128–9, KPA-18-6.

7. K. Polanyi (n.d.) "Fascism and socialism", KPA-18-7.

8. K. Polanyi (1934) 'Othmar Spann, the philosopher of fascism', *New Britain* 3:53, 7, KPA-18-4. Although Polanyi speaks straightforwardly of the "essence" of fascism, his usage may also contain irony, given the centrality in Spann's writings (e.g., in *Der wahre Staat*) of the idea that each society (or nation) has an unchanging "essence".

9. See J. Wasserman, *Black Vienna: The Radical Right in the Red City, 1918–1938* (Ithaca, NY: Cornell University Press, 2014), 11.

10. Polanyi, "Fascism and socialism".

11. K. Polanyi, "The essence of fascism", in J. Lewis, K. Polanyi & D. Kitchen (eds), *Christianity and the Social Revolution* (New York: Charles Scribner's, 1936), 259–94.

12. M. Desan, "'Order, Authority, Nation': Neo-Socialism and the Fascist Destiny on an Anti-Fascist Discourse", unpublished PhD dissertation, University of Michigan, 2016, 181–95.

13. On Cole's initial sympathy with Mussolini's corporate state, see G. Foote, *The Labour Party's Political Thought: A History* (Basingstoke: Palgrave Macmillan, 1997), 123.

14. O. Pór, *Guilds and Co-operatives in Italy* (London: Labour Publishing, 1923) 159–60, 221.

15. K. Polanyi (1934) "Spann's fascist utopia", *New Britain* 3:55, 74–5, KPA-18-5.

16. *Ibid.*

17. K. Polanyi (1934–46), "Labour movement's post-war failure", KPA-9-2.

18. Polanyi, "Othmar Spann", 7.

19. Polanyi, "Spann's fascist utopia".

20. *Ibid.*

21. K. Polanyi, "Korporatives Österreich – eine funktionale Gesellschaft?", in M. Cangiani & C. Thomasberger (eds), *Chronik der großen Transformation, Band 1* (Marburg: Metropolis, 1934), 212.

22. H. Özel, "Reclaiming Humanity: The Social Theory of Karl Polanyi", unpublished PhD dissertation, University of Utah, 1997, 78.

23. Polanyi, "Fascism: National Planning and International Anarchy", KPA-12-2; K. Polanyi (1939), "Coercion and defence", *Christian Left Bulletin*, KPA-20-16.

24. K. Polanyi (1939–40) book plan for "Common man's masterplan", KPA-20-4.

25. Polanyi, "The fascist transformation"; K. Polanyi (1936) "On the philosophy and economics of fascism", KPA-21-4.

26. K. Polanyi (n.d.) "The fascist virus", KPA-18-8.

27. *Ibid.*

28. *Ibid.*

29. *Ibid.*

30. *Ibid.*

31. *Ibid.*

32. *Ibid.*

33. *Ibid.*

34. K. Polanyi, "Die geistigen voraussetzungen des faschismus", in M. Cangiani, K. Polanyi-Levitt & C. Thomasberger (eds), *Chronik der großen Transformation, Band 3* (Marburg: Metropolis, 2005), 235.

35. Polanyi, "Fascist virus"; K. Polanyi (1961) "Annotations to a letter from Paul Medow", KPA-51-5.

36. K. Polanyi (1961), letter to Fromm, 14 January; Polanyi, "Die geistigen voraussetzungen", 218, KPP-1-4.

37. K. Polanyi (1934) "Marxism re-stated", *New Britain* 3:58/59, KPA-18-9.

38. K. Polanyi (1936–40) Lecture XXIV, "Contemporary problems and social and political theory", University of London, KPA-15-4.

39. K. Polanyi, *Europe To-day* (London: Worker's Educational Trade Union Committee, 1937), 54.

40. D. Beetham (ed.), *Marxists in the Face of Fascism* (Totowa, NJ: Barnes & Noble, 1984), 5.

41. A. Bergounioux, "L'Internationale ouvrière socialiste entre les deux guerres", in H. Portelli (ed.), *L'Internationale socialiste* (Paris: Les Éditions Ouvrières, 1983), 33.

42. Beetham, *Marxists in the Face of Fascism*, 41. For socialist debates on rationalization, see J. Moch, *Socialisme et rationalisation* (Brussels: L'Eglantine, 1927); B. Montagnon, *Grandeur et servitude socialiste* (Paris: Librairie Valois, 1929); and A. Philip, *Henri de Man et la crise doctrinale du socialisme* (Paris: Librairie Universitaire J. Gamber, 1928).

43. J. Cammett, "Communist theories of fascism, 1920–1935", *Science & Society* 31:2 (1967), 149–63; Beetham, *Marxists in the Face of Fascism*.

44. Cammett, "Communist theories of fascism", 154.

45. G.-R. Horn, *European Socialists Respond to Fascism: Ideology, Activism and Contingency in the 1930s* (New York: Oxford Univeristy Press, 1996).

46. S. Berstein, *Le 6 février 1934* (Paris: Gallimard, 1975); B. Jenkins & C. Millington, *France and Fascism: February 1934 and the Dynamics of Political Crisis* (Abingdon: Routledge, 2016).

47. G. Vergnon, *L'antifascisme en France: de Mussolini à Le Pen* (Rennes: Presses Universitaires de Rennes, 2009).

48. D. Renton, *Fascism: Theory and Practice* (London: Pluto, 1999), 77.

49. Cammett, "Communist theories of fascism", 150.

50. August Thalheimer deserves special mention as well.

51. L. Trotsky, *The Struggle Against Fascism in Germany* (New York: Pathfinder, 1971); L. Trotsky, *Fascism, Stalinism and the United Front* (London: Bookmarks, 1989).

52. Like Thalheimer and Trotsky, Bauer also attempted to apply Marx's concept of Bonapartism to fascism, although all three did so differently; see G. Botz, "Austro-Marxist interpretation of fascism", *Journal of Contemporary History* 11:4 (1976), 129–56.

53. For example, R. Hilferding, "Revolutionary socialism" in Beetham, *Marxists in the Face of Fascism*; O. Bauer, "The unification of socialism" in Beetham, *Marxists in the Face of Fascism*.

54. H. de Man, *Zur Psychologie des Sozializmus* (Jena: E. Diederichs, 1927).

55. G.-R. Horn, "From 'radical' to 'realistic': Hendrik de Man and the International Plan conferences at Pontigny and Geneva, 1934–1937", *Contemporary European History* 10:2 (2001), 239–65; G. Vergnon, *Les gauches européennes après la victoire nazie: entre planisme et unité d'action, 1933–1934* (Paris: L'Harmattan, 1997).

56. G. Cole, "Introduction", *New Fabian Research Bureau* 25, 11.

57. H. de Man, *Die sozialistische Idee* (Jena: E. Diederichs, 1933).

58. Renton, *Fascism*, 74.

59. B. Fleming, "Three years in Vermont: the writings of Karl Polanyi's *The Great Transformation*", paper presented to the Eighth International Karl Polanyi Conference, Mexico City, 2001.

60. H. de Man, *Corporatisme et socialisme* (Brussels: Editions Labor, 1935).

61. Cole cited in Polanyi, *Europe To-day*, 11.

62. K. Polanyi (1934–46) 'The Christian and the world economic crisis', KPA-8-7.

63. K. Polanyi, "The rebirth of democracy", in Dale, *Karl Polanyi: The Hungarian Writings*, 150.

64. O. Bauer, "Problems of the Austrian revolution", in T. Bottomore & P. Goode (eds), *Austro-Marxism* (Oxford: Oxford University Press, 1978), 166–7.

65. K. Polanyi (n.d.) "The eclipse of panic and the outlook for socialism", KPA-19-17.

66. Polanyi, "Fascism and Marxian terminology"; K. Polanyi (n.d.) "Five lectures on the present age of transformation: the trend towards an integrated society", KPA-31-10.

67. Polanyi, *Europe To-day*, 55.

68. Polanyi, "Fascism and Marxian terminology".

69. Polanyi, *Europe To-day*, 55.

70. Botz, "Austro-Hungarian interpretation of fascism", 135.

71. We have elsewhere discussed the merits and demerits of that argument. See G. Dale, "Karl Polanyi's *The Great Transformation*: perverse effects, protectionism, and gemeinschaft", *Economy and Society* 37:4 (2008), 495–524; G. Dale, *Karl Polanyi: The Limits of the Market* (Cambridge: Polity, 2010); G. Dale, *Reconstructing Karl Polanyi: Excavation and Critique* (London: Pluto, 2016); G. Dale, *Karl Polanyi: A Life on the Left* (New York: Columbia University Press, 2016).

72. Polanyi, "Fascism and socialism".

73. Polanyi, "Othmar Spann", 7.

74. Polanyi, "The fascist transformation".

9

DEMOCRACY

Paula Valderrama

INTRODUCTION

In this chapter, I will attempt to explain the role of the concept of democracy in Polanyi's social philosophy. This task is not so easy, as Polanyi does not provide any systematic analysis of the term. Moreover, Polanyi uses the concept of democracy in narrower and broader meanings at different points. In *The Great Transformation*, the term democracy mainly denotes existing popular governments of the twentieth century, and it is primarily used to demonstrate the inherent tension between social claims and capitalist market requirements.[1] However, in other (unpublished or less known) texts, Polanyi employs the term in its ideal meaning: democracy is hereby a vision of a future society, in which moral-political values such as freedom, equality and social justice are institutionally guaranteed.[2] Furthermore, this ideal concept of democracy involves not only a political and social transformation but also implies moral progress.[3] The development of democracy is therefore based on the "spiritual ennobling of the masses" as well as the "transformation of souls", as Polanyi states.[4]

Polanyi is not a utopian thinker, but he firmly believes in the transforming power of ideas and institutions.[5] The awareness that human beings are able to evolve is, for him, not utopian at all, but rather realistic, for the capacity of adapting to new circumstances is, in fact, an essential part of human nature.[6] One of the necessary preconditions of democracy is, therefore, the so-called "believing politics", that is the political conviction that an adequate institutional framework is able to cause socioeconomic and moral development.[7] Or, the other way round, adequate socioeconomic positions and moral practices enable the perpetuation of a democratically set institutional framework in the long run.

It is this particular aspect of Polanyi's oeuvre which I shall analyse in the next sections. The aim is to provide a better comprehension of Polanyi's concept of democracy, in particular, to present and explain his ideal vision of a free democratic society. In the second section, after this introduction, I shall present

Polanyi's view of democracy as a process. The current parliamentary democracies represent an important step towards achieving freedom, especially concerning freedom from absolutism and political totalitarianism. However, these types of democracy do not guarantee political and economic self-determination. Social freedom, that is freedom of responsibly co-shaping our own environment, can only be achieved in an advanced form of democracy.

The problem of freedom, which is for Polanyi the main issue to be solved by a real democracy, will be presented in the third section. The understanding of the concept of social freedom is crucial in order to acquire a deeper knowledge of Polanyi's insights concerning democracy. Freedom and democracy are for Polanyi both sides of the same coin. Democracy is the political-organizational form which corresponds at the moral level to the value of freedom.

In the fourth section, the relationship between the concepts of socialism and democracy will be explained, as Polanyi uses the term socialism to refer to a democracy in an advanced stage. Democratic socialism is achieved when the dominance of the market economy is overcome, and society is finally under democratic control. Polanyi's ideal model of a functional democracy will be briefly presented too. Although this model remains an ideal, it can still serve as a source of new insights concerning the direction in which democratic societies can progress.

The obstacles to this progress – the hegemonic liberal concept of freedom, market mentality and conformity – will be outlined in the fifth section. Polanyi pleads for a transformation of the mind through which old convictions concerning the alleged economic determination of human beings and society are declared to be obsolete. Furthermore, the utopian liberal concept of freedom, which identifies freedom and market agency, must be rejected and replaced by the realistic concept of freedom within a complex society. Conformity to the status quo as well as average thinking especially promoted by existing mass media will be discussed too. The last section will conclude and the contemporary relevance of Polanyi's insights concerning democracy will be briefly presented.

THE STAGES OF DEMOCRACY

For Polanyi, democracy is not only a form of government, but rather an ideal "way of life".[8] As such, it involves the application of particular decisional practices (such as majority rule or negotiations among democratic organized associations) to fundamental issues that concern human beings.[9] The ideal democracy is the societal form in which citizens consciously co-shape their environment according to their own principles and judgements. The role played by the citizen is not reduced to the political duty of electing representatives, but it mainly consists in direct citizen participation in political, economic and operational decision-making.

Especially in his later work, Polanyi prefers the term "common man" to refer to the citizen.[10] The concept of the common man does not correspond to an economic category, but it is rather a strategical term that points out to the value of the day-to-day life experiences acquired by human beings in modern societies. The "common human experience is at the back of democracy", Polanyi states.[11] The common man possesses real knowledge about the main themes that are at stake in a democracy. No special academic education is required to participate in democratic decision-making; the experience of the common man is hereby enough.[12] The political judgement of the common man constitutes, therefore, the substance of a real democracy.[13]

Polanyi is of course aware that the concept of democracy has different meanings and he is furthermore convinced that these different understandings have led to different kinds of democratic society forms.[14] The discussion about the meaning of democracy is for Polanyi indispensable, as the future of societies will depend on their actual vision of how a democratic society can function.[15]

Polanyi distinguishes between past, actual and future forms of democracy.[16] He considers the representative democracies that mostly emerged in the eighteenth and nineteenth centuries as a first step towards freedom.[17] This phase is characterized by the aspiration of the bourgeoisie of achieving political power. The aim of the democratic revolutions at that time was to achieve independence from absolutism.[18] This kind of democracy does not lead to central conflicts in the economic sphere, as the working class is not an active part of the electing population. This first stage of democracy constitutes, according to Polanyi's notes, "a phase of harmony" characterized by an "increasing self-determination under the leadership of the owners of the new means of production".[19]

In the second stage of democracy, universal suffrage is achieved.[20] This leads to a higher political power of the working classes that ends up in crucial economic-political conflicts, especially in the interwar period. The incompatibility between capitalism and political democracy becomes evident at this stage.[21] Two totalitarian systems are chosen to reverse the deadlock: communism and fascism.[22] Fascism is understood by Polanyi as the extension of the economic (industrial) principle to the political sphere.[23] It is a system that has as its main consequence the abolition of the democratic state.[24] The corporate state is ultimately an industrial-based state. Therefore, in fascism "[d]emocracy goes, capitalism becomes the whole society".[25] In (real) communism, the opposite takes place: the economic sphere is completely absorbed by the political state. However, the centralization of political and economic power in the state makes the system totalitarian too.[26]

The only democratic solution to the impasse is, according to Polanyi, social-ism.[27] Democratic socialism is hereby understood as the extension of the demo-cratic principle to the whole society, including the economic sphere.[28] Regarding this aspect, Polanyi writes: "Not in the economic, but only in the political sphere can the whole of society be reunited. This is the true meaning of democracy".[29]

The concept of socialism is, therefore, used by Polanyi in order to denominate the third and last stage of the democratic progress of societies.[30] In this phase, the people consciously decide on the main affairs of society.[31] The so-called "plastic society" is hereby achieved and the "helpless society [is] transcended".[32] That means that the socioeconomic constitution of society is in fact a result of democratic acknowledged principles and direct democratic decision-making. In an advanced democratic society, there is an intentional relation between people's judgements and social consequences. The non-intentional results of politics are diminished as much as possible. At this stage, "the philosophy of the common man [is] established", as it is his political judgement, and not the power of big corporations or anonymous market laws that defines society.[33] Thus, higher forms of freedom are thereby achieved, particularly, "freedom from the blind fate of history", as Polanyi puts it.[34] This kind of freedom – the freedom to consciously co-shape society at one's will – is only possible under a system that is ultimately under democratic control.

Democracy – in its ideal meaning – is for Polanyi the organizational form, which allows the greatest *social freedom* possible within the boundaries of a complex society.[35] Social freedom is a responsibility-based concept of freedom, one that includes the insight that the members of a society can only be free, if they are able to act assuming responsibility for the social consequences of their action. This view presupposes a transparent societal context, in which human beings and political actors are in fact capable of overseeing the social implica-tions of individual and political action.[36]

Polanyi is aware that full transparency of societal relations is impossible.[37] In order to point to this fact, he uses the terms "freedom in a complex society"[38] or "freedom in face of the reality of society".[39] These concepts are meant to demon-strate the tension between objective laws and facts on the one side, and moral, social and political principles on the other side. The polarity between power institutions and individual freedom is a crucial thought within Polanyi's theo-retical apparatus.[40] Objective systems and entities – like market prices, capital laws, or the state – restrict the sphere of freedom in society, as individual and political decision-making can only take place within these boundaries. State and markets, Polanyi states, act as an "invisible wall" that separates individuals from each other as well as the individual action from its social implications.[41] In this context, the old Rousseauian question arises: is a free society possible?[42] Or in other words: how can we achieve liberty not in the sense of independence from society, but in the sense of autonomy, of giving ourselves our own laws and living according to our own principles and responsible decisions?

The problem of freedom based on social responsibility is the key question upon which Polanyi's reflections about democracy are built. For Polanyi's main concern regarding freedom is the following:

> How can we be free, in spite of the fact of society? And not in our imagination only, not by abstracting ourselves from society, denying the fact of our being interwoven with the lives of others, being committed to them, but in reality, by aiming at making society as "übersichtlich", as family's inner life is, so that I may achieve a state of things in which I have done my duty towards all men, and so be free again, in decency, with a good conscience.[43]

Democracy is the solution to the problem of human freedom under the conditions of complexity, for it is the attempt to make society as "übersichtlich" (transparent) as possible, in order to enable responsibility for individual and political actions.

FREEDOM, DEMOCRACY AND THE "REALITY OF SOCIETY"

Democracy is the method to achieve the so-called "plastic society", that is the organizational form, in which the lives of the people depend in fact on their own moral values, political judgements, goals and visions.[44] The plastic society is for Polanyi the truly free society, for the constitution of society itself as well as its socioeconomic results depend on the will of its members.[45] Freedom understood as autonomy involves necessarily the insight that the political framework and its institutions are the result of democratic acknowledged principles and decisions. If the laws and the institutional framework of a society are given, and therefore no relevant changes are possible, political freedom becomes an empty concept.

The plastic society can therefore only be pursued by reducing the power of existing institutions that determine societal results without democratic legitimation. This purpose can only be achieved by increasing direct citizen participation in decision-making as well as by achieving a higher level of transparency within the human relationships that constitute ultimately society.[46] Transparency is the key principle in a democratic society, for political action only makes sense if its implications are largely predictable. Furthermore, assuming responsibility for one's own action is only possible in a transparent context in which human beings can judge and act according to the real individual and social consequences of their action.[47] In a context of a complete Unübersichtlichkeit (complexity, lack of transparency), political action and in general individual free action cannot take place.[48] The guiding question for Polanyi is therefore: how is it possible to achieve transparency in a context of complexity?[49] Or in other words: is it possible to reduce the power of objectively given entities such as the market or the state?[50]

Polanyi first distinguishes between facts that are inherent to complex societies and those that are institutionally conditioned, that is dependent on the institutional framework set. With the term "reality of society", he points to those entities that are implicitly given in all societies, no matter which political and economic framework they adopt.[51] Power itself is such an entity, as it cannot be completely exterminated from any society or community.[52] The "public opinion" is also an entity which arises in every community and exerts power over the members of society.[53]

The "economic value" of commodities is for Polanyi an inherent part of modern societies too.[54] The concept expresses the relationship between needs and wants on the one side, and the provision of a commodity on the other side. The social reality of economic value is unavoidable, whereas the objectivity of the market price is conditioned: it depends on the economic institutional arrangement, in this case on the institutions of private property, market distribution and division of labour.[55]

Polanyi analyses the conditional objectivity of entities such as market prices by means of the Marxian thesis of reification.[56] He argues that human decisions and human relations become in modern societies thing-like entities that exert power over human beings.[57] Institutions such as the law, the market, or the state are reified human relationships. They are human-made institutions, which, once emerged, follow their own laws and deprive human beings of having control over them. Objective entities are not natural phenomena, but they are still real in the sense that they have true consequences on human lives. In Marx's words, these entities have a "fetish" character: without human action, they do not exist, but once they do, they become independent of human will. Polanyi points out a paradox: although these entities emerge out of human decisions and actions, they are often not a direct result of human will. Mostly, they are non-intentional results of human action that end up controlling human beings. This fact sets one of the central problems of freedom in a complex society, for human beings who strive to act freely, end up as slaves of the institutions and systems they have made. Democracy, as a method to achieve transparency, is the main instrument through which this problem should be solved or at least reduced to the minimum possible.

The problem of freedom caused by the reification of human relationships arises in every society and out of any human institution. However, in capitalistic societies it is the market price, which is the main objectivation and consequently the primary barrier to freedom: "Market price, this sibylline manifestation of the fetish of commodity", Polanyi states, is "the main obstacle to the mastery of the necessary consequences of socialisation".[58] Freedom and responsibility, and therefore, freedom and transparency must go hand in hand, that is Polanyi's conviction.[59] For without the capacity of assuming responsibility for the real consequences of human action, it cannot be said that human action is free: "Responsibility to myself – this is the material out of which freedom is realized", Polanyi states.[60] The author doubts that human action can be said to be free if there is no knowledge of its essential consequences: "For where there is no over-view there is no freedom because without knowledge there can be no choice".[61]

Polanyi deals particularly with the problem of social knowledge that faces the market agent.[62] The market agent acts without any knowledge of the enormous range of consequences caused by his own action. For the consumption act has not only personal, but also social, ecological and global consequences, most of which the consumer has neither oversight nor control of. The problem of trans-parency and of lack of control over the consequences of our own action is at the basis of the question of freedom within a complex society. The institution that is at the centre of the problem is the capitalistic market price formation.

Polanyi is aware that the institution of market price building is in some respects advantageous for a modern industrial society.[63] For market price for-mation based on demand and supply provides the producer with essential infor-mation about the economic value of a commodity. The market price expresses the relationships between needs and wants on the one side, and supply on the other side. The producer can only judge according to this information, whether the commodity shall be produced or not.

However, Polanyi criticizes the false use of the institution of the market price, particularly the generalization of the market principle to all spheres of society.[64] Market price formation for commodities should, for him, therefore take place under a democratically determined economic framework.[65] That means that non-commodities such as labour, natural resources and other basic goods and services of society should be organized according to non-market principles and through democratic practices.

In this way, the institution of market price formation functions within dem-ocratically set boundaries. The partial deconstruction of capitalistic market prices is realized. The democratically determined economic framework and state regulations enables the political community to better oversee the distribu-tion process and to control its social and economic consequences. Democratic planning is here used to improve transparency. Complexity and lack of control are partially diminished. The objectivation "market price" continues to exist, but its relevance for society is reduced. Freedom is hereby increased, as the use of the democratic principle enables societal responsibility.

SOCIALISM AND THE ADVANCED DEMOCRATIC SOCIETY

The problem of freedom based on social responsibility does not only take place in the market society, but also in every complex society in which there are a high number of objective relations beyond human control. Polanyi admits that complexity is a fact in industrial societies, but he sets the partial reduction of complexity through which freedom and social justice are enabled, as one of the main goals of democratic socialism.[66] Socialism is the system that attempts to make society "an increasingly plastic medium of the conscious and immediate relationship of persons", Polanyi writes.[67] The aim of socialism as the advanced democratic society is to reach a "fuller realisation of the dependence of the whole upon individual will and purpose – and a corresponding increase of responsibility of the individual for his share in the whole."[68] As we can see, socialism and democracy are closely interrelated and interdependent terms in Polanyi's social philosophy. As Polanyi puts it: "Democracy needs [s]ocialist economies as its extension".[69] Or the other way round: socialism must be democratic, or it is no socialism at all.[70]

Of course, complexity cannot be wholly avoided; this would be utopian. Polanyi aims only to reduce complexity by replacing objective relations in some spheres of society through direct human relationships: "The more directly, the more meaningfully, the more lively the human essence emerges in social relations, the freer is the human being and the more human is his society".[71] The partial resolution of reificated entities into relations between human beings is the goal of the advanced democratic society, that is the specific goal of socialism in Polanyi's terms.

Consequently, socialism emerges out of the human striving for human freedom and the awareness that in a capitalistic market economy the freedom to co-shape society is limited by objective market relations. Capitalistic entities – market prices, interest rates, capital laws, etc. – make freedom an "illusion", for they determine the boundaries, under which human action takes place.[72] Socialism's goal is to deconstruct objective relations, particularly market institutions that are under a capitalistic framework beyond human control. Polanyi is not an anarchist and he is not at any point suggesting the abolition of commodity markets; on the contrary, he pleads for an organizational form that uses the advantages of markets, without being dominated by them.[73]

Polanyi supports a system of industrial production and distribution that is based in more transparent economic relations and direct democratic agreements.[74] This system intends to increase freedom through making *social knowledge* available: in this way, the real conditions and consequences of economic activity should at least be partially known by the members of society.[75] It is certainly impossible, and it is also not Polanyi's desire to turn back time. He instead suggests ways to reduce market complexity by using in some spheres of society alternative institutions that foster transparency into the production-consumption process.[76] Polanyi's democratic society is not a given political project. The author offers arguments and principles that can be utilized as guidelines for a democratic post-market society. For sure, Polanyi's vision is and remains an ideal created only for theoretical discussion. However, the model is important to better understand Polanyi's vision of a democratic transformation.

Polanyi's functional socialism promotes a form of direct democratic procedure not only in political but also in economic affairs.[77] Together with the existing territorial representation of current democracies, there is additionally a functional representation of interests in Polanyi's model.[78] Functional unities are those who represent partial interests of a sector of society.[79] However, these partial interests are legitimate, that is they are democratically acknowledged as being necessary for the functioning of the whole society. Functional unities are, for example, producer associations, consumers cooperatives, sectoral representations and trade unions.[80] These grassroots organizations possess what Polanyi calls "inner oversight", that is real knowledge about the needs, preferences, life and working conditions of the common man in his role as a consumer, producer, fabric worker or member of the political community.[81] The functional, democratic organized unities negotiate with one another as well as with the political representatives. They arrive at democratic agreements that determine the "economic framework" of society, that is the fundamental socioeconomic conditions, under which commodity markets function.[82] The economic framework includes public decisions about the non-market organization of non-commodities. This comprises the determination of democratically agreed prices and distributional forms for fundamental areas of society such as staple foods, energy, housing or health. Furthermore, wage scales are determined. Not only minimal, but also maximal wage levels (or maximal wage differences) can be agreed. Price fixing or regulations for the distribution of land, raw materials and other basic goods and services are also part of Polanyi's socialist framework.[83]

Polanyi considers the compromises between functional unities as an important step towards a real democracy, for these agreements express the day-to-day experience of the common man.[84] Moreover, the results of the negotiations reflect a stable society equilibrium, as the decisions are based in fact on citizen judgements. The citizen is part of each of the functional unities and therefore, in the negotiations he is represented in all his societal roles. Functional interests are ultimately societal interests, that is interests that in principle concern all citizens.

For Polanyi, the negotiations between functional unities achieve better results if the basic operational unit is not the private firm, but the cooperative.[85]

For in cooperatives and mutual-based associations, the members collectively own the organization. In this case, it is easier for the citizen to recognize that the interests of the workers are also the interests of the producers, which are at the same time the same persons as the customers.[86] General education for leadership and for self-administration at a political and an operational level is needed for the realization of Polanyi's democratic society.[87] A higher comprehension of the industrial process as well as of the roles played by the individuals in it is necessary too.[88]

Polanyi's ideal seems at first to be completely utopian, but what is relevant here is the goal of deconstructing the market system in the fundamental areas of society by replacing the market principle through organized democratic practices. This goal is followed today in some countries such as Canada, Germany or Argentina by small-scale organizations, especially in the energy and agricultural sectors.[89] In the so-called *"Erzeuger-Verbraucher-Genossenschaften"* (producer-consumer-cooperatives) or *"comunidades prosumidoras"* (prosumer communities), citizens have united together as consumers and as producers to achieve autonomy from market laws and independence from large corporations.[90]

For Polanyi it is evident that self-organization at the economic and political level must be the guiding principle to achieve transparency.[91] Regional markets for some commodities as well as smaller production-consumption circles can also increase transparency and, therefore, the freedom to consciously co-shape society.[92] Direct citizen participation in the determination of societal affairs, for example, open discussion of budget plans especially at local levels, could augment democracy, Polanyi states.[93] Market regulations that increase transparency in the market procedure are welcomed too.

Furthermore, Polanyi does not plead for one universal model to be applied globally.[94] The interpretation of moral-political values must be made democratically; the result should therefore depend on existing cultural and moral systems. Polanyi defends the idea of the *coexistence of models*, that is international cooperation among regional, highly autonomous systems.[95]

DEMOCRACY AND THE NEED OF A "REFORM OF OUR CONSCIOUSNESS"

In a manuscript written in 1957, just seven years before Polanyi's death, the author returns to the question about the main problems that face a complex modern society.[96] Polanyi is convinced that the contemporary technology-based civilization has not so much economic, but rather moral-political concerns. The key problem for Polanyi is the "loss of freedom" caused by the fact that markets' agents and political actors act without enough knowledge about the social and global consequences of their actions. The possibility of assuming responsibility for these indirect, but still real consequences is largely limited. Democracy remains in its second stage. No progress has been achieved at all. "Man's inner life is at the point of extinction", writes Polanyi in a pessimistic tone, "because he has lost hope of the individual freedom which nourished that life". He continues: "Inner and outer survival require a realism that we do not yet possess. No solution is in reach without a reform of our consciousness that postulates freedom in the face of the reality of society".[97]

Polanyi points again to the reality of complexity as well as to the tension between both poles: human freedom on the one hand, social realities on the other. Again, he focuses on the need for a reformed concept of freedom, one that can serve as political leitmotiv for an advanced democratic society. Without this reformed understanding, no democratic solution is in sight.

The reform of consciousness, as Polanyi calls it, is therefore the necessary condition in order to begin the institutional transformation into a real democratic society. The transformation of the mind is the prerequisite of institutional change. Polanyi does not work in detail his idea of a reform of consciousness, but I think that it is possible to understand it by analysing some related aspects. First, the reform of consciousness must include a modern concept of freedom, one that overcomes the liberal (and neoliberal) understanding of freedom as mere market-freedom. Secondly, the current dominant market mentality should be declared obsolete, for it is a paradigm of thought that is based on a distorted picture of human nature. Thirdly, the so-called right to non-conformity must be guaranteed in order to enable public criticism and dissent from hegemonic thought.

Polanyi criticizes the liberal concept of freedom as short-sighted, as it declares only "this side of the market" for the whole reality.[98] The implications of human action that are beyond this side of the market are considered by liberals irrelevant for reflection about responsibility, as the individual cannot know which exactly are the social and global consequences of his action.[99] This concept of freedom is for Polanyi a mere "illusion", as it ignores the reality of society and fosters a freedom "*of* duty and responsibility", whereas social freedom consists in a freedom "*through* duty and responsibility".[100] The liberal view of freedom "degenerates in a mere advocacy of free enterprise", Polanyi comments, as liberals deny the need for state regulations and controls in order to achieve societal goals.[101] Democratic planning is dismissed as it is said to lead to slavery.[102] The rejection of planning as a democratic tool is the main problem of the market-liberal concept of freedom, for it presents freedom and planning as antagonist terms, whereas they are interdependent. No modern freedom is possible without rules, regulations and controls. This is the content of the reformed concept of freedom in a complex society.

The second obstacle to achieving democracy is the so-called "market mentality".[103] The market mentality consists, at a general level, of the belief that a modern industrial society can only function under the institution of capitalistic markets. At a more specific level, it includes "axioms" about the nature of man and society.[104] These axioms are summarized in what Polanyi calls the "belief in economic determinism", which postulates at an individual level that human beings judge and act mainly according to economic-related motives (profit seeking or hunger).[105] At a societal level, it asserts that society itself is mainly determined by its economic conditions.[106] Polanyi rejects the belief in economic determinism.[107] He argues that economic determinism is only real under the condition of a market society.[108] In a market-based society, human beings become economically determined, for they have no other choice than to follow market laws in order to survive. The society itself becomes economically determined too, as the main spheres of society are controlled by market principles. However, it is a categorical mistake to apply economic determinism to every other organizational form of modern societies.[109] Market societies are industrial societies, but not every industrial society must be organized by the market principle.

Furthermore, the belief in economic determinism assumes that economic, particularly productive relations are fundamental for society, whereas moral and political ideas have a mere secondary or complementary character. Polanyi questions this assumption at a fundamental level.[110] He doubts that the question, whether being determines consciousness or consciousness determines being, is useful.[111] He instead suggests understanding social reality as the point of intersection between being and thinking.[112] Ideas are contained in social facts, these facts would not exist without human ideas and interpretation. Polanyi points at this with the aim of demonstrating that ideas can have real social consequences.[113] Not only is the market society partly the result of a political ideal, but also future democracies will depend on the development of suitable visions. However, if the market mentality prevails, no democratic transformation is possible. The transformation of the mind, particularly the rejection of accepted (false) axioms, is the first step towards institutional progress. The market society is not a fate; human beings are ultimately free to co-shape their own destiny.[114] For society, as Polanyi puts it, "depend[s] on my acts, my behaviour, my words, my thoughts, my deepest sentiments".[115] "The creative power of consciousness" (and not an alleged objectivity of economic laws) is the only certainty we need in order to progress.[116]

Conformity to the status quo represents for Polanyi another main barrier to freedom and democracy.[117] Therefore, the author postulates the institutional guarantee of the "right to nonconformity", that is the freedom to dissent from the majority and from hegemonic thought.[118] Nonconformity is the "hallmark of a free society", Polanyi states, for it is the safeguard of personal freedom.[119] The problem today is not so much the legal possibility of dissent, but the lack of individual will to differ. The market society has already reformed people's consciousness: "uniformity" and "averagism", understood as the tendency to imitation and reluctance of the individual to differ from the group, are, according to Polanyi, the results of the current institutional framework.[120] Particularly important is the widespread use of "mass media that attack the mind".[121]

Polanyi is convinced that anti-democratic systems inevitably need to create another level of human consciousness in order to achieve stability.[122] The oppression of the oppositional forces (countermovements) within an already established political democracy must be done indirectly. That is, a suitable ideology must be created and spread within society with the aim of pacifying the citizen and avoiding revolution. In other words, the citizen must be convinced that the best system is the status quo; no other reasonable alternative shall seem to him available.

In Polanyi's analysis of the philosophy of fascism, understood as the mother of all anti-democratic movements, the author deals with two strategies used by the fascist movement to transform human consciousness and foster social stability.[123] "Vitalism" and "universalism" are attempts to change democratic consciousness, which mainly consists in the awareness that society is ultimately "a relation of persons".[124] Conscious citizens know that human actions are necessarily interwoven and that society is at least a partial result of individual and political decisions. On the contrary, anti-democratic systems assert that society cannot be fundamentally changed by citizen participation. Of course, people can elect representatives and engage themselves in social and other initiatives, but the institutional framework, under which human action takes place, is declared by anti-democratic theories to be given.

"Vitalism" is the strategy that fosters a lack of reflection about the whole and about the participation of the individual in it. Universalism, on the contrary, supports reflection; however, this kind of reflection is based on the anti-democratic insight that asserts that individual action cannot fundamentally co-shape society.[125] Neoliberal theories, such as Hayek's, borrow a lot from the universalistic philosophy. The postulation of the market order as fundamental reality and as a necessary consequence of social evolution implies a vision of the global market society as unavoidable destiny. Alternative theories and political ideals seem in this context to be utopian. Cultural conformism is hereby fostered: the market order as status quo shall not be questioned at all. It is Polanyi's aim to reform this kind of false consciousness. The market society is a political project and not an economic necessity. The understanding of this view is one of the main preconditions of a real democracy.

CONCLUSIONS

I have argued in this chapter that democracy, in Polanyi's terms, is not only a form of government but rather an ideal form of society, in which the higher form of self-determination is achieved. This concept of democracy involves the insight that the socioeconomic structure of society does not primarily result from anonymous market laws, but it is rather an intentional effect of democratically acknowledged values and judgements. The common experience of human beings within an industrial society is the substance out of which democracy is built. Citizens' direct participation in political, economic and operational decision-making is the instrument through which the (at least partial) deconstruction of power institutions such as the market or the state can be achieved. This kind of democracy involves deeper forms of social integration, for the democratic procedures employed replace objective economic relations through direct human relationships. In this way, society resembles at least in some of its spheres a community. Higher levels of human consciousness are acquired by the members of society, thus leading to moral flourishing.

However, as Polanyi warned, this development could be endangered by false axioms and convictions. Particularly problematic is the belief in the economic determination of man and society as well as the liberal concept of freedom, which declares the market as the main sphere of human liberty. Polanyi criticizes this view as utopian and pleads, instead, for a realistic worldview.

Polanyi's considerations about the advanced democratic society offer arguments that can enrich the political debate and contribute to a redirection of mainstream opinion. One of the main Polanyian arguments is the one regarding the role of values and ideals for the transformation of social reality. Polanyi is convinced that society is not a fate, but a result of both non-intended societal consequences and intended individual and political action. Depending on the institutional arrangement, the balance will incline to one side or the other. In a real democracy, the constitution of society reflects, in fact, democratic ideals and decisions.

In the current neoliberal era, however, we might say that the opposite is true: it is not democracy that defines the framework, but the financial markets which set the main constraints. The political establishment acts in favour of the markets (in order to avoid "capital flight") or according to considerations of international competition. The principle of market-conformity rules political action today; even when political actors belong to social democratic or left-wing parties.[126] The main obstacle to democracy, by this account, is the current market mentality, in particular, the blindness of the politicians to their own thought axioms.[127] The belief that market-conformity has to be considered a scientific truth is the real malaise of our times. As long as the power of ideas is not really understood by the ruling elites, the market mentality will not be challenged, and therefore, neoliberalism will remain.

The analysis of Polanyi's ideal democratic society can contribute as well to the debate about future institutional agreements that overcome the market society. Polanyi's views concerning the concept of transparency and the partial deconstruction of power institutions are in this regard particularly important. The main question in this context is: which institutions are adequate in order to enable a *plastic society*? That is one whose constitution is in fact characterized by people's judgements and commonly-held moral-political values. More specifically, which organisztional forms foster transparency within complex relations? Is it possible to replace market-price formation in some spheres of society through non-market techniques? How do we increase real democratic participation in political and economic affairs? How can existing social knowledge, as the one possessed by trade unions and other functional associations be used? How can self-organization at a political but also at an operational level be promoted? Which is the role of economic planning and regulations? Do these institutions achieve the purpose of increasing transparency and, therefore, control over the consequence of our action? Finally, which is the role played by current social movements and organizations of the so-called solidarity economy? Are these efforts to overcome capitalism "from below" still marginal or should they be considered as emancipatory movements that possess already critical knowledge of a third (mutual-socialist) way?[128]

I have hopefully made clear that Polanyi's concept of democracy involves more than a democratic welfare state or a social market economy. The difference to these models results out of Polanyi's insight that decommodification should be realized without increasing state power. The citizen and his associations play a crucial role in Polanyi's theory of democracy. Academic research on this issue and on Polanyi's considerations about the need for a certain kind of *Bildung* (education) for democracy is certainly required.[129]

Notes for Chapter 9

1 A detailed review of the antagonism between democracy and capitalist markets is given by G. Dale, *Reconstructing Karl Polanyi: Excavation and Critique* (London: Pluto, 2016), Chapter 3.

2. K. Polanyi, "Believing and unbelieving politics", in G. Dale (ed.), *Karl Polanyi: The Hungarian Writings* (Manchester: Manchester University Press, 2016), 102.

3. K. Polanyi, "Civil war", in Dale (ed.), *Karl Polanyi: The Hungarian Writings*, 98.

4. *Ibid.*

5. Polanyi, "Believing and unbelieving politics", 102–05; K. Polanyi, "Being and thinking", in M. Brie & C. Thomasberger (eds), *Karl Polanyi's Vision of a Socialist Transformation* (Montreal: Black Rose, 2018), 290.

6. Polanyi, "Believing and unbelieving politics", 104f.; K. Polanyi, "Is human nature unchangeable?" (n.d.), KPA 21-17.

7. Polanyi, "Believing and unbelieving politics", 101–05.

8. K. Polanyi, "Common man's masterplan" (1939–40), KPA-20-4.

9. *Ibid.*

10. *Ibid.*

11. *Ibid.*

12. *Ibid.*

13. *Ibid.*

14. K. Polanyi, "The meaning of parliamentary democracy" (n.d.), KPA-19-8.

15. *Ibid.*

16. K. Polanyi, "The paradox of freedom" (1936), KPA-21-1.

17. *Ibid.*

18. Polanyi, "Meaning of parliamentary democracy".

19. Polanyi, "Paradox of freedom".

20. *Ibid.*

21. *Ibid.*

22. K. Polanyi, "Die wirtschaft ist für den faschismus" (1933), KPA-02-21.

23. K. Polanyi, "Marx on corporativism" (n.d.), KPA-19-11.

24. *Ibid.*

25. Polanyi, "Paradox of freedom".

26. Polanyi, "Die wirtschaft ist für den faschismus".

27. Polanyi, "Paradox of freedom".

28. *Ibid.*

29. Polanyi, "Marx on corporativism".

30. Polanyi, "Paradox of freedom".

31. Polanyi, "Common man's masterplan".

32. *Ibid.*

33. *Ibid.*

34. Polanyi, "Paradox of freedom".

35. K. Polanyi, "On freedom", in Brie & Thomasberger, *Karl Polanyi's Vision of a Socialist Transformation*, 304.

36. K. Polanyi, "Notizen: ist sozialismus eine weltanschauung?" (1919–33), KPA-3-3.

37. *Ibid.*

38. K. Polanyi, "Freedom in a complex society", KPA-37-3 (1957). See also K. Polanyi, *The Great Transformation: The Political and Economic Origins of Our Time* (Boston, MA: Beacon Press, 2001), Ch. 21.

39. *Ibid.*

40. See M. Cangiani & C. Thomasberger, "Die polarität: menschliche freiheit – markt-wirtschaftliche institutionen. Zu den grundlagen von Karl Polanyi's denken", in M. Cangiani, K. Polanyi-Levitt & C. Thomasberger (eds), *Karl Polanyi. Chronik der großen Transformation*, Vol. 3 (Marburg: Metropolis Verlag, 2005), 16.

41. Polanyi, "Notizen: ist sozialismus eine weltanschauung?".

42. K. Polanyi, "Jean Jacques Rousseau: or is a free society possible?" (1943), KPA-38-24.

43. K. Polanyi, "Letter to a friend", in K. McRobbie & K. Polanyi-Levitt (eds), *Karl Polanyi in Vienna* (Montreal: Black Rose, 2000), 317 (emphasis in original).

44. Polanyi, "Common man's masterplan".

45. K. Polanyi, "The essence of fascism", KPA-13-6 (1933), 392f.

46. Polanyi, "On freedom", 306.

47. Polanyi, "Notizen: ist sozialismus eine weltanschauung?".

48. K. Polanyi, "Das übersichtsproblem" (1919–33), KPA-3-1 and "Das übersichtsproblem, ein hauptproblem des sozialismus" (1919–33), KPA-3-2.

49. Polanyi, "On freedom", 306.

50. *Ibid.*, 301, 311.

51. Polanyi, *Great Transformation*, 266.

52. *Ibid.*, 267.

53. K. Polanyi, "Statements from Christian Left training week-ends" (1937), KPA-21-22.

54. Polanyi, *Great Transformation*, 267.

55. Polanyi, "On freedom", 300.

56. *Ibid.*

57. *Ibid.*

58. *Ibid.*, 311.

59. *Ibid.*, 302, 304, 307, 313f.

60. *Ibid.*, 302.

61. *Ibid.*, 312.

62. *Ibid.*, 308.

63. K. Polanyi, "Zur sozialisierungsfrage [On socialisation]" (1919–33), KPA-3-7.

64. Polanyi, *Great Transformation*, 74.

65. Polanyi, "Zur sozialisierungsfrage [On socialisation]".

66. Polanyi, "On freedom", 301.

67. Polanyi, "Essence of fascism", 392f.

68. *Ibid.*

69. K. Polanyi, "Fascism and Marxian terminology", KPA-18-6 (1934).

70. *Ibid.*

71. Polanyi, "On freedom", 301.

72. *Ibid.*, 305.

73. Polanyi, *Great Transformation*, 260.

74. K. Polanyi, "Sozialistische rechnungslegung [Socialist accountancy]" (1922), KPA-2-13 and "Neue erwägungen zu unserer theorie und praxis [Considerations to our theory and praxis]" (1922), KPA-12-12.

75. Polanyi, "On freedom", 313.

76. *Ibid.*, 311.

77. Polanyi, "Sozialistische rechnungslegung [Socialist accountancy]" and "Neue erwägungen zu unserer theorie und praxis [Considerations to our theory and praxis]".

78. The model is based mainly on G. D. H. Cole's theory of guild socialism (*Guild Socialism Restated*, New Brunswick, NJ: Transaction, 1920) and Otto Bauer's concept of functional democracy (*Der Weg zum Sozialismus* [The Way to Socialism], KPA-3-19).

79. See G. Dale, "Positivism and 'functional theory' in the thought of Karl Polanyi, 1907–1922", *Sociology Compass* 5:2 (2011), 148–64.

80. Polanyi, "Sozialistische rechnungslegung [Socialist accountancy]" and "Neue erwägungen zu unserer theorie und praxis [Considerations to our theory and praxis]".

81. Polanyi, "Neue erwägungen zu unserer theorie und praxis [Considerations to our theory and praxis]".

82. Polanyi, "Zur sozialisierungsfrage [On socialisation]".

83. *Ibid.* See also Polanyi, *Great Transformation*, 259f.

84. Polanyi, "Neue erwägungen zu unserer theorie und praxis [Considerations to our theory and praxis]".

85. Polanyi, "On freedom", 302.

86. *Ibid.*, 314.

87. Polanyi, "Essence of fascism", 393.

88. *Ibid.*

89. See M. Mendell, "The social economy in Quebec: lessons and challenges for international co-Operation", in D. Reed & J. McMurty (eds), *Cooperatives in a Global Economy: The Challenges of Co-Operation across Borders* (Newcastle upon Tyne: Cambridge Scholars, 2009), 226–41.

90. See P. Valderrama, "Polanyi's ideas for socio-political production and consumption cooperatives and their realization in the 'El Arca' cooperative in Argentina". Available at: http://www.academia.edu/6456653/ (accessed 28 June 2018).

91. Polanyi, "Essence of fascism", 393.

92. *Ibid.*

93. *Ibid.*

94. K. Polanyi, "Universal capitalism or regional planning" (1945), KPA-18-28.

95. *Ibid.*

96. Polanyi, "Freedom in a complex society".

97. *Ibid.* See also Polanyi, *Great Transformation*, 262.

98. Polanyi, "On freedom", 307.

99. See, for example, F. Hayek, *The Constitution of Liberty* (Chicago, IL: University of Chicago Press, 1960), 83f. Hayek states: "Freedom demands that the responsibility of the individual extend only to what he can presume to judge" and he continues, "While we can feel genuine concern for the fate of our familiar neighbours … we cannot feel in the same way about the thousands or millions of unfortunates whom we know to exist in the world but whose individual circumstances we do not know".

100. Polanyi, "On freedom", 304 (emphasis in original).

101. Polanyi, *Great Transformation*, 265.

102. *Ibid.*

103. K. Polanyi, "Our obsolete market mentality" (1947), KPA-35-6.

104. *Ibid.*

105. K. Polanyi, "On belief in economic determinism" (1937), KPA-35-8.

106. *Ibid.*

107. *Ibid.*

108. Polanyi, "Our obsolete market mentality" and "On belief in economic eeterminism".

109. Polanyi attributes this kind of mistake to Hayek. See Polanyi, "On belief in economic determinism".

110. Polanyi, "Being and thinking", 287–92.

111. *Ibid.*, 287f.

112. *Ibid.*, 289.

113. *Ibid.*, 290.

114. K. Polanyi, "Economics and freedom to shape our social destiny" (n.d.), KPA-37-4.

115. Polanyi, "Being and thinking", 290.

116. *Ibid.*

117. K. Polanyi, "Freedom and technology" (1955), KPA-36-9.

118. Polanyi, *Great Transformation*, 265.

119. *Ibid.*

120. Polanyi, "Freedom and technology".

121. Polanyi, "Freedom in a complex society".

122. See Polanyi's analysis of fascism as an anti-democratic doctrine in "Essence of fascism".

123. *Ibid.*

124. *Ibid.*

125. *Ibid.*

126. Consider, for example, the case of Syriza in Greece.

127. See M. Brie & C. Thomasberger, "Introduction", in Brie & Thomasberger, *Karl Polanyi's Vision of a Socialist Transformation*, 8.

128. See M. Mendell, "Commoning and the commons: alternatives to a market society", in Brie & Thomasberger, *Karl Polanyi's Vision of a Socialist Transformation*, 238.

129. Polanyi, "Believing and unbelieving politics", 105.

10

KNOWLEDGE

Tilman Reitz

Accounts of the capitalist knowledge and information economy promise excit-
ing theoretical innovations, and political agendas.[1] At the same time, economic
theory as such seems to face problems in the analysis of cognitive (or "immaterial") goods and resources.[2] Neoclassical as well as Marxist authors find themselves forced to rethink their fundamental categories, scarcity and labour. As
has been widely observed, knowledge and information are in many aspects
non-scarce, namely insofar as they are non-rival (i.e. not used up when used),
and excluding people from accessing them is cost intensive, difficult or even
impossible (as in the cases of digitized music or images, scientific results or published news). Neoclassical accounts thus have to introduce trade-off scenarios,[3]
network-effects promoting monopolies,[4] public spending,[5] sharing and even
gift economies in order to understand how knowledge and information work
economically. For Marxists, the equivalent set of problems is which and whose
work counts as necessary in order to achieve valuable knowledge, how this
labour is measured and where it enters processes of exploitation. Marx himself
famously argued that in an economy driven by science and technology, "labour
time ceases and must cease to be" the "measure" of wealth, so that "production
based on exchange value breaks down".[6] And while some of his followers conclude that a "post-capitalist" economy is finally within view,[7] others argue that
the mechanisms of exploitation have changed fundamentally.[8]

In contrast to neoclassical and Marxist approaches, Polanyi saw the creation
of peculiar, "fictitious" commodities at the very heart of the capitalist economy
and society. For him, three goods which are not produced for markets but are
nevertheless sold on markets – land, labour and money – explain fundamental
structures and problems of the modern market economy. Polanyi's institutionally and politically sensitive theory of fictitious commodities might also offer
clues for understanding a capitalism based on knowledge and information.
Diverse authors, more or less tentatively, have already dubbed knowledge as
the "fourth fictitious commodity".[9] Just as the commons of land were privatized through enclosures in early modernity, so common knowledge is turned

to intellectual property through laws and treaties.[10] Just as manual labour has been subjugated to the discipline of the factory, so intellectual labour is brought under dense quality control and quantified by performance indicators,[11] measuring everything from satisfaction with call centre services to the citation of publications. And as soon as measuring and (e-)valuation are trusted, the intellect, similar to money, functions not only as a medium of assessment (as Simmel argued), but can be traded as a good or asset itself. Potential parallels even go further. Michael Burawoy suggested that the "double movement" of commodification and efforts at re-regulation, which Polanyi observed in cases like the social protection of labourers, is also a key feature of the knowledge economy, making a range of contested issues from copyright conflicts to struggles about tuition fees readable as resistance to a misplaced market logic.[12]

But although parallels and analogies are striking, any closer look at the topic reveals problems of precise reconstruction. What exactly counts as the new fictitious commodity – knowledge or information (or even data)? To what extent are systemic problems due to the public good traits of knowledge, and are private-good aspects relevant? (In the important case of education, teaching time *is* a rival and expensive good, and some are taught more and better than others.) Is intellectual property the only social form through which knowledge and information can be turned into valuable, tradeable goods – or by which, in a rather Marxist perspective, their producers can be capitalistically exploited? And how to account for work performed and the workers exploited in publicly funded education and science?

I will head for a general answer to such questions by specifying, or indeed modifying, the category of the fictitious commodity for cognitive goods (including services, which will turn out to be crucial). What might distinguish these goods from land, labour and money are the strong institutional arrangements which are needed in order to make them count as *valuable* goods, and to *fund and control their production*. In both aspects, the distinction is not absolute. Private appropriation requires strong regulation in all "fictitious" cases, from legal registers of land ownership to the content and enforceability of working contracts, and it also involves negotiating value. And the problem of (costly) provision, which has been famously analysed for public goods in general,[13] also pertains to all fictitious commodities, notably to the reproduction of labour power. But whereas market valuation works at some point in the cases of land, labour and money, the value of cognitive goods remains problematic even when money is in play. How can one measure the differences between propertied software and free open source products? How much basic research needs to be funded in a technologically advanced society? Such complex conditions call for *institutionally regulated valuation*, or "a system … that assigns *value* to knowledge".[14] Moreover, this valuation allows to implement a *capitalist style of production* (e.g. in managerial universities) even where it is not feasible to commodify final products (such as published, accessible scientific insights). My definition of fictitious commodities will thus be broader than Polanyi's: in addition to goods which are not produced for, yet are regularly sold on markets, it also comprises the results of processes which are organized – measured, paid and controlled – in the same way as market-directed production.

I will first prepare these arguments in an exposition of Polanyi's concept, which will also introduce the problems of valuation and provision with regard to fictitious commodities. Secondly, I will portray and criticize existing theories of knowledge and information as new fictitious commodities. I will present my own, alternative account in a third section, which will unfold the suggested modifications of Polanyi's story. My fourth and final step will be to ask whether a commodification of knowledge which involves institutional support rather than disembedding can still be portrayed as a "double movement". This part can also profit from Polanyi's shorter texts on knowledge intensive production, the value of teaching, and the interests of the intellectual class.

WHAT ARE FICTITIOUS COMMODITIES?
POLANYI'S THEORY AND ITS BLIND SPOTS

The passages where Polanyi explicates the central structural aspects of fictitious commodities have a strong rhetorical rhythm. The first two aspects are presented as an antithetical pair, which is closely tied to the trinity of classical economic sources of income:

> Labor, land, and money are essential elements of industry; they also must be organized in markets; in fact, these markets form an absolutely vital part of the economic system. But labor, land, and money are obviously *not* commodities; the postulate that anything that is bought and sold must have been produced for sale is emphatically untrue in regard to them.[15]

For present purposes, it does not matter how strict the "postulate" and therefore the paradox or contradiction is. If something not produced for markets on a regular basis is continually sold on markets, at least a certain tension can be assumed – even if it still needs to be explicated. Polanyi does this in a sweeping way. In describing the respective non-commodity aspects, he uses the most general and meaning-laden terms possible, which makes his return to the factual (or now "fictitious") commodity status of labour, land and money especially striking:

Labor is only another name for a human activity which goes with life itself, which in its turn is not produced for sale but for entirely different reasons, nor can that activity be detached from the rest of life, be stored or mobilized; land is only another name for nature, which is not produced by man; actual money, finally, is merely a token of purchasing power which, as a rule, is not produced at all, but comes into being through the mechanism of banking or state finance. None of them is produced for sale. The commodity description of labor, land, and money is entirely fictitious. Nevertheless, [...] [they] are being actually bought and sold on the market; their demand and supply are real magnitudes; and any measures or policies that would inhibit the formation of such markets would *ipso facto* endanger the self-regulation of the system.[16]

A third and final structural element, societal countermovements to commodification, follows almost necessarily from this tension. Polanyi immediately hints at the destructive dynamics implied in fictitious commodification: "To allow the market mechanism to be the sole director of the fate of human beings and their natural environment, indeed, even of the amount and use of purchasing power, would result in the demolition of society".[17] Faced with such a threat, it seems only natural and unavoidable that society (which survived, after all) has found counter-measures:

Social history in the nineteenth century was thus the result of a double movement: the extension of the market organization in respect to genuine commodities was accompanied by its restriction in respect to fictitious ones. While on the one hand markets spread all over the face of the globe [...], on the other hand a network of measures and policies was integrated into powerful institutions designed to check the action of markets relative to labor, land, and money.[18]

It would be tempting to probe how far the general and basic concepts of this rhetoric find complements in the sphere of knowledge. Knowledge, after all, is just another name for the symbolically and technically organized conscious relationship of human beings towards their world and themselves, cultivated and passed over to new generations throughout our history, systematically expanded in modern science. Moreover, as Polanyi himself stated elsewhere: "Education in the broadest sense is just another name for society".[19] Subjecting this complex to market mechanisms and profit interests can only mean a complete disorientation of human beings, a loss of their shared world as such, a serious attack on scientific progress and truth.

Such terms are not necessarily wrong or over-general, provided that additional distinctions among knowledge, cultural patterns, information, implicit and explicit knowledge are made. And as we will see, structural changes of knowledge today surely make it attractive to reflect on its apparent commodification. Yet there are reasons to not simply follow this line. Most importantly, Polanyi's generalist existential style distracts attention from concrete productive relations in the environments of markets. Not unlike Marx, he stresses that capitalism destroys its own preconditions (nature, the worker, the stability of exchange), but offers no closer analysis of the activities and processes which are thus destructively exploited, from human care to natural reproduction. He only adds apocalyptic scenarios[20] and refers to the welfare state, or a network of "powerful institutions designed to check the action of the market"[21] as a solution. The various other factors that are addressed in feminist, ecological and postcolonial critiques of Marx,[22] remain absent or marginal in Polanyi's picture as well. Unpaid female care work, the exploitation of nature and of the (post) colonial periphery have not only generally enabled capitalist accumulation, but have also played a vital part in the provision of the fictitious commodities. An account of parallel processes in the sphere of knowledge should keep this productive side in view, too.

Reflecting on the actual social neglect of unpaid work and reproductive processes leads to an additional problem. If the agents of the productive side – women, nature, or even indebted state administrations – do not have a real say in the pricing of fictitious commodities, how is the price of these goods determined? The question is less pressing insofar as property relations and a practice of buying and selling are firmly established, so that (however volatile) market prices exist. Where labour, real estate and financial markets have grown out of traditions of hiring, transferring and lending, the only thing to be explained is how the "individual interest in the possession of material goods"[23] came to trump all other aspects of transfer. The process might simply follow Polanyi's trajectory of disembedding, destructive effects and re-embedding: in some countries, weakened hereditary traditions of land-owning first led to an exchange-driven fragmentation of space and then to problem-solving state regulation. The basic argument remains intact even when the zero level of the commodity, the reduction to nothing-but-market price, is achieved by political coercion, as when British workhouses stripped potential labourers of social support for a decent life.[24] But in still other cases, most notably money, systems for *regulating value* partly preceded and systemically *enabled* the commodification of the respective goods. "Capitalist credit-money" especially requires a state and (central) bank apparatus which ensures social trust, from money creation over routinized exploitation to interest rates.[25] Polanyi himself holds that central banks and "a centrally managed currency"[26] had to be established before capitalism took off: "Modern central banking … was essentially a device developed for the purpose of offering protection without which the market would have destroyed its own children, the business enterprises of all kinds".[27] It is not hard to conclude that the modern financial industry, too, became possible only after this regulatory innovation.

In the sphere of cognitive goods, even more basic devices of assessing value and establishing trust could be necessary. In terms of use value, putative knowledge, especially new insights or problem-solving capacity, and information, especially information relevant for the success or failure of action, are high risk bets on the future. Nor can valuation in exchange be taken for granted: traditions of selling knowledge on markets are weak; the supply of knowledge claims and well-educated workforce tends to exceed demand, whereas the need for generic intellectual competences, knowledge and information exceeds the propensity to pay for their provision. Thus, an analysis of knowledge as fictitious commodity not only has to address productive activity, but also the valuation of knowledge and information as such.

WHAT MAKES KNOWLEDGE A FICTITIOUS COMMODITY? THREE INCOMPLETE STORIES

Existing accounts of knowledge as a fictitious commodity are far from homogeneous. The arguments and authors referred to in the introduction can be associated with at least three different stories, whose lowest common denominator rather reveals a conceptual weakness: empirical evidence is very often derived from the theorists' own academic lifeworld, so that "academic capitalism" frequently enters the scene.[28] At least one story, however, can also be presented without academic examples.

- *The (post-)Marxian story of intellectual property.* Knowledge, information and data are products of a genuinely collective activity, which can only be brought under the rule of capital by an artificial enclosure of cultural commons. The main instrument of this process is intellectual property, which allows legally backed owners of knowledge to draw private profits or rents from the results of collective cognitive labour. Bob Jessop offers a Polanyian version of this story, focusing less on work than on selling conditions: "just as wages are the market price for the use of labor power, rent is the market price for the use of land, and interest is the market price for the use of money capital, so we can interpret royalties in their different forms as the market price for the use of knowledge as a … commodity".[29] According to Jessop, this involves "more traditional intellectual property rights (including patents, trademarks, trade secrets, design rights, and copyright)" as well as "newer forms", specific to the "information economy. These include database rights, protection for semiconductor topographies, plant breeders' rights, protection for indications of geographical origin, rights in performances, and protection against circumvention of copy protection devices."[30]

- *A Mills-inspired story of the taylorization of white-collar work.* With Marx in view, Jessop also argues that the commodification of knowledge presupposes "the process whereby workers' tacit knowledge is formalized and integrated into expert systems or smart machines".[31] A recent analysis of commodification as control of intellectual labour, however, rather draws on C. Wright Mills.[32] In this story, Antonino Palumbo and Alan Scott accentuate a shift of institutional power from white-collar workers to management, and the close control of work (or neo-Taylorization) which is thereby enabled. Besides knowledge-intensive enterprises,[33] the paradigmatic contexts of this strand of digital capitalism are public administration and higher education, reshaped by New Public Management:

  > By using different combinations of privatization, liberalization, and marketization, clerical and intellectual work is parcelled in discrete sequences and routinized; *ex-ante* and *ex-post* forms of assessment are then used to measure the degree of conformity of each civil servant and academic [...] located along the production line. In this model of mass production, conformity is rewarded by allowing a tiny minority to move up the ranks, whereas non-conformity is strongly discouraged by the ease with which an individual could be replaced along the digital conveyor belt by a growing number of part-time and temporary workers seeking a more secure position.[34]

- *The (neo-)Polanyian story of commodification and resistance.* Where the commodity form is imposed upon common activity, and new forms of discipline are introduced, resistance aiming at re-regulation is to be expected. In this spirit, Michael Burawoy has tied his story of knowledge as a fourth fictitious commodity to wrongs and unrest in institutions of higher education:

  > The theorists of postindustrial society [...] did not [...] anticipate the way that the production and dissemination of knowledge would be commodified, leading the university to sell its knowledge to the highest bidders [...]. Knowledge has become a commodity, and universities now cultivate students as customers who

pay ever-increasing fees for instrumental forms of knowledge. The university reorganizes itself as a corporation, which maximizes profit not only through increasing revenues, but through the cheapening and degrading of its manpower, reducing tenured faculty, and increasing the employment of low-paid adjunct faculty [...].[35]

In short, "The university, once a taken-for-granted public good [,] has become a private good subject to the dictates of the market. [...] The struggle for the university [...] has a central role to play in any countermovement to [...] marketisation"[36] today.

Some of the obvious differences between these stories may be complementarities, some of them probably hint at incompatible understandings of commodification or of fictitious commodities. In order to arrive at a structured comparison, however, it is helpful to first tackle a number of errors and shortcomings of the respective stories. I will proceed in reverse order.

The quotes representing Burawoy's story[37] immediately reveal two weaknesses. On the one hand, hinting at the putative commoditization of academia is simply not sufficient to understand the advanced knowledge economy in general. The booming sectors and business models of information technology, biotechnology, platform capitalism, etc., have to be analysed in themselves, as well as the ailing cultural industries, mass media and other content producers in the age of the internet. Whatever characterizes markets and profits in these parts of cognitive capitalism, it is highly unlikely that the specific institutional landscape of higher education provides the model.

On the other hand, analyses of "academic capitalism"[38] usually question whether marketization works as smoothly as Burawoy suggests. From the UK to the US, from Scandinavian to central European countries, most products of academic research are still *not* sold to commercial bidders. They are largely funded by public money (often co-ordinated with private funding, and distributed in competitive processes), and extra money is invested to pay for their publication, in order to increase the reputation of the respective university, department or scientist. Research for patents has been increased and pays out at some places, but not in general, because costs for technology transfer and legal advice staff roughly equal the gains.[39] The other big feature of "academic capitalism", tuition fees, is strongly regulated and often heavily state subsidized. While countries like Germany provide higher education for virtually no fees, others have (or had) set maximum rates; repayment of student debt is either contingent on income (such as in the UK and Australia) or assisted by state aid and reduced by stipends (such as in the US). Under such conditions, profit-oriented institutions are not the new normal, but extreme cases of a predatory capitalism. For-profits in the US earn money at the expense of the state and of students "in search of vocational credentials that guarantee them little but lifetime debt";[40] these institutions were put under scrutiny by the Obama administration and have begun shrinking after initial successes. In contrast, rich and successful players from Cambridge to Harvard are usually public institutions or endowments with long-standing property due to historical public grants. The other measures which Burawoy rightly highlights – the exploitation of (adjunct) faculty and the rise of an academic managerial class – are thus not so much examples of a knowledge capitalism but of a *capitalist* or *neoliberal style* in which knowledge economies apparently try to save some of the exploding costs of an ever-widening, near universal higher education.

In one respect, however, academia obviously partakes in a general development of cognitive capitalism. As Scott and Palumbo point out, the standardization and measuring of intellectual work is both a general trend and a specific development in the academic sector.[41] Especially the avalanche of performance indicators – journal impact factors, citation counts, student numbers, graduate income, reputation scores, university rankings, etc. – documents a will to impose market-like discipline on intellectual work. It remains to be discussed below how the rise of performance indicators relates to real market valuation. In any case, the commodified object has already been categorized by Polanyi himself: not as knowledge, but as labour. Changes in this context are interesting enough. On the one hand, new obstacles to the commodification of labour are being tackled in the non-manual sectors. There is "a renewed attempt to commodify labour, which has as its main target administrative, managerial, and intellectual activities".[42] On the other hand, the qualification of the workforce tends to become more cost intensive and income relevant than ever before in the history of capitalism.[43] Yet nothing in all this makes it necessary to talk of knowledge as a fictitious commodity. Conceptual parsimony suggests that one instead simply extends the analysis of the fictitious commodity labour. Regarding labour power, such a move immediately brings analytical insights. In whichever way knowledge may yield private profits, the cultivation of intellectual labour power primarily entails private or public costs.

Where Palumbo and Scott directly speak of an "enclosure" of the intellectual "commons", they correctly address a different set of problems: "The various attempts to separate and measure individual contributions to a common scientific enterprise are producing ... a number of conflicting legal claims, which inevitably give the most powerful actors the opportunity to acquire exclusive entitlements".[44] If appropriation on the basis of legal claims is the pivotal point, it fits with Jessop's thesis that knowledge and information are generally commodified by the expansion of intellectual property rights (IPRs). A central function of IPRs has been suggested in various accounts: by post-operaists who see an exploitation of the cultural commons,[45] in the theory of a rent-extracting "information feudalism",[46] in the critique of "biopiracy" exerted by transnational agrobusiness,[47] and in conventional theories of incentives for research work.[48] Examples are wide-ranging, too. A slightly systematized version of Jessop's list could include patents and business secrets in advanced industries, especially information technology (IT), protected software, rights over "green" and "red" knowledge goods – pharmaceuticals, genetic codes and genetically modified life – copyrights in the cultural industries, legal arrangements around (big) data collected by internet firms. However, in nearly all of these fields counterexamples to IPR rent-seeking also abound:

- In the bio-pharmaceutical sector, the bigger players tend to open access or shared databases in order to reduce dependency on and payments to small research start-ups.[49] These market leaders also engage in public--private product development partnerships, where economic gain perspectives are abstract (entering new or future markets), and property titles like patents might primarily matter for reputation.[50]
- In the IT and software sector, ecologies of open-source communities and corporations have evolved, from the IBM and Linux ecology to the world of free Android licences (conditional on the use of other Google/Alphabet products).
- Rather than selling propertied information and content, the biggest firms in the internet economy generally rely on a mix of offering free services and hosting user-generated content.[51] The most important assets in control of enterprises such as Google and Facebook, besides a number of algorithms, are the attention of billions of users and masses of user data which are prevalently employed in contexts of advertising and marketing. Even platform capitalists who offer information based paid services – Uber, Airbnb, dating platforms, etc. – do not need strong property rights; like the advertising giants, they count instead on a maximally extended clientele.[52]
- Part of this logic even affects the very tangible role of intellectual property rights in agrobusiness. In spite of US-led efforts at global IPR unification and enforcement, national governments and local farmers in many parts of the world reject or neglect rent claims on biological substances. Indian peasants gratefully use improved seed varieties without paying fees to the US and European "owners".[53] Corporate profits in these contexts rather rest on non- or para-legal factors, such as the reputation of firms for seed quality – possibly another example of an indirect function of patents[54] – or their strategies to make farmers dependant on a set of interconnected services.[55]

The (non-)development referred to in the last example offers an especially strong reason to rethink the role of IPRs. While debates of the late 1990s and early 2000s typically anticipated a global knowledge economy dominated by TRIPS (the Agreement on Trade Related Aspects of Intellectual Property Rights) or stronger future regulations, the establishing of such rights has apparently met its limits. Follow-up agreements such as the EU Copyright Directive (1996) or ACTA (the Anti-Counterfeiting Trade Agreement of 2011) have been restricted to smaller groups of technologically advanced countries, while the most recent global post-TRIPS round in Doha (2002) was mainly concerned with medical needs of countries in the South. If knowledge and information capitalism nevertheless kept expanding, it seems to have found alternative pathways and mechanisms.

The stories of a commodification of knowledge and information thus need substantial revision. First, if knowledge and information only become fictitious commodities through the legal force of IPRs, the role of cognitive fictitious commodities is rather limited. Real and profitable control of knowledge assets often involves more than just legal ownership, from reputation to service monopolies. Secondly, a bigger picture can be drawn if fictitious commodification also characterizes the ways in which economic and public actors tackle problems of the public provision of knowledge and the control of intellectual work. However, the existing accounts of neo-taylorization and of academic capitalism fail to show why the concept of the fictitious commodity applies in these contexts. And thirdly, a similar observation can be made concerning resistance against cognitive capitalism. Even if such resistance takes place, from open source activism over struggles against global agrobusiness to contested academic employment and tuition fees, the relation of these conflicts to commodity production remains conceptually unexplored.

This set of problems shows two rather different things. On the one hand, crucial factors may yet be missing in the analysis, such as the role of highly valued intellectual services. On the other hand, instead of only revealing weaknesses, the theoretical problems hinted at may be closely related to actual social problems. The features which Polanyi ascribes to fictitious commodities might even reliably lead to these problems. In a capitalism which increasingly depends on knowledge and information, it turns out to be highly problematic to sell the respective goods on markets, not least because much knowledge and information is not simply produced in order to be sold on markets, so that many people involved tend to resist efforts to implement profit goals, property rights and price logic. In order to develop a clearer view of these zones of difficulty and conflict, it is helpful to return to Polanyi's conceptual framework.

COMMODIFICATION, THE ASCRIPTION OF VALUE
AND ITS INSTITUTIONAL PRECONDITIONS

With differences to Polanyi already in view, I will ask once more: (a) to what extent and in which ways is it possible to buy and sell knowledge and information; (b) to what extent and in which ways are knowledge and information already produced for markets; and (c) how do institutions *prepare* these goods for markets. As indicated above, the obvious point of departure from Polanyi will be (c), but the new direction will be already prepared in (a) and (b), where a curious reversal takes place: commodity logic may be more important for the production than for the selling of knowledge and information. In many cases, their profitable employment demands economic discipline and control, but not necessarily knowledge and information commodities.

The selling of knowledge and information on markets

Polanyi's observation that land, labour and money are sold on markets with often devastating effects is more evident than ever before: real estate and financial speculation ignited the latest global crisis of capitalism, labour markets in southern Europe were among the main victims, and people all over the world have been suffering from the loss of their homes, of jobs and purchasing power. It is much harder to see in which ways and with which effects knowledge and information are sold.

Obviously, *knowledge based* or *knowledge intensive* goods play a vital role today, but they might only gradually differ from cars and industrial farming. What is new, of course, is the development and relevance of *information technologies* – and yet also big firms like Apple mainly sell tangible, rival and mass-produced hardware. Even the large network of software and services that often comes with them may not radically differ from service networks for cars, washing machines or industrial technology.[56] In contrast, cases in which knowledge or information as such are commodities may be quite limited. The first case (on which theories almost exclusively focus) concerns the objects of intellectual property rights, with their wide blurry margins of accepted free access. A second, at least equally important sector are specific intellectual or informational *services*. Some of them, such as financial or legal consultancy, are in themselves knowledge-centred activities; others, such as the implementation of software or supervision of the use of transgenic seed, also interact with knowledge and information products. Still another variety is the fully automatized processing and connecting of data, be it on internet trading sites or flat sharing platforms. Characteristic of all these services is that the concrete needs of the clients make intellectual property mostly redundant – since everyone's case is specific, solutions and match-making processes can be standardized, but not simply organized outside the platform. What matters is the (processing and thus control of) specific information and data which enter the processes.[57] The key economic problem of knowledge and information for sale thus shifts significantly: it is not how to protect non-rival goods, but how to signal superior services. Wherever this problem is not solved by quantitative network dynamics – in which even non-paying additional users rather count as gains than as losses – complex social mechanisms are needed.

The production of knowledge and information for markets

Strong instances of valuing mechanisms can be seen where the problem of free-floating costs of intellectual labour is pressing as well. Similar to land, labour and money, knowledge and information are not simply produced for markets. However, in important gradual differences to the classical cases, increasing numbers of people are regularly employed in order to produce and administrate knowledge and information. The difference to social activities directed to labour and nature is far from general: there is paid and unpaid knowledge work as well as paid and unpaid care work and (as already mentioned real overlapping) education; natural reproduction takes place with and without organized social support. Even the problem of increasing public costs is partly common to knowledge and care work. Some of the reasons, however, differ sharply. While all personal services whose quality depends on expended labour time suffer from a "cost disease",[58] knowledge work also partakes and expands in the course of rationalization, or the reduction of labour time. And whereas care work is always in the service of concrete persons (who often do not have sufficient resources to pay), a lot of knowledge work has the opposite function of augmenting the general intellect (for which private actors usually have no sufficient economic reason to pay). This cluster of cost problems stands behind a large part of the processes which are discussed as commodification: taylorization, managerialism, tightened controls, outsourcing and precarization as strategies of cost reduction, increased fees and the harnessing of peer production as efforts to make private households and unpaid workers carry the costs.

It should be noted that nearly all of these strategies can work on an ideological as well as on an economic level. Often the introduction of competition, auditing and quasi-markets does not serve to save time or money, but only to justify continued public spending for lofty research and teaching. More generally, the notion of quasi markets hints at a curious trend: in the case of knowledge and information, it may be more precise to speak of fictitious commodity production than of fictitious commodities. What is actually *not* sold on markets (academic research and publications, in-house training and self-training of job-transcending skills, the free services of internet monopolists) is in many ways treated *as if* produced with the main goal of market sale. This redescription might have the advantage to cover different cases which previously could not be conceptually unified: state and business led commodification, knowledge incorporated in workers and information circulating in the public domain. In all of these cases, capitalist knowledge societies seem to have to cheat themselves in order to provide for their necessary knowledge and information.

The institutional validation of knowledge

Of course, the strategies and mechanisms just reviewed in large parts operate at the expense of knowledge workers, even if public and business resources are mobilized in order to fund some of their activity. Examined more closely, these disadvantages (and related advantages) belong to another set of economic problems and social mechanisms. The crucial question of who works for whom, or how labour time is socially distributed in capitalism is posed in new ways when price mechanisms are suspended. If the point of cognitive capitalism is less that knowledge and information goods are sold, but that intellectual labour is mobilized, measures have to be found to regulate payment and maintain the disciplining force of market rewards. The explosion of systems of evaluation and performance measuring can be seen as an answer to this cluster of questions. Among other functions, these systems serve as a socially instituted mechanism to determine the value of cognitive work in a wide range of contexts. At a basic level, rules are needed to register whether tasks are performed in due time; at the top level, formalized reputation attracts those who are able to pay for high quality intellectual services; throughout the system, popularity of cognitive work can be documented and translated into systemic rewards, from research grants to donations.

Over the years, reflection on the knowledge economy has produced for-mulations which help to capture the institutional validation of knowledge and information. As early as 1988, Dan Schiller observed that "information is not inherently valuable but that a profound social reorganization is required to turn it into something valuable".[59] Even earlier Alvin Gouldner, speculating about the distribution of intellectual labour and gains, anticipated "a cultural bourgeoi-sie who appropriates privately the advantages of an historically and collectively produced cultural capital".[60] More recently, the spread of academic performance indicators, evaluations and rankings brought Simon Marginson to assume that the "chaotic open source flows of knowledge" had at last found an institutional answer: "knowledge flows are vectored by a system of status production that assigns value to knowledge and arranges it in ordered pattern".[61] Yet more than good formulations is needed. The exact (or fuzzy) coordination of performance measuring and status systems with the distribution of money and work still has to be analysed. Presumably, the ascription of value to knowledge involves hierarchies (for example in higher education), exclusion (from the ranks of professionals, etc.), trusted organs of evaluation (from performance indicators to rating agencies), and reward systems (which transfer reputation into funding, a willingness to pay fees, etc.). Two general observations can already be put down. In addition to market valuation, cognitive capitalism has generated circuits in which knowledge and information (work) are valued previous to market exchange. And if cognitive goods have become fictitious commodities, these commodities are strongly embedded from the outset.

RESISTANCE TO THE COMMODIFICATION OF KNOWLEDGE: A MOVEMENT AGAINST DISEMBEDDING?

In the light of these results, resistance to commodification in the intellectual sphere has to be rethought. The old model of free-market forces which need to be countered by institutional embedding no longer works. A passage of Jessop's text shows how this model collapses when confronted with the developments of cognitive capitalism:

> [...] despite increasing resistance [...], states have not yet responded with active and massive intervention to protect the intellectual commons and thereby prevent the treatment of knowledge as if it were a simple commodity [...]. Indeed, the leading capitalist states are intervening to subordinate knowledge as a collective resource to the profit-oriented, market-mediated logic of economic competitiveness.[62]

The rupture between the first and second sentences demonstrates a shift from textbook notions to observed reality. There *is* massive and active state intervention in the knowledge economy, but mainly to establish the institutional embedding necessary for commodification. What remains to be discussed are the political implications of the state powered subordination of knowledge and information to profit production.

With regard to potential countermovements, the most important point probably is that discontent with raw market logic does not automatically threaten the new institutions, hierarchies and exclusions of knowledge and information capitalism. The reasons can be seen in a final modified list of economic-institutional arrangements of cognitive production:

1. *The more or less successful implementation of profit-directed management and competition without real price mechanisms.* Examples include publicly funded research in managerialized contexts, state subsidized private schooling and for-profit higher education. In such cases, main actors are driven by a profit motive, so that the productive process is characterized by fictitious commodification, but this motive is (meant to be) harnessed by the welfare state or other non-capitalist organizations who carry (most of) the costs. Resistance is thus almost programmed and marginalized at the same time. It usually cannot turn to politics and public administration, but has to be directed against them.

2. *The more or less integral implementation of systems of competition based on performance indicators.* In some aspects, this is simply the complementary process to directing the flows of public money. But a system of performance indicators can also steer the propensity of private actors to pay for cognitive goods and services. The latter can thus be analysed as fictitious commodities based on pre-market valuation. Examples range from professions like law to investment decisions and management methods at technological frontiers. The immediate goal of producers is success in non-market competition, usually closely coupled to economic rewards, but sometimes also autonomized as reputation fetish – such as when scientists compete for prestigious publications. In these contexts, renouncing direct market orientation often only means turning to elevated prestige competition which pays out better in the long run.[63]

3. *Networks of voluntary production, sharing and free provision of cognitive goods and services with functional relations to commercial production and services.* In this bright part of the knowledge and information economy, producers are primarily driven by a use value orientation, the will to create and improve functional cognitive goods (most famously software). The commodity form only plays a parasitical or secondary role here: in the result, when commercial actors manage to derive profits from the unpaid common cognitive labour, or as the enabling condition, because the workers have to earn something somewhere. The bigger picture, however, is claustrophobic: instead of offering an alternative to the capitalist knowledge economy, contexts of voluntary peer-production (have) become its subordinate part.

4. *Networks of intellectual cooperation, cooptation, privilege, exclusion and dependence with a strong overlapping to the distribution of capitalist profits.* Although intertwined with the bright scenery of (3), this functional nexus represents the dark side of capitalist economies: the distribution of gains among circles who are powerful enough to serve themselves. Standard receivers of research grants, management strata of monopolistic

information firms, highly paid university presidents, CEOs equipped with credentials and networks from highly selective educational institutions all owe their privileges to an overlapping of capitalist and knowledge hierarchies. Insisting on a genuine value of knowledge is not likely to destabilize this connection; it only ideologically invokes purity where intellectual authority and institutional power are inseparable.

The political lessons to be drawn from this list are not obvious. An anarchist conclusion would be that resistance to cognitive capitalism has to attack both information markets *and* hierarchical knowledge institutions. The opposite, affirmative conclusion would be a relative satisfaction with the open and communal elements that are already part of the knowledge economy: universal higher education with some support of the welfare state, rising amounts of funding invested in a somehow still autonomous scientific community, a fair amount of peer production and masses of free services in the internet economy.

The Polanyian conclusion probably lies in between. Since the late 1930s, Polanyi observed that labour in almost all sectors is becoming more and more knowledge intensive. He strongly endorsed the North American version of this process which in his eyes avoided the old European cleavage between mental and manual work:

> In America, the job itself is changing under the influence of the better education of those who perform it. [...] It [...] will become a job performed by intelligent people, conscious of the technological and commercial implications of their work, *i.e.*, possessing some measure of real understanding of the consumers' needs the job caters for and of the factors governing its discharge.[64]

Ten years later, as he saw socialist opportunities in Britain, Polanyi added that such a solution would need strong efforts in overall education, extending to adults, and reversing established divisions between politics and economics, individual and collective cultural competences:

> Education for leisure catered for the student's wish to study for personal ends, and there was but scant reason why tuition should take account too much of his social background and natural interests. [...] Emphatically, the opposite should apply, once adult education is to help the individual working man or woman to be more effective *as a worker*, especially if this is to include no less than the active and responsible participation in a change in our industrial system.[65]

It is tempting to relate these ideas to the changes taking place in transition to a "post-industrial" system – especially since Polanyi's vision includes political claims which would radically alter today's knowledge and information economies. On the one hand, he apparently presumes that funding education (and, we can add, knowledge production) belongs to the core tasks of regulative states. This can be taken as a strong and valid claim. No matter where a society is situated in the spectrum between New Deal welfarism and New Public Management, economic rationality speaks against efforts to install markets for knowledge. The most important effect of such markets will be to feed new and renewed oligarchies, not to improve productivity[66] – and the cost problems of providing general intellect for a private economy can only be shifted between different overburdened groups, but not solved by fictitious commodification. On the other hand, knowledge-intensive production also points beyond hierarchical capitalist relations of control in the work process. Polanyi's notion of education as contextual knowledge anticipates this insight in remarkable ways. The "active and responsible participation" of cognitive workers has been spurred with all sorts of partial autonomy and corresponding indirect control, but it still remains to be seen which productive force could be developed should the capitalist limits to cognitive workers' self-responsibility be removed.

What precludes steps towards a responsible knowledge and information economy might therefore be less substantial problems than issues of class struggle. In general terms, Polanyi allows us to see that cognitive capitalism took shape under the hegemony of (capital fractions with) a radical market ideology, imposing the commodity form even where it is clearly misplaced. More specifically, an early text on a non-reconcilable cleavage between manual and cognitive work might be of help. It is not only material interests which separate white- from blue-collar workers, the service precariat from schooled project teams, but a different relationship towards interests as such. In a very schematic analysis of revolutionary potentials after the First World War, Polanyi contrasts the "physical labour", "tangible results" and "working hours" which matter for manual workers with the different focal points of intellectual employees: "mental labour" and "the intangible benefit that it brings for the productive system or society as whole", as long as it is endowed with a "sphere of authority and responsibility".[67] As a result, manual workers demand the product of their work, while intellectual workers strive to extend their responsibility and authority. As schematic as the distinction is, it still has not lost explanatory power. The prestige competition, hierarchies, privileges and exclusions which have proven to be essential for the fictitious commodification of knowledge and information are obviously supported by cognitive workers who strive to be recognized in their authority. As long as this struggle for recognition goes on, the fictious commodification of knowledge will hardly meet effective resistance.

Notes for Chapter 10

1. I wish to thank Gareth Dale, Anna Saave-Harnack and Barbara Brandl for their helpful comments.

2. The more usual term is "immaterial goods", but since the (im-)materiality of symbolic structures is a difficult topic and since some authors also count affective labour as "immaterial", I use the term "cognitive" in this text. A remaining problem is that information technology is not exactly "cognitive".

3. For example, J. Stiglitz, "Knowledge as a global public good", in I. Kaul, I. Grunberg & M. Stern (eds), *Global Public Goods: International Cooperation in the 21st Century* (Oxford: Oxford University Press, 1999), 311.

4. In contexts where every additional user increases the value of the product, the networks which serve almost all users are in a monopolistic position; cf. H. Varian & C. Shapiro, *Information Rules: A Strategic Guide to the Network Economy* (Boston, MA: Harvard Business School Press, 1999), 173–86, 301–05.

5. S. Scotchmer, "The political economy of intellectual property treaties", National Bureau of Economic Research working paper 9114 (2003).

6. K. Marx, *Grundrisse* (Harmondsworth: Penguin, 1973), 705.

7. See (with strong references to knowledge and information) P. Mason, *Postcapitalism: A Guide to our Future* (London: Allen Lane, 2015).

8. This is a central claim of "post-operaists". See, for example, A. Negri & M. Hardt, *Commonwealth* (Cambridge, MA: Harvard University Press, 2009), 131–64; C. Vercellone, "From formal subsumption to general intellect: elements for a Marxist reading to the thesis of cognitive capitalism", *Historical Materialism* 15 (2007), 13–36.

9. M. Burawoy "From Polanyi to Pollyanna: the false optimism of global labor studies", *Global Labor Journal* 1:2 (2010), 310.

10. B. Jessop, "Knowledge as a fictitious commodity: insights and limits of a Polanyian perspective", in A. Bugra & K. Agartan (eds), *Reading Karl Polanyi for the Twenty-First Century* (Basingstoke: Palgrave Macmillan, 2017), 120ff.

11. A. Palumbo & A. Scott, *Remaking Market Society: A Critique of Social Theory and Political Economy in Neoliberal Times* (New York: Routledge, 2018), 175–8.

12. M. Burawoy, "Marxism after Polanyi", Rhuthmos, 9 October 2014; Available at: http://rhuthmos.eu/spip.php?article1321 (accessed 1 August 2018).

13. The most important account is probably M. Olson, *The Logic of Collective Action: Public Goods and the Theory of Groups* (Cambridge, MA: Harvard University Press, 1965).

14. S. Marginson, "A funny thing happened on the way to the k-economy: the new world order in higher education: research rankings, outcomes measures and institutional classifications" IMHE, OECD (2008), 8; available at: http://www.oecd.org/site/eduimhe08/41203671.pdf (accessed 7 May 2019).

15. K. Polanyi, *The Great Transformation: The Political and Economic Origins of our Time* (Boston, MA: Beacon Press, 2001), 75.

16. *Ibid.*, 75f.

17. *Ibid.*, 76.

18. *Ibid.*, 79.

19. K. Polanyi, "Adult education and the working-class outlook", *Tutor's Bulletin of Adult Education*, November 1946, 8; KPA-18-32.

20. The "demolition of society" quoted above is explained as follows: "Robbed of the protective coverings of cultural institutions, human beings would perish from the effects of social exposure; they would die as victims of acute social dislocation through vice, perversion, crime, and starvation. Nature would be reduced to its elements, neighborhoods and landscapes defiled, rivers polluted, military safety jeopardized, the power to produce food and raw materials destroyed" (*ibid.*, 76).

21. *Ibid.*

22. As a prominent example of the feminist critique, with references to the others, see S. Federici, *Caliban and the Witch: Women, the Body and Primitive Accumulation*, second edition (Brooklyn, NY: Autonomedia, 2014), 12f.

23. Polanyi, *Great Transformation*, 48.

24. Polanyi describes the process in *Great Transformation*, 86f., 105–07.

25. Cf. G. Ingham, *The Nature of Money* (Cambridge: Polity, 2004), 107–33.

26. Polanyi, *Great Transformation*, 204.

27. *Ibid.*, 201.

28. As will become clear, I use "academic capitalism" here in a deliberately open way, referring to a range of related phenomena instead of a clear-cut economic logic. Sheila Slaughter and her co-authors, who developed the term, already emphasized that it does not signify the transformation of universities into real enterprises, but rather a mixture of heightened budget orientation, managerial governance, competition and quasi-markets in higher education. It is in this sense that "research" and "education … become commodities"; see G. Rhoades & S. Slaughter, "Academic capitalism and the new economy", in R. Rhoads & C. Torres (eds): *University, State, and Market: The Political Economy of Globalization in the Americas* (Stanford, CA: Stanford University Press, 2006), 105, 127–9.

29. Jessop, "Knowledge as a fictitious commodity", 121.

30. *Ibid.*

31. *Ibid.*, 120.

32. Palumbo & Scott, *Remaking Market Society*.

33. On the industrialization of work in IT and commercial office work, which is not analysed by Palumbo & Scott, see, for example, A. Boes *et al.*, *"Lean" und "agil" im Büro. Neue Organisationskonzepte in der digitalen Transformation und ihre Folgen für die Angestellten* (Berlin: Transcript, 2018), 13–16, 174–82.

34. *Ibid.*, 177.

35. M. Burawoy, "A new sociology for social justice movements" (2012), 12. Available at: burawoy.berkeley.edu/Recent%20Pubs/A%20New%20Sociology.docx (accessed 4 May 2019).

36. Burawoy, "Marxism after Polanyi".

37. The story appears in several texts, for example, M. Burawoy, "Facing an unequal world", *Current Sociology* 63:1 (2015), 5–34, 19; Burawoy, "From Polanyi to Pollyanna", 310. As far as I see, however, the versions quoted above give the most detailed accounts.

38. See note 28.

39. Even in the US, "most university technology transfer offices barely break even, once full costs are taken into account" (W. Powell, J. Owen-Smith & J. Colyvas, "Innovation and emulation: lessons from American universities in selling private rights to public knowledge", *Minerva* 45 (2017), 121–42; 128).

40. Burawoy, "Marxism after Polanyi". For a short overview of the situation of for-profit students, see T. Schulze-Cleven & J. Olson, "Worlds of higher education transformed: toward varieties of academic capitalism", *Higher Education* 73:6 (2017), 813–31; 822. For detailed numbers, see A. Looney & C. Yannelis, "A crisis in student loans? How changes in the characteristics of borrowers and in the institutions they attended contributed to rising loan default", Brookings Institution, 10 September 2015; 28–32, 36–9; available at: https://www.brookings.edu/bpea-articles/ (accessed 20 February 2019).

41. Palumbo & Scott, *Remaking Market Society*, 176–8.

42. *Ibid.*, 176.

43. Years spent in education systems and GDP shares of money spent on (higher) education keep rising around the globe, as well as the average income premium on degrees; for a US centered overview see C. Goldin & L. Katz, *The Race between Education and Technology* (Cambridge, MA: Harvard University Press, 2009). The causal relationship between both sides is heterogeneous. The exponential growth of income in US elite jobs, which are traditionally reserved for elite graduates, was obviously *not* caused by equally increasing intellectual challenges; see, for example, L. Rivera, *Pedigree: How Elite Students Get Elite Jobs* (Princeton, NJ: Princeton University Press, 2015).

44. Palumbo & Scott, *Remaking Market Society*, 180.

45. See the works cited in note 8.

46. P. Drahos, with J. Braithwaite, *Information Feudalism: Who Owns the Knowledge Economy?* (London: Earthscan, 2002).

47. As a classical example, see V. Shiva, *Biopiracy: The Plunder of Nature and Knowledge* (Boston, MA: South End Press, 1997).

48. Cf. Stiglitz, "Knowledge as a global public good", 309–16.

49. K. Sunder Rajan, *Biocapital: The Constitution of Postgenomic Life* (Durham, NC: Duke University Press, 2006), 39–76.

50. J. Lezaun & C. Montgomery, "The pharmaceutical commons: sharing and exclusion in global health drug development", *Science, Technology, & Human Values* 40:1 (2015), 3–29.

51. See D. Elder-Vass, *Profit and Gift in the Digital Economy* (Cambridge: Cambridge University Press 2016).

52. See (among others) N. Srnicek, *Platform Capitalism* (Cambridge: Polity, 2017), 43–60, 75–92.

53. B. Gill *et al.*, "Autorisierung. Eine wissenschafts- und wirtschaftssoziologische perspektive auf geistiges eigentum", *Berliner Journal für Soziologie* 22 (2012), 407–40; 426f.

54. *Ibid.*, 412f.

55. J. Schubert, S. Böschen & B. Gill, "Having or doing intellectual property rights? Transgenic seed on the edge between refeudalisation and Napsterisation", *European Journal of Sociology*, 52:1 (2011), 1–17.

56. In this sense, the "platform economy" is a rather old structure, especially if it is defined in the sense of Isabell Gawer, who coined the term for goods such as computer chips; cf. I. Gawer & M. Cusumano, *Platform Leadership: How Intel, Microsoft and Cisco Drive Industry Innovation* (Boston, MA: Harvard Business School Press, 2002).

57. Cf. Srnicek, *Platform Capitalism*, 51–88.

58. The reason for this "disease" is different potentials to save labour time. While the progressive reduction of necessary labour is a central characteristic of (capitalist) industrial production, the time necessary to perform an opera cannot be compressed much without reducing the quality of the performance; W. Baumol & W. Bowen, *Performing Arts: The Economic Dilemma* (New York: Twentieth-Century Fund, 1966). The same holds for care work or teaching – whose comparative costs therefore keep rising.

59. D. Schiller, "How to think about information", in V. Mosco & J. Wasko (eds), *The Political Economy of Information* (Madison, WI: University of Wisconsin Press, 1988), 27–44; 32.

60. A. Gouldner, *The Future of Intellectuals and the Rise of the New Class* (New York: Oxford University Press 1979), 19.

61. Marginson, "A funny thing happened", 8.

62. Jessop, "Knowledge as a fictitious commodity", 118.

63. This is, in another context, the main point of P. Bourdieu, *The Rules of Art* (Stanford, CA: Stanford University Press, 1996).

64. K. Polanyi, "The educated workman: what he is contributing to industry," *The Technology Review* 39:5 (1937), 198–210; 199, 210; KPA-18-19.

65. Polanyi, "Adult education", 9.

66. For an extended version of this argument see M. Mazzuchato, *The Entrepreneurial State: Debunking Public Vs Private Sector Myths* (London: Anthem, 2013).

67. K. Polanyi, "Manual and intellectual labour" (1919), in G. Dale (ed.), *Karl Polanyi: The Hungarian Writings* (Manchester: Manchester University Press, 2016), 197–203.

11

AFTERWORD:
RESOLVING POLANYI'S PARADOX

Michael Burawoy

Over the last 30 years Karl Polanyi's *The Great Transformation*, first published in 1944, has become a canonical text in several inter-related social sciences – sociology, geography, anthropology, international political economy, as well as making in-roads into political science and economics. Undoubtedly, part of its appeal lies in the resonance of his theories with our times which have been marked by the deregulation of markets and their extension into new realms. Polanyi argued that the rise of market fundamentalism had devastating consequences for society, leading to protective countermovements that could be of a progressive or reactionary character. From the perspective of today's market fundamentalism, Polanyi's countermovement effectively frames, on the one hand, the democratic social movements of 2011, including the Arab Spring, Occupy, and Indignados, and, on the other hand, the more recent advance of illiberal democracies, often veering toward dictatorships, in Turkey, Poland, Hungary, the Philippines, Brazil, Italy, Israel and Egypt. It also frames an understanding of such popular movements behind Brexit, Trumpism, the Five Star Movement, and the Yellow Vests as a reaction to an expanding market that commodifies, denigrates and excludes. It is the obvious appeal of Polanyi's argument that now leads commentators to evaluate his writings critically and with renewed intensity, searching for answers to crises of a global scale.

CRITIQUES OF POLANYI

The most common criticism of *The Great Transformation* is Polanyi's failure to anticipate another round of market fundamentalism beginning in the 1970s that has continued virtually unabated for nearly 50 years. Attributing colonial atrocities, two world wars, and the rise of fascism to the repercussions of a market fundamentalism, Polanyi believed that humanity would never be so irrational and irresponsible as to take another plunge toward a market utopia. Yet this is precisely what happened. I call this "Polanyi's Paradox" – a mistaken idealistic response to a materialist diagnosis. He failed to recognize the mighty economic forces driving marketization.

This calls for a twenty-first-century reconstruction of *The Great Transformation* very much as *The Great Transformation* can itself be seen as a twentieth-century reconstruction of *The Communist Manifesto*. Polanyi's reconstruction of Marx and Engels' treatise moved the centre of gravity from production to exchange, from exploitation to commodification, from struggle against capital to countermovement against the market. Just as Marx and Engels saw competitive capitalism as the end of all capitalism and thus failed to see the rise of organized capitalism, Polanyi saw the rise of organized capitalism and the possibility of socialism but failed to anticipate the renewal of market fundamentalism.

Grappling with Polanyi's Paradox has led to an impressive array of criticisms, levelled against *The Great Transformation*. Thus, the chapters of this book interrogate Polanyi's overdrawn binary division between substantivist and formal economics; the idea of fictitious commodities; an inadequate and contradictory theory of the state; an elusive agent of social change with too little attention to class struggle; a misleading theory of money together with a misconception of the origins and mechanisms of the gold standard; a too thin conceptualization of fascism and democracy.

The authors would not have bothered to undertake such trenchant criticisms did they not think that there is much to redeem from Polanyi's writings. But what exactly is there to redeem? Why should we read *The Great Transformation* today? How can we use the criticisms to develop a historically informed reconstruction of *The Great Transformation*, leading to new visions of the past, present and the future?

In this afterword I try to reconstruct Polanyi's framework by elaborating two tensions running through these chapters and through Polanyi's writings. The first tension is between market and society in which the former threatens to destroy the latter through the commodification of so-called fictitious commodities – land, labour and money. In Polanyi's view these entities were never intended to be commodified. In their commodification they undermine human livelihood, human capacities and human agency, commodification disembeds land, labour and money from their necessary social supports. Society, then, springs back in self-defence.

The second tension is between capitalism and democracy. Here, too, the tension is between the economic and the extra-economic, between the interests of capitalists in accumulation and the interests of workers in democracy. Polanyi claims that the unstable equilibrium between capitalism and democracy results either in the democratic transformation of capitalism (socialism) or the capitalist dissolution of democracy (fascism).

My hypothesis is that in *The Great Transformation* as well as in reality, the first tension, between market and society, is propelled by a first wave of marketization in the nineteenth century, whereas the second tension, between democracy and capitalism, is propelled by a second wave of marketization in the twentieth century. Each wave, therefore, gives rise to different countermovements – crystallizing around localized social movements in the nineteenth century and around the state in the twentieth century. The question we have to ask, then, is how these two sets of tensions play themselves out in the present third wave of marketization that begins in the 1970s, calling for a reaction of a global character. Human fate depends not only on the possibility of such a global reaction but also on the form it might take, whether authoritarian or democratic. Polanyi was concerned with the alternatives of fascism and socialism on a national scale, we have to be concerned about them on a global scale.

FIRST-WAVE MARKETIZATION: MARKETS VS SOCIETY

Like so many classics written by independent scholars, *The Great Transformation* has its idiosyncratic side. It often leaves readers scratching their heads about the intricate logic of his argument. Thus, Polanyi devotes an inordinate space to Speenhamland, the obscure English system of parish wage supplements that brought wages up to a minimum level, first introduced in 1795. It blocked the development of a national labour market. Polanyi claims that Speenhamland was eventually abolished under the influence of political economists who saw this as encouraging indolence. Wage labourers have to be forced to work hard under the economic whip of the market, which happens with the abolition of local relief and the passing of the New Poor Law of 1834. Unregulated commodification of labour power, with the hated workhouse as support of last resort, leads to a spontaneous reaction from society that assumes diverse forms – the movement for the reduction of the working day, cooperatives, community self-organization, and eventually trade unions and parties. There is a double movement: the rise of the market and the reaction of society. Let us examine each in turn.

Christopher Holmes and David Yarrow argue that the political economists (particularly, Ricardo and Malthus), whom Polanyi saw as condemning the labour protection of Speenhamland, did not originate the idea of market fundamentalism. Polanyi relied on them too heavily in his account of the rise of the market in nineteenth-century England. Holmes and Yarrow find Polanyi's reliance on the economists as responsible for his overdrawn distinction between the "formalist" (disembedded) description of the market economy and the "substantivist" (embedded) pre-industrial economy, based on redistribution, reciprocity and household. This divide between substantivist and formalist economies does not map onto market and pre-market society. Even the most disembedded of market economies still rely on such non-market production as domestic labour. They conclude that the market did not emerge spontaneously from the brain of the political economists, ideas do not drive the market economy. Even so, economic *theory* does have its "performative" effects by conceptually reducing all economic activities to the market, excluding, for example, the unpaid household labour essential for a modern economy. Economic theory creates a national accounting system that distorts the calculation of such indices as GDP, leading to faulty claims and misguided policies.

Hüseyin Özel takes a similar approach, but justifies Polanyi's focus on economic theory as an immanent critique of neoclassical economics, showing that a textbook market economy does not take into account the dehumanizing consequences of commodifying labour, land and money. Neoclassical economics becomes, therefore, an ideology in the Marxian sense, simultaneously expressing but also hiding the underlying features of capitalism. Just as Marx's analysis of commodity fetishism reveals underlying relations of exploitation, Polanyi's use of fictitious commodities highlights the destructive objectification of human relations.

Polanyi has much to offer on the consequences of marketization, but what drives the expansion of the market? In casting out Marxian theories of accumulation and history, Polanyi is left only with the force of ideas, paradoxical for someone so concerned with the material consequences of marketization. The obvious driver of marketization is the emergent capitalist class. As Sandra Halperin makes clear, for Polanyi class is only a significant actor if it organizes itself in defence of society. By this criterion the struggles of the working class and sometimes of the landed classes can become effective agents of history, but the manufacturing class is ruled out as a significant force as it is in the business of destroying society. Halperin makes a cogent argument that class forces were behind both the expansion and the opposition to the deepening market.

The only way to reconcile Halperin and Polanyi, is to argue that the capitalist class becomes effective when it becomes *hegemonic*, when it advances its own interests as the interests of all, which would require the regulation of commodification. Broadly speaking, one can argue with Antonio Gramsci, the great Italian theorist of hegemony, that the English capitalist class went through his three stages: economic-corporate (sectional interests, in particular, commerce vs manufacture), economic class (as against landed classes) and, by the last quarter of the nineteenth century, it reaches a political or hegemonic level which the capitalist class takes into account material interests in civil society. But note, this is still different from Polanyi for whom society is prior to class whereas for Gramsci class is prior to society.

In the Gramscian scheme the orchestration of hegemony is conducted by the state in its relation to civil society. What does Polanyi have to say about the state? Maria Markantonatau and Gareth Dale point to Polanyi's very different conceptions of the state – the utopian vision associated with guild socialism, the realist turn of the twentieth century, but also the liberal state and its ambiguous relation to the market. Reading Polanyi's account of the nineteenth century, it would seem that the state spontaneously represents the interests of society – there is an identification of state and society. In Polanyi's view the state is not a contradictory entity recognizing, organizing and taking into account multiple class interests. To the contrary Polanyi offers us a Hegelian or Durkheimian view of the state as an expression of a largely homogeneous society.

Invoking Gramsci raises an ambiguity with regard to the countermovement as so many of the struggles against the market – from cooperatives to trade unions, from the factory movement to Owenism – are not necessarily struggles against capitalism, and were successfully absorbed into the emerging hegemonic order. Thus, Polanyi's "counter-movement" diverges from Gramsci's "counter-hegemony", the one organized against the market and the other against capitalism. Although the former *might* be part of a Gramscian war of position, a prefigurative movement for socialism, it is not necessarily anti-capitalist. If Polanyi's account of the relationship between state and society is undeveloped, Gramsci's account of the relation between market and society is equally undeveloped.

There are other sources of ambiguity in Polanyi's countermovement, as the (de)commodification of one fictitious commodity may affect the (de)commodification of another. Take money. Fixing the relation of a currency to some metallic commodity has the effect of commodifying money but the fluctuating price of the metal can radiate disturbances through the rest of the economy, thereby putting pressure on businesses, fearful of profit turning to loss, to intensify the commodification of labour. As Kurtuluş Gemici argues, the commodification of money has a destructive effect *within* the economy in contrast to the commodification of land and labour that are examined for their consequences outside the market system.

Samuel Knafo goes further. He argues that Polanyi has a thin and abstract account of the gold standard, projecting its operation in the interwar period of the twentieth century onto the nineteenth century. If in the twentieth century the gold standard was intended to stabilize the international financial order, it would also impose such restrictions on national economies that lead countries to exit from that order. But, actually, that belies the history of the gold standard.

In the nineteenth century the gold standard was designed to bring order to national economies, opposing banks that created their own local paper currency. The commodification of money, by attaching it to the gold standard, allowed central banks to displace local currencies with a single national currency. It was only as central banks in different countries adopted singular currencies linked to the gold standard that the interwar system emerged to eventually sow the seeds of its own destruction. Thus, the gold standard originated in the nineteenth century with the state orchestrating the decommodification of money, to advance a national market economy. Knafo is effectively calling into question the very meaning of the double movement, suggesting we need to simply focus on the institutional foundations of the market.

Do we have to abandon the idea of the double movement, the dynamic part of Polanyi's theory, in favour of the more sociological proposition of the always embedded market? To hold on to the double movement as it applies to the nineteenth century, on the one hand, requires the restoration of Marx's account of *capital accumulation* as driving commodification. But the destructive powers of commodification are held in check by a state that is compelled to recognize the plurality of interests in society, in particular the interests of the working class. On the other hand, and here we depart from Marx, the interests of those workers congeal around the *experience of commodification*, that is around the sale of labour power, rather than exploitation that Marx himself claimed is mystified. What happens to this argument when we take it into the twentieth century?

SECOND-WAVE MARKETIZATION: CAPITALISM VS DEMOCRACY

Marking the expansion of civil society and the advance of democracy toward the end of the nineteenth century, Polanyi's analysis shifts its focus. His account of the dialectics of market and society, gives way to the tension, even the irreconcilability of capitalism and democracy, expressed as the antagonism of capital and labour. Now Polanyi leaves the singular focus on the UK and moves toward different national compromises between capitalism and democracy.

Gareth Dale and Mathieu Desan dissect Polanyi's writings of the 1920s and 1930s, before he wrote *The Great Transformation*, pointing to fascism as the negative resolution of the incompatibility of capitalism and democracy and socialism as a positive resolution. They show how Polanyi's interest in the origins of fascism focuses largely on the hostility of capitalist class toward democracy, a hostility that had its origins in the nineteenth century. Polanyi misses, they claim, the popular basis of fascism. In particular, the analysis of the lived experience of commodification disappears from Polanyi's account. As regards the socialist resolution, they show how Polanyi was influenced by the ideas of guild socialism, the Austro-Marxists and the Viennese municipal socialism that advanced through the 1920s. Crucially, for Polanyi, fascism arises from capitalism and its crises rather than from socialism's failure to deliver on its promises.

Polanyi returns to the question of capitalism and democracy towards the end of *The Great Transformation*. The argument is spelled out by Paula Valderrama as follows: in the nineteenth century when democracy was still embryonic, excluding the working class, it was deployed by capitalism in opposition to the old order. But with universal suffrage that spawned political parties and civil society, democracy could not be sustained and the tension was resolved through authoritarian means, either fascism or communism. Socialism as the extension of democracy to the whole society, including the economy, is presented as a utopian project, but one essential to Polanyi's vision of a possible future as well as a reference point to evaluate political orders.

Valderrama spells out the meaning of socialism as the realization of democratic freedoms, her interpretation of Polanyi's conclusion to *The Great Transformation*. Democratic freedom in a complex society is the very antithesis of the economists' market freedom. For Polanyi freedom can only be realized under socialism – a collective self-determination defined by individuals assuming responsibility for the social consequences of their action. This requires a transparency of those consequences, a transparency made impossible by the "invisible hand" of the market economy. Under socialism the unintended consequences of market action must be contained within democratically set boundaries. Above all socialism must set limits on the commodification of fictitious commodities, although Polanyi makes no mention of them in that last chapter. Beyond the market, democracy must reduce the power of unreflexive institutions, that is, those institutions that are not transparent to themselves. With socialism social relations turn from reified relations to human relations that are collectively controlled. This is, of course, the essence of Marx's understanding of communism.

In reality the countermovement to second-wave marketization in advanced capitalism did not end up with socialism or fascism but a compromise between capitalism and democracy that took the form of electoral politics, founded on the substantial concessions extracted from capital, concessions that don't touch the essential but are nonetheless meaningful to contesting political parties and their constituencies. As Markantonatou and Dale argue capitalism proved to be unexpectedly flexible in adapting to democratic regimes. Recognizing the way markets, such as the European Monetary Union, impose limits on the realization of social demands, they also ask whether democracy, such as it is, can last.

In his *Capital in the Twenty-First Century*, Thomas Piketty, argues that for advanced capitalist countries the era of diminishing inequalities was a blip of no more than half a century, and beginning in the 1970s we see a return to late-nineteenth-century patterns of unrestrained accumulation. We can project this view of capitalism onto the political terrain – the three waves of capitalism correspond to three phases in the relation between capitalism and democracy: in the first wave democracy is underdeveloped and limited in its constraining power; in the second wave, various forms of social democracy manage to redistribute wealth, making democracy a meaningful terrain of politics; in the third wave of capitalism inequality deepens, democracy becomes ineffectual in constraining accumulation, electoral politics loses credibility and enters a crisis and politics increasingly moves onto an extra-parliamentary terrain. How can Polanyi's notion of countermovement shed light on this politics of third-wave marketization?

THIRD-WAVE MARKETIZATION: POLANYI'S PARADOX

We must now return to Polanyi's Paradox – why did Polanyi not anticipate another round of market fundamentalism? Quite simply, he failed to take into account the imperative of capital accumulation. In rejecting Marxism's teleology Polanyi rejected accumulation as the driving force behind the expansion of markets. As David Harvey has underlined, accumulation through the deepening and extension of commodification cannot be confined to the genesis of capitalism. It is a perpetual feature of all capitalism, generating successive periods of commodification that can be distinguished in terms of the creation and articulation of fictitious commodities.

Focused, as he was, on the "origins of our time" – in particular, the rise of fascism – Polanyi saw a long arc of marketization, beginning at the end of the eighteenth century, leading to the reaction against the market, culminating in the ascendancy of state regulation. We have argued there were actually two periods. In the first period the tension between marketization and society prevails, which emphasizes social movement reactions to commodification. In this period Polanyi is unclear as to the driving forces behind marketization. In the second period, the driving imperative of capitalism overwhelms democracy, resulting in fascism, or alternatively, democracy reacts to overwhelm capitalism, resulting in some form of socialism. In between are a variety of social democratic resolutions.

If, in the first period, it is not clear what drives marketization, in the second period it is not clear what drives the diverse countermovements, that is what combination of forces give rise to one political regime rather than another. Very different from the response to first-wave marketization, Polanyi gives little attention to popular reactions to marketization, and there is no mention of fictitious commodities.

In analysing third-wave marketization, we need to see how the market–society tension comes together with the capitalism–democracy tension. For much of the period after the Second World War, at least in advanced capitalist countries, some form of democracy prevailed. To be sure it was not the radical democracy Polanyi proposed, but a liberal democracy based on elections and party politics. It channelled substantial popular participation into electoral politics, attracted by the significant material concessions that could be distributed among different capitalist and non-capitalist groups – concessions that depended, in part, on the balance of power within the legislature and between the legislature and the executive. Which party ruled mattered for material as well as ideological reasons, even if it didn't touch the essential, that is the capitalist order. Success in democratic competition could advantage the dominated classes, in terms of benefits, conditions of work and job security, at the expense of capital. You might say with Seymour Martin Lipset that electoral politics was a peaceful form of class struggle.

However, beginning with the recession of the 1970s, capital took the offensive against workers. Increasingly, the class compromise at the basis of democracy, was turned against workers who now made concessions to capital in the hope of holding onto their jobs. The great recession of 2008 and its denouement created a legitimation crisis not so much for capitalism but for the steering capacity of democracy. The compromise between capitalism and democracy eroded in favour of capital, democracy lost its credibility, and the dominated classes increasingly turned to extra-parliamentary struggles.

How should we think of those struggles? Marxian struggles are about exploitation, about the dependence of capital upon labour and the leverage or structural power this gives to the working class. The third wave of marketization has effectively destroyed labour's leverage power. On the one hand, global labour markets have supplied labour from foreign lands or capital has simply moved abroad. On the other hand, states have undermined protections of labour whether in the workplace or in the labour market. Labour is on the back foot as it moves from a proletariat to a precariat, manifested, for example, in the dramatic decline of strikes. At this point Polanyi comes into his own as we turn from Marxian-type struggles around exploitation to Polanyian-type struggles around commodification of labour, land and money.

With regard to labour, it means that the focus is on struggles against the commodification of labour, against subjecting "labour power" to unregulated exchange, leading to struggles for living wage, for social benefits and pensions, for basic income, but also the search for alternative and supplemental means of livelihood, for example, in the gig economy. This is very different from the struggles against capital in the era of the countermovement to second-wave marketization – the most radical forms of which attempted to expropriate the capitalist class, as for example in the Swedish Meidner-Hedborg Plan for wage-earner funds and even more remote from the struggles around state socialism.

From the commodification of labour power we can turn to the commodification of land, whose effects we see all around us in the rising prices of real estate and soaring rents, increasing the cost of living that has far outstripped incomes. Here the resulting struggles are against eviction and for rent control, and, more rarely, for public housing. We see processes of land commodification in the Special Economic Zones of India as well as in the urbanization of rural China that have given rise to their own forms of collective resistance.

The commodification of land only exacerbates the desperation that stems from the commodification of labour power. The bottom begins to fall out of the middle class that gradually (and sometimes precipitously) descends into the working class, thereby enlarging the precariat at the bottom of society. At all levels survival turns on borrowing. So finance capital, the making of money from money, made possible by the commodification of money, deepens the indebtedness of the dominated classes through micro-financing, sub-prime mortgages, and credit cards. All of which results in an intricate mutual re-enforcing of the destructive effects of the commodification of land, labour and money. The study of the articulation of modes of production meets its complement in the study of the articulation of the commodification of fictitious commodities.

I am suggesting that with third-wave marketization, the focus on fictitious commodities comes into its own as an experience of dispossession. Polanyi played down the role of violence even in his discussion of the English enclosure movement, but violence is part and parcel of commodification. What is important is not simply the *existence* of an object that is bought and sold, but the process of producing something that is bought and sold, a commodity. The process of commodification, a process of dis-embedding, can be very violent, as in the expulsion of peasants from their land, which simultaneously turns land and labour into commodities.

Fictitious commodities go beyond labour, money and land – and now we can say nature so as to include water and air as well as land. We can also think of the commodification of the body, whether its physiological organs or its sexualization. Tilman Reitz's essay takes us in another direction to various attempts at formulating *knowledge* as a fictitious commodity. He argues that the importance of the sale of knowledge has been exaggerated: the most that can be said is that there has been an increased classification of knowledge in readiness for commodification that has yet to occur in any major way. He doesn't take into consideration, however, the rise of what Shoshana Zuboff calls surveillance capitalism that constitutes everyone as producers of information that is expropriated, organized and sold. Here the process of commodification is actually not a violent process, but one in which all enthusiastically participate through digital technologies that record our every move, our every sentiment, our every taste. This is the prototype of symbolic violence – the simultaneous securing and obscuring of behavioural surplus – that results in massive commodification of information.

Another issue raised by third-wave marketization is the scale of commodification. The process of commodification may be local but the commodity can have a global character. Randall Germain addresses this question in his chapter where he argues that the state is at the fulcrum of the globalization of money and, indeed, of labour. While there are financial institutions such as the IMF and World Bank that regulate the global commodification of money, states are key to the facilitation or obstruction of a global labour market. Third-wave marketization, working through states, has proved to be very disruptive of populations, generating vast flows of refugees, creating a global reserve army of labour. Although the commodification of land is impelled by global forces, bought and sold on a global market, land itself is locally rooted. Moving from land to nature we see how capitalism is destructive of air and water as well as land with global consequences, such as climate change. Commodification only enters, however, with the calibration of emissions, so-called carbon trading that displaces or redistributes the destruction of the environment with its own inequities. Whether the commodification of waste actually reduces the amount of waste is doubtful.

If Polanyi's centring of commodification illuminates the dire threats to the planet as posed by third-wave marketization, one has to ask whether there is a comparable account of countermovements. With the wave of movements of 2011, most famously Occupy, Arab Spring and Indignados, there was a temporary renaissance of older movements – labour, environmental, feminist, indigenous and racial justice movements. These movements had a common character in their disparagement of liberal and illiberal democracies, and a broad scepticism toward the state. Unlike the anti-globalization movements of the 1990s, however, they had national objectives. They may have been anti-state but still national in scope. The movements spread from country to country but that did not make them global in orientation. They, therefore, could not tackle finance capital, climate change, the flow of refugees. We might say, therefore, that these movements were second-wave responses to third-wave marketization. That, in part, explains their short lives.

Just as it may be said that it was the failure of socialism that gave way to fascism in Germany and Italy, so perhaps it can also be said that it was the failure of left-wing populism of 2011–14 that contributed to the right-wing populism that followed – a right-wing populism that appears to be more enduring, manifested in popular support for a series of so-called illiberal democracies in such countries as Hungary, Poland, Russia, the Philippines, Brazil, Argentina, Turkey and

Israel. The popularity of these regimes lies in targeting outsiders – whether they be immigrants, racial and ethnic minorities, women, or LGBTQ – who are held responsible for the ills experienced at the hands of third-wave marketization. If left-wing populism shirked leadership and rejected liberal democracy in favour of autonomous movements, right-wing populism rejects liberal democracy in favour of popular leaders and ideologies that disparage "outsiders". Right-wing and left-wing populism each dismisses the problems identified by the other as false problems, but they share the rejection of the state (and the politics associated with the state) as manipulated by ruling elites. Each populism sees the other as part of the problem, yet they are also expressions of common underlying tendencies.

Thus, I return to my essential point: to understand the countermovement to commodification, one has to appreciate the force driving commodification, namely the imperative of capital accumulation. Without appreciating that underlying imperative one cannot fully comprehend the countermovement – neither its shape nor its consequences. For Polanyi, ideas drove marketization, so, with human foresight, marketization could be contained or reversed. That, you might say, was Polanyi's mistaken determinism. He rejected Marx's determinism, but he substituted a determinism of his own – the inevitable defence of society against commodification.

We have inverted the Polanyian scheme: marketization is no longer a contingent outcome of history, but the inevitable product of capital accumulation. Furthermore, with marketization, liberal democracy no longer guarantees minimalist decommodification or material concessions, thereby making party politics less effective. In this alternative interpretation, what is contingent is not the market but the appearance of a countermovement. Polanyi may be correct that commodification forms the experience of capitalism, and it may even provide the basis of a countermovement, but there is no inevitability to that countermovement. Third-wave marketization may lead to fascism, to the renaissance of a deeper democracy, to some form of socialism, but it may also lead to no sustained countermovement at all, to a great involution.

INDEX

Page numbers in **bold** refer to tables

Nazi Germany 55, 60, 158, 159
neoclassical economics 123, 135, 140–41, 144, 191, 216
neoliberalism 27, 30, 49, 184–5
non-market labour 20–21
non-market societies 16, 123

Offe, Claus 65
organized capitalism 158, 214
Özel, Hüseyin 4, 216

Palumbo, Antonino 197, 199
parliamentary democracy 50, 60–61, 64, 172
Paterson, Matthew 17
Peel, Robert 98, 155
performance indicators 192, 199
Piketty, Thomas 219–20
planism 162–3, 164
planned economies 17, 155, 164
plastic societies 174, 175
Polanyi, Karl 1–3, 39
political democracy 167, 173, 183
political economy 5, 11–12, 36, 41, 104–5, 135
    classical 90, 93, 94, 99, 100, 101, 113–17, 123
    global 28, 31, 37, 40, 41
political power 40
political repression 3
politics 4, 5, 7
Poor Law Amendment Act (1834) 34, 72, 78, 89, 215
Popular Front 160, 161, 162, 163, 164
Pór, Odon 153
price determination theory 140–41
price mechanism 8, 10, 16, 18
prices 135–6, 176–7, 195
private property 12
protectionism 75, 78–9, 138
protective countermovement 9, 58–9, 70, 74, 75, 132, 133, 134, 135, 136, 138, 165, 194, 217
public choice theory 18
Pufendorf, Samuel 12
purchasing power 35, 36, 43, 110, 113, 114, 120
purchasing power economies 119, 123

real democracy 172, 173, 179, 181, 183, 184
regional planning 39
regulated markets 70, 76
reification 142, 144, 145, 176
Reitz, Tilman 4, 222
representative democracy 4, 173
revolution 80
Ricardo, David 7, 10, 12, 58, 99, 100–101, 115–16
right-wing populism 223–4
Ruggie, John 28, 30, 31

Schaffer, Felix 119
Schiller, Dan 204
Schumpeter, J. 81, 114
Scott, Alan 197, 199
self-interest 14, 15, 17
Smith, Adam 11–12, 75, 100
social change 71, 72–3, 81
social democracy 62, 63, 82, 158–9, 160, 161–2, 164, 167, 172, 174, 220
social freedom 172, 174, 181
social institutions 51–2, 56, 75
social knowledge 177, 178
social protection 9, 10, 11, 21, 27, 59, 61–2, 69–70, 72, 136
social reality 176, 181, 182, 184
social totality 132, 133, 154, 167
socialism 51, 53, 61, 63, 76, 152, 153, 157, 158, 164, 167, 172, 174, 178, 214, 218–19
socialist economies 118–19
socialist functional democracy 52
socialist societies 52–3
Somers, Margaret 10, 12
soulless institutions 69, 75, 78
Soviet Union 39, 55, 164
Spann, Othmar 152, 153, 154, 167
special-purpose money 17, 109, 110, 121, **122**, 123
Speenhamland Law (welfare provision system) 10, 12, 72, 215
state power 3, 50, 51, 52, 59, 64
states 3, 13, 17, 37, 43, 49–54, 55–63, 64–5, 75, 78–9, 82, 83, 217
    capitalist 50, 60, 61, 64
    democratic 61, 62, 173
    expansive 28–9, 32, 34, 41